OUTBACK
PIONEERS

Evan McHugh's previous books include *Shipwrecks: Australian Maritime Disasters*, *Outback Heroes: Australia's Greatest Bush Stories* and *Red Centre, Dark Heart*. He writes a weekly column, 'Dry Rot', in the *Sunday Mail* and has written for television and radio. He is married and lives in Sydney.

OUTBACK PIONEERS

EVAN McHUGH

VIKING
an imprint of
PENGUIN BOOKS

VIKING

Published by the Penguin Group
Penguin Group (Australia)
250 Camberwell Road, Camberwell, Victoria 3124, Australia
(a division of Pearson Australia Group Pty Ltd)
Penguin Group (USA) Inc.
375 Hudson Street, New York, New York 10014, USA
Penguin Group (Canada)
90 Eglinton Avenue East, Suite 700, Toronto, Canada ON M4P 2Y3
(a division of Pearson Penguin Canada Inc.)
Penguin Books Ltd
80 Strand, London WC2R 0RL England
Penguin Ireland
25 St Stephen's Green, Dublin 2, Ireland
(a division of Penguin Books Ltd)
Penguin Books India Pvt Ltd
11 Community Centre, Panchsheel Park, New Delhi – 110 017, India
Penguin Group (NZ)
67 Apollo Drive, Rosedale, North Shore 0632, New Zealand
(a division of Pearson New Zealand Ltd)
Penguin Books (South Africa) (Pty) Ltd
24 Sturdee Avenue, Rosebank, Johannesburg 2196, South Africa

Penguin Books Ltd, Registered Offices: 80 Strand, London, WC2R 0RL, England

First published by Penguin Group (Australia), 2008

10 9 8 7 6 5 4 3 2 1

Text and cover design by Karen Trump © Penguin Group (Australia)
Cover photograph copyright © Corbis

Typeset in 10/16pt Linotype Centennial by Post Pre-press Group, Brisbane, Queensland
Printed and bound in Australia by McPherson's Printing Group, Maryborough, Victoria

National Library of Australia
Cataloguing-in-Publication data:

McHugh, Evan
Outback pioneers / Evan McHugh.
ISBN: 9780670072491 (pbk.)
Pioneers – Australia. Frontier and pioneer life – Australia.
Australia – History – 1788–1900.

994.02

penguin.com.au

We shall not travel by the road we make.
Ere day by day the sound of many feet
Is heard upon the stones that now we break,
We shall but come to where the cross-roads meet.

For us the heat by day, the cold by night,
The inch-slow progress and the heavy load,
And death at last to close the long, grim fight
With man and beast and stone: for them the road.

For them the shade of trees that now we plant,
The safe smooth journey and the ultimate goal
For us day-labour, travail of the soul.

And yet the road is ours, as never theirs;
Is not one thing on us alone bestowed?
For us the master-joy, oh, pioneers
We shall not travel, but we make the road!

(Violet) Helen Friedlander

Quoted in the Inlander, *Vol. 5, No.1, 1918.*

CONTENTS

1 **THE FIRST PIONEER**
John Wilson (c. 1770–1800)   1

2 **HUNGRY JIM**
James Tyson (1819–1898)   25

3 **OLD BLUEY**
Nat Buchanan (1826–1901)   45

4 **THE QUIET ACHIEVER**
Dervish Bejah (c. 1862–1957)   71

5 **THE WATER BRINGER**
C.Y. O'Connor (1843–1902)   97

6 **A BOND OF IRON**
The Trans-Australian Railway (1912–1917)   117

7 **NO PLACE FOR A WOMAN**
The Country Women's Association (1922–)   147

8 **BUSH NURSE**
Grace Francis (1892–1959)   163

9 **NO BETTER SOUND**
John Flynn (1880–1951)   187

10 **THE PEDAL RADIO MAN**
Alfred Traeger (1895–1980)   **207**

11 **THE SCHOOL OF THE AIR**
Adelaide Miethke (1881–1962)   **225**

12 **THE LAST BUSHMAN**
R.M. Williams (1908–2003)   **241**

13 **OUTBACK RESCUE**
Peter McRae (1951–) and Frank Manthey (1938–) **257**

SOURCES   **275**

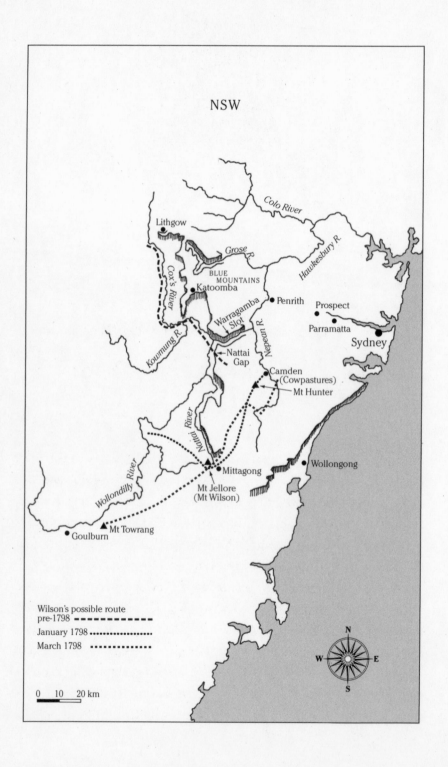

NSW

Colo River

Lithgow

Grose

BLUE
MOUNTAINS

Cox's River

Katoomba

Warragamba
Slot

Kowmung R.

Nattai
Gap

Haukesbury R.

Penrith

Prospect

Nepean R.

Parramatta

Sydney

Camden
(Cowpastures)
Mt Hunter

Nattai River

Wollondilly River

Mittagong

Mt Jellore
(Mt Wilson)

Wollongong

Goulburn

Mt Towrang

Wilson's possible route
pre-1798 ▬ ▬ ▬ ▬ ▬ ▬
January 1798 ∙∙∙∙∙∙∙∙∙∙∙∙
March 1798 ▬∙∙▬∙∙▬∙∙▬

N
W   E
S

0   10   20 km

Detail from Juan Ravenet's
Convicts in New Holland, 1789–1794
(Dixson Galleries, State Library of New South Wales)

I

THE FIRST PIONEER

John Wilson (c. 1770–1800)

In January 1788, the anchors of the sea-battered ships of the First Fleet rattled down into the sparkling waters of Sydney Cove and 780 of England's most unwanted were herded ashore by their guards, British Navy Marines. The convicts were bullied into some semblance of order to view the raising of the English flag as Australia became the farthest outpost of the largest empire the world has ever seen.

Convicts and gaolers then turned their eyes upon the untamed wilderness that lay before them. Nothing, not a single plant or animal, bore any resemblance to the place they had called home and many recoiled from the oppressive silence of the Australian bush. Eventually a contingent of soldiers explored the country 10 kilometres south to Botany Bay. Naval officers navigated the upper reaches of Port Jackson until they found soils reasonably suitable for agriculture,

whereupon most of the colony decamped to Parramatta, 20 kilometres inland. After that, exploration stalled as the colonists focussed
their attention on cultivating the virgin land.

*

The spread of the first European settlement in Australia was halt-
ing at best, but there was one member of the First Fleet who eagerly
embraced this strange new country. In him there was a sense of
adventure, a natural curiosity and the first stirrings of the pioneering
spirit. What's remarkable is that despite his considerable achievements, which were documented in several of the journals of the First
Fleet, this man has been almost ignored by history.

His name was John Wilson. His date of birth isn't known, but in
October 1785 he was probably in his mid-teens when he was con-
victed of stealing 'nine yards of cotton cloth called velveret, of the
value of tenpence' and sentenced at Wigan Assizes to transportation
for seven years. The former mariner arrived in Australia with the
First Fleet aboard the convict transport *Alexander* and served out
the remainder of his sentence. In 1792 he became a free man. The
government's usual expectation for newly freed convicts was that
they would go to work on one of the farms in the Parramatta district.
Wilson had other ideas. He weighed the grinding toil of his fellow
settlers against a life of freedom among the semi-nomadic local Aborigines and decided to go bush.

This was easier said than done. The people who had enjoyed possession of Australia for the previous 40000 years were at that time
contesting the legal notion that it was terra nullius (no-man's-land).
Their spears didn't discriminate between convict, free man or guard
and they weren't about to welcome Wilson with open arms. Yet in
the 'outback' beyond the western fringes of Sydney's settlements he
gradually built a relationship with members of the Bidjigal people.
He learned enough of their language to be able to communicate

effectively and they named him Bun-bo-é. Over the next three years he was spotted from time to time, but had little or no contact with other European settlers.

That all changed early in 1795 when Wilson voluntarily emerged from the bush and asked to see the acting governor, Captain William Paterson. Wilson informed Paterson that the settlers along the Hawkesbury River, which had become the front-line in the war with the Aboriginal defenders, had been engaging in outrageous behaviour that had provoked conflict. He named the offending settlers as Michael Doyle, Robert Forrester and a man named Nixon. He explained that the Aborigines were intent on payback and had attacked two other settlers, George Shadrach and John Akers, mistaking them for Doyle and Forrester.

Despite the value of the information, the authorities didn't hesitate in deriding the messenger, particularly as he'd been living with the Aborigines. The colony's judge advocate, David Collins, described Wilson in his *Account of the English Colony in New South Wales* as a 'wild, idle young man' and that 'in herding with these people, no good consequence would come of it'.

That didn't stop the authorities putting Wilson's skills to good use. Shortly after he emerged from the bush, Wilson was taken by Deputy Surveyor Charles Grimes on an expedition to explore Port Stephens, 200 kilometres north of Sydney. There the initial contact with the Aboriginal inhabitants was peaceful. When Grimes went ashore from his schooner he was welcomed with a tribal dance, but then one of the warriors attempted to lure Grimes away from the party. Grimes allowed himself to be led, but Wilson saw what was happening. He watched as the warrior raised a spear and prepared to use it on Grimes. Wilson was armed with a double-barrelled gun. When he was sure Grimes was about to be speared, he fired at the Aborigine. The man fell, then rose and made another attempt to throw a spear at Grimes. Wilson fired a second shot, hitting the man once more. He fell again. This time, he stayed down. (It was later learned, through a group of escaped convicts who were living among the indigenous people in the area, that the warrior survived and had the scars to prove it.) Grimes was sure he owed Wilson his life.

After the expedition returned to Sydney, Wilson found life in the European settlement unappealing and returned to his former life among the Aboriginal people, this time in the company of another man named Knight. In mid-August 1795 they came to the attention of the authorities once again. The pair appeared in Sydney town with a group of Aboriginal men, and the following day made clear the reason for their visit. They were seeking wives. Unfortunately, the tribal custom of kidnapping women from rival groups didn't go down well with the authorities, especially because the partners Wilson and Knight fixed upon were only girls. Wrote Collins:

> In the midst of a considerable uproar, which was heard near the bridge, Wilson and Knight were discovered, each dragging a girl by the arm . . . assisted by their new associates. The two white men being soon secured, and the children taken care of, the mob dispersed. Wilson and Knight were taken to the cells and punished, and it was intended to employ them both in hard labour; but they found means to escape, and soon mixed again with companions whom they preferred to our overseers.

There was something about Wilson's preference for life in the Australian bush that offended Englishmen driven by the ambition to establish their brand of civilisation throughout the world. As the warfare against the settlers along the Hawkesbury continued, the authorities were only too ready to believe that Wilson and Knight were the instigators of the Aboriginal attacks, although they also lay responsibility at the feet of warriors such as Pemulwuy. Collins considered the ex-convicts capable of 'every kind of mischief'. In

February 1796 he wrote: 'They demonstrated to the natives of how little use a musket was when once discharged, and this effectually removed that terror of our firearms with which it had been our constant endeavour to inspire them.' It didn't occur to Collins that the Aboriginal people had been shot at for the previous eight years and might have worked it out for themselves.

The running battle continued, much to the chagrin of the colony's newly arrived governor, John Hunter. He, too, was certain that much of the trouble was provoked by escaped and former convicts, rather than an indigenous population fighting for their land. On 13 May, 1797, he issued a proclamation declaring four men, including John Wilson, outlaws. It read in part:

> That [if] the said John Jeweson, Joseph Saunders, John Wilson and Moses Williams do not within the space of fourteen days from the date hereof deliver themselves up to the nearest peace officer they will be consider'd as having lost the protection of his Majesty and the aid of the law; consequently, if taken, will be considered not only accessory to the death of those natives who may suffer in the unlawful plunder already mentioned, but as accomplices with them in the mischiefs and cruelty so frequently committed by them, and be liable to be immediately executed without the form of a trial, having by their unlawful conduct forfeited the protection of those wholesome laws under which they have been born and bred.

The proclamation was based on flimsy evidence at best, but the consequences of ignoring it were clear. After some delay, Wilson obeyed the proclamation and turned himself in, in November 1797. Hunter's deadline had long since passed, but instead of hanging Wilson without the form of a trial, he gave him a job.

Wilson had changed a great deal from the English convict who'd arrived in Australia nine years before. When he surrendered, all he was wearing was a kangaroo skin loincloth. The skin of his chest and shoulders was deeply scarred, the marks made as part of an initiation ceremony that indicated he'd been honoured with full membership of his tribal group.

David Collins still conveyed his contempt for Wilson and his tribe by describing him as 'herding with the savages in different parts of the country', but even he had to acknowledge that the information Wilson had to impart was superior to anything that had so far come to hand.

Wilson claimed to have travelled up to 160 kilometres from the settlement in every direction. As proof, he described two animals that no one in the colony knew about. One was a 'bird of the pheasant species', which is now regarded as the first European sighting of a lyrebird (*Menura novaehollandiae*). The other was a 'quadruped', which he said was 'larger than a dog, having its hind parts thin, and bearing no proportion to the shoulders, which were strong and large'. Wilson had travelled far enough into the interior to encounter a wombat (probably *Vombatus ursinus*).

Even more interesting is the place where he claimed to have seen these wonders. Collins wrote: 'to the northwest of the head of the Hawkesbury, [Wilson] came upon a very extensive tract of open and well-watered country'. Fortunately, the country surrounding the headwaters of the Hawkesbury-Nepean River has changed little since 1797, so it's still possible to identify the location. What's remarkable is that it's on the other side of the supposedly impenetrable barrier of the Blue Mountains.

The Cox's River, which branches off from the Hawkesbury-Nepean (the river winds around so much that it was discovered and named twice before it was realised the two were one), dramatically cleaves the mountains before widening into the expanses of the Megalong and Kanimbla valleys just down the hill from the memorials to Gregory Blaxland, William Wentworth and William Lawson – the people who got the credit for discovering the first route through the Blue Mountains in 1810.

The reason Wilson didn't get the credit for such an extraordinary feat can be found in the writings of David Collins: 'It is not improbable that Wilson invented these circumstances in the hope of obtaining some attention, and thereby averting the punishment which he expected, and well knew that he had long deserved.' The fact remains that you can still find lyrebirds and wombats, which don't inhabit the Sydney coastal region, in the Cox's River valleys.

Fortunately, Governor Hunter took Wilson's claims seriously. In particular, Hunter had learned that some convicts were escaping into the bush in the mistaken belief that it was an easy walk to China, where they would be free. Wilson's story verified just how wrong they were. As Collins noted:

Occasional desertions of one or two people at a time had occurred since the establishment of the settlement; but the first convicts who arrived from Ireland in the Queen in the year 1791 went off in numerous bodies, few of whom ever returned. They too were prepossessed with the possibility of penetrating through the woods to China, and imparted the same idea to all of their countrymen who came after them, engaging them in the same act of folly and madness. It was not then to be wondered at, that Wilson, who lately came in from the woods, should, among other articles of information, mention his finding more than fifty skeletons, which the natives assured him had been white men who had lost their way and perished. This account was corroborated by different European articles which were scattered about, such as knives, old shoes, and other things which were known not to belong to the natives.

In January 1798 another rumour was found to be circulating among the Irish convicts. It was believed that between 500 and 600 kilometres to the south-west of Sydney there was another colony of white people. The settlement was rumoured to be a kind of utopia where, according to Hunter, 'They were assured of finding all the comforts of life, without the necessity of labouring for them.'

Hunter learned of this fabled place when he uncovered a plan for a mass escape by up to sixty convicts. Armed constables staked out the convicts' rendezvous point and captured twenty. Found among the convicts' stocks were written instructions on how to reach the colony and a 'compass' given to them by someone who had no qualms about preying on their inexperience. The compass was drawn on a piece of paper.

The source of the rumour was never discovered, but Hunter noted his suspicion that 'some wicked and disaffected person or persons lurk somewhere within this colony'. Collins thought it had come from 'some strange and unintelligible account which one of these men, who had left his work, and resided for some time with the natives, had collected from the mountain savages'. He probably meant John Wilson.

The day after the convicts were captured Hunter went to see them in prison and tried to convince them of the foolishness of their beliefs. He'd been the commander of the warship HMS *Sirius* and well knew that the maritime exploration of Australia had revealed a continent of almost uniform desolation. When he realised his attempts to enlighten the convicts were getting nowhere, he forsook the voice of reason. In a letter to his masters in England he explained, 'I conceived there could be no better argument used to convince them of their misconduct than a severe corporal punishment, which was inflicted.'

Seven escapees were given 200 lashes each.

The governor attempted to quash the conspiracy by scattering its ringleaders among the work gangs throughout the colony. To his dismay, all he succeeded in doing was spreading the belief in a promised land even further. So Hunter conceived a new plan. He wrote:

For the sake, therefore, of humanity, and a strong desire to save these men, worthless as they are, from impending death, I ordered four of the strongest and hardiest of their numbers to be selected by the people themselves, and to prepare for a journey of discovery for the satisfaction of their associates, in order that they might have an opportunity of relating, upon their return, whatever they saw and met with.

Australia's history of exploration has seen nobler motives than proving to convicts that escape was futile. Yet the plan provided an opportunity to test John Wilson's claim that he knew the country for 160 kilometres in every direction. He was one of three guides selected for the expedition. Hunter instructed them to lead the convicts on until 'fatigued and exhausted with their journey over steep and rocky mountains, through thick and extensive woods, and fording deep and rapid rivers, they should feel disposed to abandon their journey'.

The plan was barely announced before Hunter, who must have had a particularly good informant working among the convicts, learned that a new plot was afoot. The convicts not chosen for the expedition were planning to ambush it, murder the guides, take their guns and provisions, then carry out the original escape plan. Hunter sent four soldiers to escort the expedition to the edge of the wilderness.

On 22 January, 1798, Wilson, the other guides, four soldiers and four convicts set out from The Cowpastures (so named because it was where the descendants of the First Fleet's herd of two bulls and four cows were found in 1795, seven years after they'd escaped, fattening on the verdant meadows and then numbering sixty). The identity of the other two guides isn't entirely clear. One was probably a servant of Hunter's, nineteen-year-old John Price, who fancied himself a bit of a bushman and asked to go on the journey. If it was Price, who could read and write, Hunter instructed him to keep a journal (which has survived but is unsigned). The identity of the third guide isn't known at all. It may be that the third person in the group was actually one of the convicts, named Roe, who pressed on after the expedition reached the edge of the known world, which was Mount Hunter, a mere 8 kilometres south-west of The Cowpastures. There, three of the convicts decided they'd already had enough and asked to return with the soldiers.

Hunter thought the calibre of the remaining expeditioners was less than ideal. He wrote to Sir Joseph Banks some years later: 'I wish I had been fortunate enough to have had officers in the colony who would have volunteered for such excursion but sorry I am to say that too many of them were employed in a way less to the advantage of the Public Service.'

As it was, the ex-convict, the manservant and the convict set their course from Mount Hunter south-south-west. There had been no fanfare for their departure; the streets had not been lined with cheering crowds as was the case with later expeditions such as that of Burke and Wills. Instead Wilson and the others slipped quietly into the bush with their meagre stock of provisions. They were on foot since the colonial administration wasn't about to lavish horses on men so low in the social order.

The expedition covered 20 kilometres of undulating country until it hit the first obstacle, the meandering Hawkesbury-Nepean River. The river had cut deeply into the relatively soft sandstone that forms the dominant rock of the Sydney region and it took the men some time to find a way past the cliffs on both sides. Wilson, Price and Roe eventually crossed the river and, continuing south-south-west, managed to cover nearly 30 kilometres for the day. Along the way they were rewarded with a glimpse of two of the 'pheasants' Wilson had mentioned earlier. Price's journal provided independent corroboration.

The next day, 25 January, they continued into the wilderness noting large numbers of kangaroos and emus. They also met and spoke to a group of Aborigines who, according to Price, 'gave a very good account of the place we were in search of, that there was a great deal of corn and potatoes, and the people were very friendly'.

Here was the story that had inspired the Irish convicts to attempt their escapes – exactly what Governor Hunter did *not* want the expedition to discover. Yet the fact remains that the story wasn't true, which suggests, curiously, that the local Aborigines made it up. Why? One explanation is that the story is based on a translation provided by Wilson, who may have played fast and loose with the truth for his own advantage. Another possibility is that when the Aboriginal people found three strange white men on their land, they realised the easiest way to get rid of them was to confirm everything they asked about and speed them on their way. As it was, the Aboriginal people suggested they head farther west, possibly to keep them on the easiest and fastest route out of their country.

The time spent with the Aboriginal people meant the expedition only covered 10 kilometres that day, but there was one success. Before they made camp they also found 'a great deal of salt', at that time used for preserving food and a discovery of considerable value in a colony where nearly everything had to be imported.

On 26 January, Wilson pointed out the dung of a 'whom-batt' and described it to Price as 'an animal about 20 inches [50 centimetres] high, with short legs and a thick body forwards with a large head, round ears and very small eyes. [It] is very fat and has much the appearance of a badger.' He also mentioned a creature the Aborigines called a *cullarine*. This was the first reference to the koala (*Phascolarctos cinereus*), which was previously unknown. That day, Price also managed to shoot one of the 'pheasants', which he described:

The tail of it very much resembles a Peacock with two large long feathers, which are white, orange and lead colour, and black at the ends; its body betwixt is brown and green, brown under its neck and black upon his head, Black legs and very long claws.

This was the first detailed description of the lyrebird, which is such a remarkable bird that it's featured on the Australian 10 cent piece. After shooting the bird, Price and Wilson carefully wrapped it and took it with them, hoping the specimen would survive the journey relatively intact. In the ensuing days, as they continued west-south-west, they passed through country that at times was rocky, scrubby and barren, at other times open, gently undulating and meadow-like, with kangaroos and emus in abundance.

In one such place they saw another group of Aboriginal people. Wilson caught one of them as they fled, a young girl, but was unable to understand her language. By Price's account, the men actually had another Aborigine with them (who only rated a single mention in all the references to the expedition) who couldn't understand her either. The girl was held all night, crying the whole time. In the morning they gave her a tomahawk and let her go. Price also noted that the locals in the area wore large skins that hung down to their feet, which suggests they had reached the Southern Highlands, where even in summer the nights are much colder than on the coastal plains.

After only five days, the journey was starting to take its toll on Price and Roe. According to Price, they'd run out of food and for the previous two days they'd caught only one small rat to eat between them. He and Roe were both sick. Roe had hurt his leg and found walking difficult. Wilson, on the other hand, 'was well and hearty'. Roe's injury must have healed quickly, for on 29 January Price esti-mated that they still managed to cover 36 kilometres.

The following day they reached the head of a river that was nearly as big as the Hawkesbury-Nepean. This was most likely the Wollon-dilly River, which lies 20 kilometres west of present-day Mittagong, itself 100 kilometres south-west of Sydney. The three explorers gazed down on the river that had carved a deep, wide valley into the sand-stone over millions of years. The other side of the valley seemed to hold the promise of open rolling country, and Wilson was all for carrying on by making a canoe to get across the river. However, his two companions had had enough. Price wrote:

> The other man and myself were so faint and tired, having nothing to
> eat but two small birds each, we were afeared to venture on the other
> side of the river for fear we should not be able to procure any thing
> to subsist on, likewise our shoes was gone and feet were very much
> bruised with the rocks so that we asked Wilson to return.

They hadn't found the fabled white settlement, but nor had their progress been barred by the sheer ramparts of stone that were to become the official reason for many subsequent expeditions giving up on their exploration of the Blue Mountains west of Sydney. On their trek to the Wollondilly, Wilson and the others had simply bypassed the barrier.

Wilson managed to convince his companions to go a little further by altering their course to the south-east. By doing so they found themselves among the fertile rolling grasslands of the Southern Highlands. Price described 'many meadows with scarce any trees upon them'. Wilson managed to shoot two parrots the size of cockatoos. They were probably king parrots (*Alisterus scapularis*).

As Price's condition deteriorated, the journal ceased to detail the daily courses, distances and events. Instead, a single entry for 2 February, 1798, covers the whole of the return journey, much of it through areas he described as having meadows and lakes. Again they found themselves among a vast number of kangaroos, one of which Wilson managed to shoot.

The next morning, right on sunrise, Price heard what sounded like two gunshots to the south-east of their camp.

Wilson asked, 'Did you hear that gun fire?'

'I did,' Price confirmed.

Price got his weapon and fired a signal shot. There was no reply.

He fired four more times but got no answer. It's possible there were escaped convicts hunting in the vicinity and Price's signal alerted them to the presence of the expedition. It's more likely they were taken in by the incredible mimicry skills of a lyrebird, which were unknown to the men. Wilson had been shooting at a kangaroo the afternoon before. A lyrebird could easily have added the sound to its repertoire for its dawn chorus.

For the next six days the three men journeyed towards the settled areas around Sydney, their return track about a dozen kilometres east of their outward path. Soon Wilson was in familiar country – barren, full of deep ravines and littered with sandstone outcrops protruding from infertile soil. All Wilson could find for food was a few grubs and roots. In his journal, Price paid tribute to Wilson's bush skills.

> We must all have perished with Hunger, which certainly would have been the case had it not been for the indefatigable zeal of Wilson to supply us with as much as would support life . . . We were all but starved and were obliged to cut up all our clothing to cover our feet which was cut with the rocks.

When Price and Roe were sure they couldn't go on, Wilson realised they were only 16 kilometres from the nearest settlement, at Prospect, 20 kilometres west of Sydney Cove. By then they'd left the rocky country and were travelling easily on the plains country of the Sydney Basin. Wilson encouraged the other two to make one last effort, knowing food and rest weren't far off. They made it back to civilisation late in the afternoon on 9 February, 1798. Price and Roe were so sick from their ordeal that when they were given something to eat their stomachs reacted with such violence it nearly killed them. Price noted that Wilson was still as fit as a fiddle.

Considering what they'd achieved, the men might have expected more than the lukewarm reception they received. Governor Hunter, who'd been hoping the trip would prove escape was impossible, instead found the rumour of paradise apparently confirmed by a group of Aborigines. And rather than being hemmed in by rugged wilderness, his strife-torn colony had pockets of fertile, well-watered land stretching away for more than 100 kilometres to the south-west. However, there were some consolations for Hunter. A potential source of salt had been found a short distance from the settlements on the upper Hawkesbury-Nepean. Also, the terrible condition of convict Roe on his return reinforced the official view of how hard the country could be.

Wilson's discoveries were enough to encourage Hunter to send out another expedition a month later. Wilson was asked to guide surveyor Henry Hacking to the salt deposits and to search for the cattle known to be wandering free beyond The Cowpastures. Price, assuming it was he, appears to have recovered sufficiently to accompany the expedition and again keep a journal (the handwriting was the same).

This time they left Prospect Hill, just south of the settlement at Prospect, on 9 March, reaching the Hawkesbury-Nepean River the following morning. The river was in flood and they spent almost the entire day finding a way to get across. The next day, 25 kilometres south-west, and well south of The Cowpastures, they found some of the cattle. On Sunday 11 March, Price wrote: 'We fell in with the cattle in a fine open country, having a pleasant sight of them. We counted a hundred and seventy, but was not able to make out how many calves.'

Wilson once again demonstrated his knowledge of the country when he altered their course slightly and brought them back to the Nepean River within 2 kilometres of their previous crossing. It was still running very high so the next day Hacking and Wilson swam across and went in search of the salt. They found several deposits up to 3 metres thick in the vicinity of the Nepean and several branch creeks that ran into it. They spent a couple of days exploring the labyrinth of rocky gullies, some 400 metres deep, and finding more salt. Then Hacking seems to have concluded that finding salt deposits wasn't particularly rewarding and returned to Sydney.

On 14 March Wilson set out with another man named Collins (who may have been another of Hunter's servants) to hunt for animal skins. On his return he made Price a proposal. 'Are you willing to go to the south-west part of the country for nine or ten days?' he asked.

Price had put his life in Wilson's hands a month before and found it a gruelling experience. Yet the youngster was toughening up. 'I'm willing to go to any part you think proper,' he replied.

With that, Wilson, Price and possibly Collins set out on a fresh adventure. At first they followed the tracks of the cattle to the south-west as they progressed through fine open country for nearly 15 kilometres. After a difficult creek crossing they got into rugged sandstone country with deep gullies and steep mountains. They struggled on for four days, covering up to 20 kilometres a day by Price's estimation. Their journey brought them in sight of a mountain that Wilson said was the highest in the country. They crossed a small river, the Nattai, and camped at the mountain's foot on the afternoon of Saturday 17 March. They began their ascent the following morning.

In places the mountain's flanks are sheer cliffs. The rest of it rises at an angle approaching 45 degrees. The summit of what is now known as Mount Jellore is 834 metres above sea level (nearby mountains are actually higher) and the view is certainly worth the effort. To the north-west, north, east and south the lay of the land can be seen for up to 100 kilometres. Much of it is unchanged from the day in 1798 when young John Price wrote:

> We took a view to the N and NW which is nothing but exceeding high mountains on a rise one above another, so that the clouds is lost. We

likewise saw a river bearing NNE and SSW, Wilson told me that this river runs into Tenches (or Nepean) River for he was well acquainted with it. We saw that the river that we had cross't before came into it and discovered a brook which runs through the mountains, I supposed it to be a river so I asked Wilson if it was a river or not, he told me that he was certain that it is the river that runs clear through the mountains to the Hawkesbury.

Wilson's information about the river running through the mountains to the Hawkesbury-Nepean suggests that he'd been to the area where the Nattai, Wollondilly and Cox's Rivers combine to form the Warragamba River, which then cuts spectacularly through the Warragamba Slot to join the Hawkesbury-Nepean just downstream from the present-day wall of Warragamba Dam. From the summit of the mountain that Price named Mount Wilson (it was later named after one of the region's first settlers), the Slot isn't visible. Yet Wilson clearly knew which way the rivers ran.

The conversation with Price on the summit of Mount Jellore corroborates Wilson's story given to the governor three years earlier – that he'd been to the headwaters of the Hawkesbury-Nepean and found good open country. If he'd travelled up the Cox's River, an easy journey along the banks if it isn't in flood, he'd have done just that. If he'd gone up the Wollondilly River he'd have reached what became known as the Colong Stock Route, which was 'pioneered' for most of the way by the wandering cattle that were spreading to any place that offered good pasture. From Mount Jellore they could also see a third route through the Blue Mountains, the ridge line that would become the route 'discovered' fifteen years later by the 'explorers' Blaxland, Wentworth and Lawson. Mount Jellore was itself only a few kilometres west of the easiest route past the obstacle of the Blue Mountains (it's now the route used by the Hume Highway), the one Wilson and Price had been travelling. The only route Wilson and

Price couldn't see was Bell's Line of Road, out of sight behind the distant Blue Mountains ridge.

Price's journal suggests the day was cloudy, which probably limited how far the men could see. However, on a clear day they'd have been able to make out the smoke rising from the chimneys of Sydney, 95 kilometres away. Over on the south-western side of the summit, the fertile rolling plains of the Southern Highlands stretched into the distance. Far to the south a solitary peak rose from the plains. Over the ensuing days, Price and Wilson made their way towards it.

As they travelled on, Price started getting used to Wilson's economical diet. Their remaining provisions amounted to thirty biscuits each, and they decided to restrict themselves to two a day, which would allow them to explore for at least another week and still have enough supplies for the return journey. They hoped to go even further if they could supplement their diet with game.

As it happened, as they made their way through the lush meadows that were destined to become the estates of wealthy Sydneysiders who would turn the area into a little piece of England with scarcely a eucalypt in sight, they saw plenty of ducks on the waterways but chose to preserve their gunpowder. Instead, Wilson spotted 'a large green, yellow and black snake he quickly run and caught by the head, which made us an excellent dinner'. It was probably a diamond python (*Morelia spilota spilota*).

The journal entry for 19 March reported on the country in glowing terms (and makes it evident that a third person was present, contributing to the journal):

We saw an exceedingly high hill about five miles [8 kilometres] from us. We concluded to go and see how the country seemed to look towards the SW as this hill bore SE and E from us. We walked about a mile, when we came into a most beautiful country, being nothing but fine large meadows, with ponds of water in them, fine green hills, but very

thin of timber. We got to the top of this hill where we had a most delightful prospect of the country and in my opinion one of the finest in the
known world. It certainly must be a pleasure to any man to view so fine
a country. We found by altering our course as we did, that we had mist
all the creeks that we met with when we was going our SW course, we
likewise saw to the S a most beautiful country, more particular to the
SE. It is not in my power to lay it down fine enough, the E it is mountainous, but fine green Hills to the north and we saw the mountains and
Mount Wilson, for we brought it to bear due N from us. We likewise saw
to the W and SW a good level and low country, we perceived that Wilson and Price was at before, and all the Creeks that we met with runs
into the river. Being satisfied from our view from off the hills we gave
it the name of Mount Pleasant, leaving it to your Excellency, to name it
as you think most proper.

This is thought to be 800-metre Mount Gingenbullen, 4 kilometres
west of the town of Moss Vale, 19 kilometres south of Mount Jellore.
From here the men continued to the south-west for four days, enjoying duck and lyrebirds shot by Wilson as they went. The country
was easy going and they estimated that they covered 30 kilometres
a day. The country gradually became stony and hilly again, until on
24 March they came to a high mountain, probably Mount Towrang,
10 kilometres east-north-east of the town of Goulburn. There they
decided to turn their steps towards home. Not only had they penetrated further into the country than anyone before them, but it would
be nearly twenty years before their feat was equalled.

The return journey was made easier thanks to their new knowledge of the land. They'd found that the country west and east of
their outward track was mountainous and riddled with steep gorges
and cliffs. Between the two, a wide 'ramp' gently sloped down to the
plains of Sydney.

Heavy rain on the return trip meant the skins they'd collected soon spoiled. However, they kept coming upon excellent grazing country with huge numbers of kangaroos. The explorers were so well fed that they made occasional side trips that revealed more excellent country.

As the terrain on either side of them grew more mountainous, they managed to keep to the ridge and still make good distances. On 30 March they shot two more lyrebirds to replace one that had rotted in the rain. Continuing down the ramp they reached the plains south of The Cowpastures on 1 April. The following day they came upon the cattle 'about four miles [6 kilometres] nearer than we saw them the first time'. At the Nepean, which was in flood, Wilson shot several ducks and that night they enjoyed a feast in the supposed wilderness. They reached Prospect the following day, Tuesday 3 April, 1798.

Wilson and Price had not only travelled more than 200 kilometres from the settlement at Sydney Cove, they'd also found a route that skirted the problem of the Blue Mountains. They'd indirectly confirmed Wilson's assertion that there was good grazing land on the other side of the Blue Mountains, at the head of Cox's River. They'd found a place they considered paradise on Earth (although without any white settlements). They had even returned to civilisation fat and healthy, still licking the juices of barbecued duck from their fingers.

It was terrible news for Governor Hunter, who was trying to run a prison. Now, it seemed, right on his doorstep there was a land of milk and honey just waiting for anyone who chose to escape. What's surprising is that no one pounced on the land. However, in 1798 the European population of Sydney was less than 5000 and there was still plenty of good land much closer to civilisation (unless your perspective was that of the dispossessed Aboriginal owners). Without the pressure of population, the need for such country wasn't urgent.

In the years immediately following Wilson's journeys, few official expeditions into the interior were organised. In 1803, Francis Barraillier was sent out to locate the wandering cattle. He tracked them through the Nattai Gap and down to the Wollondilly River. From there they'd spread well along what is now the Colong Stock Route. Barraillier followed for some way but turned back when his supplies ran low. Significantly, he didn't turn back because of impassable cliffs.

It was only during the drought of 1813, when most of the available land close to Sydney was taken up, that the growing population increased the pressure to settle new areas. It was then that Blaxland, Wentworth and Lawson suddenly found a way across the Blue Mountains. Their route was less than ideal. They'd camped every night in fear of Aboriginal attacks, having been followed (and possibly guided) throughout their journey by indigenous inhabitants long familiar with the paths through the mountains. By the time they reached the ramparts of Mount York, on the western side of the Blue Mountains, their horses were starving because they'd followed the stony ridges rather than the fertile valleys. Necessity forced them to find a way down from the treacherous heights to the Cox's Valley to get the animals enough feed for the return journey. According to Gregory Blaxland's journal: 'They contrived to get their horses down the mountain by cutting a small trench with a hoe, which kept them from slipping, where they again tasted fresh grass for the first time since they left the forest land on the other side of the mountain. They were getting into miserable condition.'

The governor at this time, Lachlan Macquarie, immediately had a road hacked through the mountains by William Cox (from whom Cox's River takes its name) using convict labour. This was the most direct route to the open plains west of the Great Divide, but the Colong Stock Route remained the preferred route for cattle which had, for the most part, found the better-pastured way themselves.

As for the Southern Highlands, after Wilson's expeditions the government actually forbade anyone from going there. It wasn't until 1814 that John and Hamilton Hume explored the area. In 1818 Charles Throsby revisited the area and his reports persuaded Macquarie to open it up for settlement. By then, Wilson was long dead. In reporting his death, Collins remained true to form:

> The natives who inhabit the woods are not by any means so acute as those who live upon the sea coast. This difference may perhaps be accounted for by their sequestered manner of living, society contributing much to the exercise of the mental faculties. Wilson presumed upon this mental inability; and, having imposed himself upon them as their countryman, and created a fear and respect of his superior powers, indulged himself in taking liberties with their young females. However deficient they might be in reasoning faculties, he found to his cost that they were susceptible of wrongs; for, having appropriated against her inclinations a female to his own exclusive accommodation, her friends took an opportunity, when he was not in a condition to defend himself, to drive a spear through his body, which ended his career for this time.

Wilson quickly slid from history's view. Credit for the discovery of the Southern Highlands and the various routes through the mountains went instead to proper English gentlemen more suited to the idealised view of explorers. Nevertheless, Wilson's route to the Southern Highlands is now one of the most heavily trafficked road and rail corridors in Australia, a vital link between its two largest cities, Melbourne and Sydney. The whole of the road route to the Southern Highlands is a high-speed dual lane expressway. By comparison, in many places the Great Western Highway – which follows Blaxland, Wentworth and Lawson's route – is still a single lane in each direction, winding and climbing through steep and difficult terrain.

There are no memorials to John Wilson. There are no cairns on the peaks he ascended. There are no known images of him. History has struggled to reconcile his convict stain with the heroic image of the explorer. Wilson was certainly no angel, but in turning his back on the drudgery mapped out by his English masters he faced the challenge of the Australian bush and became one of the first Europeans to come to terms with it. Rather than dismiss the indigenous population as ignorant savages, he embraced their culture, benefited from their knowledge, and lived and died by their rules. His exploration appears to have been motivated by a genuine curiosity about his adopted home. He was resourceful, a consummate bushman. Many of his qualities are those now prized among the people of the bush and outback. In John Wilson the seeds of the outback spirit can be traced to the very beginnings of European settlement. It was there, in chains, when the anchors of the First Fleet plunged into Sydney Harbour in January 1788.

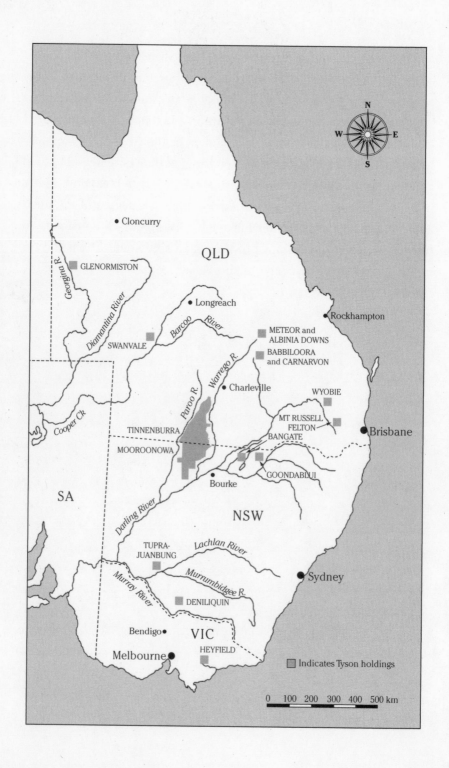

N
W   E
S

• Cloncurry

QLD

Georgina R.

■ GLENORMISTON

Diamantina River

• Longreach

• Rockhampton

Barcoo   *River*

■ SWANVALE

■ METEOR and
ALBINIA DOWNS

■ BABBILOORA
and CARNARVON

Cooper Ck

Paroo R.

Warrego R.

• Charleville

■ WYOBIE

TINNENBURRA

MT RUSSELL
FELTON
BANGATE

■ ● Brisbane

MOOROONOWA

■ ■

SA

■ GOONDABLUI

• Bourke

Darling River

NSW

TUPRA-
JUANBUNG

Lachlan River

■

Murray River

Murrumbidgee R.

● Sydney

■ DENILIQUIN

Bendigo •

VIC

Melbourne ●

■ HEYFIELD

■ Indicates Tyson holdings

0   100   200   300   400   500 km

James Tyson, circa 1890
(John Oxley Library, State Library of Queensland)

2

HUNGRY JIM

James Tyson (1819–1898)

Few kings have origins as humble as James Tyson. The man who would come to be called The Cattle King by some and Hungry Jim by others started life in a rough bush shack at The Cowpastures, the place first discovered by escaped cattle from the First Fleet. He was born on 8 April, 1819, the seventh of eleven children. His mother, Isabella, was a convict transported for theft in 1809. His father, William, worked his passage aboard the same ship. On their arrival, Isabella was 'assigned' to her husband.

Typical of many bush kids, as soon as James Tyson was old enough he went out to work. At age fourteen he was labouring on local properties. In 1837 he got a job working for a bootmaker in Sydney, but the country boy only lasted six months before heading back to the land. As he later recalled, bush life was 'hard work and small wages' but it made a man of him – 188 centimetres tall (just over 6 feet), broad-shouldered and incredibly strong. A full dark beard gave him a handsome, striking presence, the look of a true bushman with the skills to match. Soon he was made an overseer, then a station manager, on properties in southern New South Wales.

By the mid-1840s, while still in his mid-twenties, Tyson was looking to strike out on his own. The inland was opening up as people from around the world realised they could get a foothold on the land that was beyond their reach anywhere else (albeit at a terrible cost to the displaced indigenous population). In 1845 he and his older brother William took up a lease on a property called Bundoolah, near Moulamein between the Murray and Murrumbidgee rivers in southern New South Wales. Unfortunately, at that time prices for wool were down and sheep in the district were stricken with disease. The Tysons' funds were soon exhausted and they lost control of Bundoolah. They may have been down but they weren't out and the following year they were back for another try, this time squatting on land at the junction of the Murrumbidgee and Lachlan rivers.

Toorong, on the outer edge of the settled areas of the colony of New South Wales, was so far 'outback' that parts of it hadn't actually been released by the government for settlement. When it was, the Tysons had to buy out the speculator who successfully tendered for the lease. In the meantime they'd flung up basic bush shacks for William and his family, and two other brothers (John and Peter). The young men started clearing what would become the nucleus of the Tyson holdings.

By all accounts the early years were incredibly tough. The property was extremely isolated, the lack of money a constant worry. Years later, Sidney Kidman recalled Tyson's reminisces of the time: 'He said he was one of the hardest working men in Australia. He drove a mob of bullocks himself. When they lay down to sleep he slept, and when they woke up he did likewise. He took them over the

Blue Mountains to Sydney, and got 25/ a head for the best, and 15/ a head for the others.'

To make extra money, the Tyson boys also drove stock for other land-holders. The brothers are reputed to have also tried their hand at making cheese, which they transported to Sydney twice a year. Stock agent Harry Peck recalled another of Tyson's trips, one that may be more legend than truth:

> He had one shilling to finance the trip, and when he came to the punt at Forbes the river was in flood. The puntman offered to take him across for the shilling when he found that was the extent of the lad's finances, but Jim decided to keep his shilling and swim for it. He did, but nearly lost his life in the crossing. He got the cattle and landed them safely at Juanbung [a later addition to Toorong], a good 500-mile [800-kilometre] journey from there and back, and the shilling still in his pocket. That trip was characteristic of Jim Tyson as a young man, when he denied himself many a necessity in order to save money, and no doubt was the origin of his reputation as a 'possum eater', of which he was not ashamed, for many another good and hard pioneer had eaten possum and, when properly grilled, relished it, too.

Everything changed for the Tyson fortunes in the year 1851. For a couple of decades larger land-holders had been managing to keep the presence of gold deposits on their properties secret, for fear of losing their labourers to a rush. In this they were entirely justified. When gold was 'discovered' at Bathurst, then across New South Wales and Victoria, labourers deserted the countryside and cities become ghost towns as people flocked to make their fortunes.

Out at Toorong, the dramatic shifts in population didn't go unnoticed. At the end of 1851, before gold was found at Bendigo, the population could be counted on one hand. By February 1852, it had exploded to 26500. Some miners struck it rich, others went broke,

but rich and poor had one thing in common: they all had to eat.
The gold strike was 300 kilometres from the Tyson property as the
crow flies, 350 by the shortest route that provided sufficient water
for stock. That distance presented no difficulties for a family that had
been crisscrossing the outback for years. They mustered all the fat
cattle they could find and headed for the goldfields. They arrived in
the middle of the year.

There James Tyson and his brothers did something inspired.
Instead of simply selling the cattle to the local butchers and heading
back to the farm, they set up their own slaughter yard and butchering
business and sold their beef directly to the miners. It was a business
model that 150 years later would be termed 'vertical integration'.
Back then, the idea proved such a goldmine their business became
known as Tyson's Reef (a cafe in the town still bears the name).

Even before they'd run out of their own cattle, the Tyson boys
were scouring the surrounding districts and buying cattle from anyone who'd sell. Kidman recalled: 'They bought cattle for about £2,
and got £20 a head for them.' Eventually, the boys were ranging
as far away as Queensland, buying stock and droving them back to
the goldfields. It took great skill and involved considerable risk to
move cattle such long distances and have them arrive in good enough
condition to sell, but it was worth it. By 1855 the highly profitable
business had made the whole family a fortune.

It was then that the canny Tysons made yet another extraordinary
move. They put the business on the market. It was a bit like selling
the goose that laid the golden egg, but the brothers knew enough
about gold strikes to understand that sooner or later the gold would
run out and the miners would move on. Rather than watch their business slowly decline, they sold at the top of the market. Estimates of
the price paid for Tyson's Reef range from £80 000 (as much as $10
million in present values) to suggestions that James Tyson's share
alone was £200 000. No matter what the figure, when added to what

they'd earned over the preceding years, all the Tyson boys were now extremely wealthy.

A lot of people might have retired at that point or gone back to their property to enjoy the comforts of life. Instead, James and John Tyson bought three run-down sheep stations that had contributed to the ruin of the mercurial entrepreneur Ben Boyd (his ambitious plans to develop the harbour at Eden, on the New South Wales south coast, hadn't done him any good either). The properties were South Deniliquin, Deniliquin and Conargo – all located around the present-day town of Deniliquin.

The brothers set about developing the properties with extensive irrigation works, which they could easily fund with their now considerable capital reserves. Massive channels were dug, possibly by Chinese labourers who were starting to look for work as the gold diggings began to wane. Dams were built on the watercourses, to capture water for diversion to the properties' dry backblocks. The works increased the amount of useable land by extending the areas where sheep could graze and still be within range of water.

Such pioneering irrigation works, which became widespread in the late 1850s and the 1860s, soon generated animosity among landholders downstream who saw their water sources thus diverted. Angry meetings were held. On some dark nights dams were attacked and breached. The essence of the controversy, water rights, is still hotly debated today.

The Tyson brothers also pioneered construction of water storages (called tanks) to capture the runoff from rain, and considered the possibilities of drilling wells to find artesian or other underground water sources. It didn't take long to realise that land without river frontage could still be developed to carry stock, effectively raising the value of their properties (and those of other land-holders).

James Tyson's fortunes received another boost with the untimely death of his brother in 1860. John, single like James, left nearly everything to his brother, virtually doubling overnight his already considerable wealth. Tyson decided to consolidate. He sold the Deniliquin properties and concentrated his efforts on irrigating the original Toorong property that had been expanded by the acquisition of adjacent properties to form Tupra-Juanbung, a station that bestrode the Lachlan and Murrumbidgee rivers and extended over more than half a million acres (200 000 hectares).

By now in his early forties, Tyson was one of the most eligible bachelors in the country – tall, handsome, healthy and incredibly wealthy. Several of his other siblings had already married and were raising families of their own. Tyson, who had spent almost all of his life in the bush, remained single. It may not have been because he never found the right woman. One story that Tyson apparently repeated throughout his life was recalled by stock agent Harry Peck in his memoirs. Tyson was on a train trip with a group of stock agents when he recounted meeting 'one of the finest women he had ever set eyes on' at a wayside shanty perched on a hill in the upper Murrumbidgee, where he was buying cattle for the Bendigo market:

His description was one of those rare occasions on which he came out of his shell and fairly let himself go. She was his ideal woman, tall, clear eyed, rosy cheeked, the embodiment of blooming health and constitution. The agents, who had met him for the first time, listened with surprise as they had always thought him to be 'a woman hater', but [stock agent] Tom Mates, irrepressible as usual, and who would not have been abashed in the presence of an Emperor, said: 'Well, Mr Tyson, I have always heard that you never tasted alcohol, smoked tobacco or kissed a woman in your life, but what about that lass at the top of the hill? I guess you relaxed your rule in the third degree that time.' Tyson made no reply and, treating the question with contempt, went right back into his shell.

Tyson appears to have been genuinely smitten, but like many out-back men, who often outnumbered women by more than four to one, he may have been too socially inexperienced to begin courting her. However, while in his later years he held some extraordinary ideas about women, including their use as breeding stock, he is also noted as being respectful around women and always proper in his dealing with them as his employees. And he appears to have been a model uncle to his growing number of nieces.

In the place of marriage and family life, Tyson focussed his entire attention on his business – acquiring and developing cattle and sheep properties. Key among his acquisitions was the property Hey-field, in Victoria's Gippsland. The initial purchase, in 1865, was 8000 hectares. It was such prime grazing country that Tyson declared, 'Heyfield can fatten anything.' However, he got the property cheap because the roads to Gippsland, across the southern flanks of the Great Dividing Range, were extremely poor. Nevertheless he now had two good properties where he could fatten cattle for the rapidly expanding Melbourne market. Now what he needed was a source of cattle needing to be fattened. His eyes turned to Queensland.

In later years poet Banjo Paterson would sing the praises of Queensland's 'sunlit plains extended' but when Tyson started buy-ing land along the Warrego River in the mid-1860s, the plains had plenty of sunshine but not much else. They lacked the vital ingredi-ent – water. But Tyson had a plan.

Once he'd established himself along the Warrego, he started acquiring holdings out on the sunlit plains. Next he hired bore con-tractors and sank wells. Wherever he struck water, he stocked the backblocks. As with his earlier successes, the idea sounds simple. All Tyson had to do was apply the lessons learned from his irrigation of the backblocks of Tupra-Juanbung, and before that at Deniliquin.

The big difference was the scale of his plans. In 1868 Tyson held 13 000 hectares along the Warrego. Over the next decade hardly a year went by without him acquiring blocks ranging from 36000 hectares to 500000 hectares on the Queensland and New South Wales sides of the border. By 1879 he had created a super-station along the Warrego that covered over a million hectares.

It was easily the biggest station Australia had ever seen. It was known on the New South Wales border as Mooroonowa, but the Queensland property gave the vast complex the name that has become part of legend, Tinnenburra. Everything about the place, which primarily bred cattle but also carried sheep, was big. The shearing shed was the biggest in the country. Sidney Kidman (who eventually created the 2.2 million-hectare Anna Creek station in South Australia, still the world's largest) noted: 'His huge station used to run right down to Brewarrina in New South Wales on the Bourke Road. He put up a fence about 140 miles [224 kilometres] long to keep the wild horses off the Warrego, and left gaps in it in order to lead the cattle through to water.'

Harry Peck recalled:

On Tinnenburra, which extended from the Warrego on the east to the Parroo on the west, musterings, owing to seasonal conditions and the great area of the place, were sometimes very incomplete. The result was that often old bullocks up to 10 to 15 years old, which had perhaps never been mustered since they were branded as calves and had become very wild and 'real old pikers', were sent down to Heyfield to fatten. The Heyfield managers regularly protested but in vain, for the 'Old Gentleman' always replied, 'Heyfield can fatten anything.' He was about right, for in those days [stock auctioneers] T.K. Bennett and John Woolcock fought each other keenly for the heaviest prime bullocks at Newmarket [the Melbourne saleyards until 1987]. The big weighty extra prime TY1 brand Tinnenburra-bred bullocks from Heyfield, loading only eight to the big truck, often averaging 1000 to 1200 lb. [450–550 kilograms], and constantly topping the market, were

bullocks to conjure with, and a great pleasure and pride for any auc-
tioneer to sell.

Tinnenburra was also considered to be one of the best irrigated stations in the country. During an interview he gave in 1893, Tyson
offered a journalist from the *Brisbane Courier* a drink of water. 'This
is a sample from the ninth bore just put down on my Tinnenburra
run,' he explained, 'which was previously destitute of surface water.
It is beautifully soft water, and the bore yields between three and
four million gallons a day . . . I have spent a great many thousands of
pounds on these bores, but must spend a great deal more in distributing the water over the run to utilise all the grass of the country.'

Big as it was, Tinnenburra wasn't Tyson's only acquisition. Between
1867 and 1872, he also bought land and took up leases on what
became the Queensland properties Felton and Mount Russell, in the
lush Darling Downs, which he used to fatten cattle for the nearby
Brisbane market. Numerous other properties in New South Wales
and Queensland were added to his holdings, some of them when
their owners defaulted on loans that Tyson had given them.

There are suggestions Tyson used debt as a means to get hold of
properties cheaply. It wasn't that simple. It's more likely Tyson's initial motivation was to help out a neighbour or friend. As Harry Peck
wrote:

On one occasion, when making a search through old papers left on one
of his stations, the manager and I came across a number of cheque
butts of the '60s and '70s, and were surprised at the number of loans
they represented to well-known station holders. Amounts ran up to
tens of thousands each, and at interest generally around 7 and 8 per
cent. Apparently many of such loans were without security, as memos
on the butts simply read, "Lent to Mr. So-and-So at so much per cent.,
to be repaid by proceeds of fat stock or wool".

The problem, according to Peck, was that 'once Tyson lent money on a property luck seemed to desert it and bad seasons set in until he took over, when the hoodoo would lift'. In reality, Tyson sometimes found himself holding properties abandoned by their owners because they couldn't generate any income.

As he pointed out in 1893: 'The Glen Ormiston run [in far-western Queensland, now Glenormiston] has given me no return whatever for five years . . . Another northern station has never paid me a penny; of course they are not all so; I have so many stations in all the colonies that some of them are always paying. The several Governments of Australia get from £18 000 to £20 000 a year from me in rents.'

Those same governments had Tyson in their sights. From the early 1860s onwards, state governments passed legislation aimed at giving small selectors access to the land as well. In some circumstances it allowed them to apply for selections on unimproved leasehold land (unfenced, unwatered, without buildings), even if it formed part of an existing station. Unfortunately, the effect was often to encourage speculators who took up selections purely in order to disrupt a station's operations.

Tyson complained of the New South Wales' Robertson Act of 1861: 'It made selectors for the purpose of plunder, and not for founding homes or developing the land. Fancy selectors taking up areas between the squatter's homestead and his run for the purpose of cutting him off from his country and compelling him to pay blackmail by buying the selections at a high price!'

Despite his reservations, Tyson still supported the idea in principle, in part because the small selections provided a source of workers. Indeed, many of his managers had their selections around his larger runs. Others trained on his stations before going on to build their own, just as he'd done in the 1840s. He actually went as far, according to the *Brisbane Courier*, 'as to advocate that river and creek frontages should be held by farmers and small graziers, leaving the back lands to the capitalists who can sink for artesian water and make surface reservoirs'.

The growth of Tyson's empire also gave him a public profile. He was dubbed by newspapers The Cattle King, the first time that title had been applied to anyone, let alone the son of a convict mother, born and raised in Australia. However, the convict stain and the disparaging 'possum-eater' reference also remained. As the years passed, Tyson's voracious appetite for land led to *The Bulletin* giving him a new title: Hungry Jim. Given his early years of struggle and hardship, it may have been more appropriate than *The Bulletin* intended.

Great wealth doesn't seem to have changed Tyson's way of life. Kidman recalled travelling with Tyson (unlike many absentee landlords he was still riding around his properties while in his seventies) during the strikes of 1891: 'He used to wear a beautiful big gold watch-chain – a bootlace. I do not care what they say about Tyson, I like him. He was a very reserved and humble man. Tyson arrived at Glenormiston station in Queensland one day, and asked the manager's wife where her husband was. She replied that he would not be back for a day or two, and he said, 'When he returns tell him Tyson is here, and that he is down the creek.' That was nothing unusual for him. I was once at a beautiful place, 40 miles [60 kilometres] from Mount Kosciusko, and the woman there asked me if I had ever met Mr Tyson. She said he had stayed there but had slept outside. There was plenty of hot water at the house, but Tyson said he always washed in the creek as the sand cleaned his hands better than soap.'

Kidman also noted Tyson's complaints about endless approaches from people asking for donations. He'd been supporting his mother for years and helping out various relatives (usually with jobs or loans rather than cash handouts) but the world believed he had a duty to it as well. Here, Tyson could get prickly. Asked for a donation to construct a church on the Darling Downs, he paid the full amount. Then it was realised they'd forgotten a lightning conductor. The priest went back to Tyson to ask for another donation. 'No,' came the answer. 'If God thinks proper to strike the church with lightning, I am not going to attempt to interfere.' Another priest, from a parish near Heyfield, got a 5 pound donation with a note: 'I think if you would use as much starch on your congregation as you do soft soap, you have a fair chance of getting all you want without applying to outside sources for support.'

For some recipients of the Tyson largesse, it must have been hard to bank the cheque. In 1890 he was asked to help establish a women's college at Sydney University. His response:

> I very much doubt whether any good can be done by educating women upwards seeing we have too much Frills and Starch amongst them now. Women should be educated up to be useful to assist their husbands and children rather than spending their husbands' resources in worthless trinkets and wasting their time in shopping. However as I feel assured your intentions are honourable and pure in the interest of your sex, I send you my cheque on the Commercial Bank for One hundred pounds with the condition that the name of the donor is not to be revealed.

Tyson's preference that his donations be kept anonymous means the extent of his philanthropy, or lack of it, will never be known. However, his greatest charitable act was impossible to hide. In 1892 he bailed out the state of Queensland. At the time the colony was riddled with land speculators. They borrowed to pay inflated prices, but when the bubble burst, as it did in other states at the same time, the slew of loan defaults threatened to topple the banks that had done the financing. In Queensland, that included the Bank of Queensland. As the state bank teetered on the brink, innocent account holders faced ruin until Tyson stepped in and bought £250000 worth of government bonds. It wasn't a gift, but at an interest rate of between

4 and 6 per cent (sources vary on the figure), it kept the bank, the government and state afloat.

The following year a grateful government appointed Tyson to the Legislative Council. He reputedly made only one speech, and an unremarkable one at that. Apparently he preferred to lecture the government in private or in writing. He held little back in expressing his opinions on matters that were in his area of expertise or which affected his interests. This included land bills, the taxes charged on moving cattle over state borders and the charges for transporting stock by rail. He was a strong supporter of Federation, which would remove trade barriers between states.

Many of the border taxes and freight charges deliberately targeted men like Tyson, who had succeeded on the land, while protecting those who were failing. It didn't matter to governments that Tyson had established a chain of stations that efficiently supplied cattle from Tinnenburra to the tables of Sydney, Melbourne and Brisbane. His management practices were so advanced that he had stock weighed as they left Tinnenburra and when they arrived at market. He found, as expected, that stock sent on the hoof (relatively cheaply) lost far more condition than those sent by rail. However, by comparing the prices equivalent Tinnenburra cattle got when they reached the market, he was able to work out which form of transport gave the best return. Depending on the level of the charges, it was generally better on the stock and his hip pocket if they went by rail. Droving cattle may have romantic connotations, but long before motor vehicles and the trucking of cattle all but wiped out droving (in the 1920s), Tyson realised its days were numbered.

Tyson's acute intellect was just as sharp when it came to his managers, even if they were relatives. In a letter to a nephew, William Tyson III, regarding William's purchase of sheep at too high a price, Tyson wrote:

I have to call your attention to the fact that you had no authority from me to use my money in the purchase of a thing you don't understand. Ram-breeders are an able lot to deal with generally and an expert in the trade would have little difficulty in palming off their greatest trash to a greenhorn like you. The fact is you get into a hotel amongst thimble riggers, sharps and card shufflers and like to hear yourself talk largely . . . in exposing your weakness in company with any such people I don't see you had any right to go to the length of buying rams.

He may have been tough on his staff, but it appears he was also fair. He asked a lot of them, but when they delivered, he rewarded their efforts. Bonuses often followed hard on the hooves of a successful droving trip. While the 1890s were characterised by confrontations between employers and employees (particularly miners and shearers) that led to the rise of the Australian Labor Party, the Tyson properties saw few disputes. Tyson also had a high regard for Aboriginal people, whom he employed on his stations, and there is some evidence he respected their traditional rights to the lands he leased. The Wiradjuri people, for instance, appeared to have remained on Juanbung and were sufficiently well treated that they formed a guard of honour when his brother Charles died in 1884.

By then, though, Tyson had seen and done it all. During a boom, a colleague reputedly said to him: 'I don't hear of you running around like so many just now on the buy, and you must have lots of feed to spare.' Tyson answered: 'When others run, I walk.' On another occasion, the view was expressed to him that the country was going to the dogs. 'I have heard that lament many times in my life,' he said, 'but I haven't yet heard them barking.'

In his final years, when asked about his great wealth, he tended to dismiss it with a few words. 'I'm happiest under the stars of heaven, with a bluey for my pillow, and a billy of tea by my side.' He was telling the truth. It's another Tyson legend that at his final home, Felton

on the Darling Downs, his tea was always served on the sideboard in
a billy. His housekeeper tried serving his tea in a pot with a tea cosy,
but a lifetime of bush living meant he wasn't used to tea piping hot.
He burnt his mouth. He asked her to go back to the billy, but she per-
sisted. When he burnt his mouth again, he threw the pot and cosy out
the window, got his old billy back and enjoyed 'tea as it should be'.

Tyson's love of the outback ran deep. In the rare interview he gave
the *Brisbane Courier*, he opened his heart. Not for him the nostalgia
of 'home' and Mother England; he was Australian-born and proud
of it:

> Our dry, pure, rarefied air, our genial sun, and our boundless space
> combine to promote the development of animal life in its most vigorous
> and perfect forms. The rather scanty rainfall, with the almost incessant
> sunshine, produces sweet and nutritious grasses and herbage such as
> are found in no other part of the world to my knowledge. Even the
> physical health of the animal is conserved as its natural functions are
> stimulated by the great expanse of country usually in the line of vision.
> Body and mind are both cultivated through the eye . . .
>
> The men of Central Australia will be among the picked men of the
> world, physically and mentally; the horses will be the fleetest and most
> enduring; the cattle and sheep yield the most tender, succulent and
> toothsome meat. England is little more than a manure heap whose soil
> is poisoned by the animal droppings of centuries, and whose vegeta-
> tion is at least less wholesome for stock than the health-giving native
> grasses of inland Australia, whose pastures are constantly purified by
> a tropical sun and occasionally renovated by bush fires.

That last sentence might explain why Tyson never received a knight-
hood. Certainly men with smaller holdings who did less for the
pastoral industry and their state got honours, but the real reason
may be that none of them had Tyson's past. He was still the son of

a convict and the disgrace of the convict stain didn't fade with the passing of the years or the accumulation of wealth. It probably didn't matter to Tyson.

In November 1898, approaching his eightieth birthday, Tyson was taken ill at Felton. His manager reputedly took him in a buggy to see the doctor in nearby Pittsworth, but along the road Tyson roused himself and asked where they were going. When the manager told him, Tyson replied, 'Pull up and drive back home; I have never consulted a doctor in my life and am not going to do so now.'

Back at Felton, his illness continued for the next fortnight, Tyson still refusing to see a doctor. He was in the habit of rising early, but on the night of 3 December he told a servant he might get up a little later the next morning. He still wasn't up when his manager came in for breakfast. A check of his room revealed he had died in his sleep.

Tyson's fame ensured a great deal of media comment after his death. Most newspapers referred to him as 'eccentric'. His most vehement critics went much further. *The Bulletin*'s obituary was the most damning of all:

Hungry Jimmy and his millions have focused Australian eyes for a quarter-century; and now the earth which he grabbed has grabbed him, and given 7ft. × 4ft. in exchange for odd hundreds of square miles. As the old man apparently died intestate, the addition and division of his property among scores of heirs and heiresses – chiefly nephews and nieces – will keep the interest lively for quite a while. If Tyson had owned a sense of humor, he might have supplied a secret marriage and a thunderbolt of a buxom wife to help things; but he wasn't built that romantic way. Probably Tyson was the only natural-born Australian over 12 years old who never hugged a woman in his life; anyway, the woman who can say Tyson hugged her hasn't been found at date of writing. The only goddess he ever adored was Diva Moneta; and to her he clove faithfully. His money may have made him happy; but he never looked like it. Tyson never smoked – 'couldn't afford it'; but, when travelling, he always patronised the smoking compartment, where petticoats couldn't hurt him . . .

He 'couldn't afford' marriage either. He 'couldn't afford' liquor, or theatres, or society, or a bit on the Melbourne Cup, or any of the things that the ordinary £200-a-year person takes his pleasure in. He was like the high-class Maori chief who thoughtfully chopped off his toes in order to get his fine new European boots on. Tyson lopped his passion, and smothered that appetite, and sacrificed yonder human satisfaction; but he made money. Six foot and a bit he was; but a pretty stunted specimen of humanity all the same, Bulletin reckons. He died so much while he lived that it's no wonder he wouldn't let a doctor try and deprive him of the economy of being dead altogether. But he made money – or gathered dead leaves – there was no difference. In his daily life, and in a small way, Tyson was a mean man – he gave nothing for nothing; but occasionally he could be generous in a large way – that is, as he grew older he gave away considerable sums, and knew himself as rich as he was before. The widow who gave her mite was more generous. Just, Tyson was, but hard. 'He assisted Queensland by purchasing £250000 Treasury Bills' – at a safe 4 per cent. They made him a Q. Legislative Councillor (it meant free rail travelling); and he was merely another nominee nonentity. Grit, industry – these were his virtues; and in reclaiming land and breeding stock he helped others, but his chief end was to help himself. Many a millionaire has made money to spend in noble actions: Tyson made money to keep it – and he kept it as long as ever he could. There is need of such men to enforce the gospel of work in this country of shirk; and Tyson's was not a bad life. But, considering his powers and opportunities, how far from the best!

Other publications protested his virtues. The *Brisbane Courier*, which got closer to him during his life than any other newspaper, admitted his attitude to money was unconventional, but given he had acquired more of it than almost anyone else, who could say it wasn't the right one. During his life there were plenty of people telling stories about Tyson refusing to help them. It was only after his death that stories about Tyson's often anonymous donations (including those mentioned above) started circulating, and the picture of the man gradually shifted.

Eventually, his pioneering qualities were recognised. His irrigation projects, the vertical integration of his operations and his realisation that rail transport was easier on stock than droving were years ahead of their time. His profound understanding of conditions in the outback, love of the bush and resourcefulness in dealing with its challenges typified the outback pioneer spirit. His efforts to nurture similar qualities in the people who worked for him meant that they were much sought after once they left his employment. Most of them didn't leave until after he died. Many went on to manage Kidman properties. As for his generosity, the shy old bushman tried to keep it hidden but it was not to be. Shortly after Tyson's death, Banjo Paterson, an occasional contributor to *The Bulletin*, wrote a poem for the *Australasian Pastoralists Review*, 'T.Y.S.O.N.'. It concludes:

> But in that last great drafting-yard,
> Where Peter keeps the gate,
> And souls of sinners find it barred,
> And go to meet their fate,
> There's one who ought to enter in,
> For good deeds done on earth;
> Such deeds as merit ought to win,
> Kind deeds of sterling worth.
> Not by the strait and narrow gate,
> Reserved for wealthy men,
> But through the big gate, opened wide,
> The grizzled figure, eagle-eyed,

Will travel through – and then
Old Peter'll say: 'Let's pass him through;
There's many a thing he used to do,
Good-hearted things that no one knew;
That's T.Y.S.O.N.'

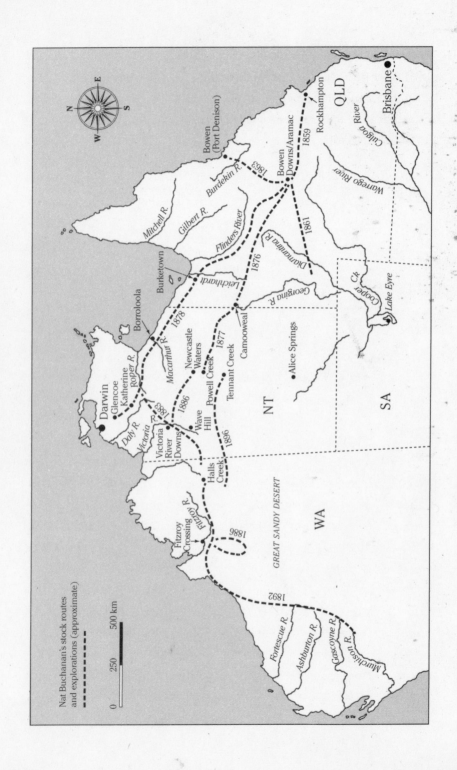

Nat Buchanan's stock routes
and explorations (approximate)

0   250   500 km

N
W — E
S

Darwin
Glencoe
Katherine
Roper R.
Borroloola
Daly R.
Victoria R.
Victoria
River
Downs
Wave
Hill
Halls
Creek
Fitzroy
Crossing
Fitzroy R.
Newcastle
Waters
Macarthur R.
Powell Creek
Tennant Creek
Camooweal
Alice Springs
Burketown
Mitchell R.
Gilbert R.
Flinders River
Burdekin R.
Bowen
(Port Denison)
Bowen
Downs/Aramac
Rockhampton
Brisbane
Leichhardt R.
Diamantina R.
Georgina R.
Cooper Ck
Lake Eyre
Warrego River
Culgoa River

GREAT SANDY DESERT

Fortescue R.
Ashburton R.
Gascoyne R.
Murchison R.

QLD
NT
SA
WA

1859
1861
1863
1876
1877
1878
1886
1888
1891
1892
1896

Nat Buchanan, circa 1863
(John Oxley Library, State Library of Queensland)

3

OLD BLUEY

Nat Buchanan (1826–1901)

It's hard to imagine how anything in Nat Buchanan's early years could have prepared him for his future life as the greatest drover the Australian outback has ever seen. He was born in Ireland in 1826, the Emerald Isle's forty shades of green as far from the red sandhills and bone-dry gibber plains of the bush as it's possible to get. Even after he arrived in Australia with his parents and four brothers aboard the *Statesman* in January 1837, their move to the well-watered pastures of the aptly named New England Plateau of New South Wales was a gentle introduction to the harsh conditions of the Australian bush.

In his twenties, after a foray to the California goldfields in 1849 with his brothers Andrew and Frank failed to make their fortunes, Buchanan took to the road. He worked droving cattle to the New South Wales and Victorian goldfields, always hungry for the opportunity that would set him up on the land. He had plenty of competition. Good land was being seized by speculators and squatters. He eventually realised the only option, as James Tyson had found just a few years earlier, was to go 'run hunting' and head 'further out'.

In 1859, with the explorer William Landsborough, he set off from Rockhampton, on the coast of Queensland, to examine inland possibilities for raising stock. The men penetrated more than 400 kilometres to the present-day Thomson River and the site of what would become the town of Aramac, where they found superb downs country that a succession of good seasons had given the appearance of being well watered. Encouraged by what they found, they pressed on until they were running critically low on rations. As the food gave out, they reputedly resorted to eating the greenhide hobbles they'd been using to restrict their horses' movements at night. They put them on to boil when they went to bed at night, reducing them to a chewy jelly by morning.

There was little question as to who was the more capable navigator. According to a series of articles written by Buchanan's son, Gordon, in *The Sydney Stock and Station Journal* (later compiled in the book *Packhorse and Waterhole*), Buchanan's natural ability was akin to that of a homing pigeon. 'Landsborough on the other hand was in this respect very ordinary. Probably he could not "get lost" in a forty acre [16 hectare] paddock, but some of the paddocks now in Queensland would, without a compass, be enough to "bush" him. He, however, could stand almost any hardship, and was brave and cheerful withal.'

Buchanan got the party back to the coast and returned in 1861 with a land speculator, Edward Cornish, who agreed that the land around Aramac was perfect for sheep. With Cornish, they pressed on across the downs to see how far they extended. They reached the Diamantina River and found fresh tracks which, they realised, had been made by the Burke and Wills expedition. The explorers had been the first through the region little more than a month ahead of the 'run hunters'.

On Buchanan and Cornish's return, leases covering almost 3000 square kilometres of what was to become Bowen Downs station were taken up by a consortium comprising Landsborough, Cornish, Buchanan and the financiers of the Scottish Australian Investment Company, led by Robert Morehead. In 1863 Buchanan was appointed the station's manager. His first job was to drove thousands of sheep from properties in southern Queensland up to the vast new station. He also blazed a new stock route from present-day Bowen, then Port Denison, 483 kilometres inland. When that stock route is considered alongside his previous journey from Bowen Downs to the Diamantina, at that point he'd personally pioneered from the coast of Queensland across the state to the Northern Territory border (it was still part of South Australia at the time). Buchanan had no way of knowing, but that was just the beginning.

There are few instances of Buchanan having any trouble with the indigenous inhabitants whose lands he crossed during his early expeditions. It's thought the reasons were that he had some knowledge and respect of their customs, stayed calm when there were confrontations and tried to be fair in his dealings with them. He was also careful about how he set up his camps. If he was alone or in a small group, he'd stop for the evening meal then move on after nightfall, making his new camp harder to find in the dark.

He also had a habit of telling new men harrowing tales of what had happened to stockmen who'd nodded off during their night watches. They were sufficiently bloodcurdling to leave his audience spending most nights jumping at the slightest sound, whether they were on watch or not. Buchanan, meanwhile, slept soundly.

Despite his care and his warnings, there were still clashes. On the first trip to stock Bowen Downs, Buchanan was scouting for water and the next day's camp site when a group of Aborigines (their bodies painted in what some of the drovers thought was 'war paint') appeared near the evening camp. They showed no signs of hostility, but as they approached some of the drovers panicked and opened fire. The rest, probably mindful that Buchanan had admonished them not to shoot Aboriginal people unless provoked, held back. As the shooting continued and the others shouted for help, everyone joined in. How many Aborigines were shot isn't known.

Buchanan's son later wrote that his father believed the shooting was justified. There's no record of the consequences for those involved, but it was typical of incidents that poisoned relations between Europeans and Aboriginal people. The idea that the indigenous inhabitants had a claim to the country and a right to defend what was theirs never entered most Europeans' minds. Massacres of Europeans at central Queensland properties (notably Cullen-La-Ringo in 1861 when nineteen were killed) had led to reprisals and the establishment of the Queensland Native Police Force (in 1848), whose members often hunted their own kind ruthlessly or were forced to do so by their European superiors.

In 1863 Buchanan married Kate Gordon, the daughter of a grazier with properties in northern New South Wales and Queensland. He was sixteen years her senior. Kate had grown up on the land and could ride as well as any man. She was no stranger to the hardships of the bush, but even she must have been daunted by the prospect of following her husband to the isolation of newly established Bowen Downs. When she arrived she was the only white woman on the only property for hundreds of kilometres.

When he was not droving stock from the south to build up the flocks and herds of Bowen Downs, Buchanan continued roving north and west, spying out new country with potential for stock. His old exploring companion, William Landsborough, had identified country between Bowen Downs and the Gulf of Carpentaria as being particularly promising, and the Scottish Australian Investment Company had taken up leases on a block known simply as The Paddock, between the Albert and Nicholson rivers. Like other speculators, they hadn't done anything with them, but that changed in 1864. News came that another syndicate was on the road with stock bound for the Gulf Country, and Bowen Downs was alerted to beat them to it.

Buchanan set off with a droving plant and as many as 2000 head of cattle, pioneering a new stock route north along the Flinders River. He got there first, establishing the first stage of what would become known as the Old Gulf Track to the Northern Territory.

Amid the feverish activity of stocking stations, Kate Buchanan discovered she was pregnant. When she was nearing full term she moved back to the coast, to her father's station near Gladstone, where she gave birth to Gordon Buchanan on 29 May, 1864. When mother and child were well enough to travel, they returned to the isolation, dangers and hardships of Bowen Downs. How Kate dealt with the challenges of being a new mother – far from the support of more experienced women and any hope of medical support – can only be imagined. Like many outback women, she didn't have time to write her experiences down. Yet the proof of her resourcefulness and courage was her child – the youngster thrived.

Unfortunately, Gordon was about the only successful Buchanan venture on the station. Drought and falling prices saw Bowen Downs fall deeper and deeper into debt. Up at The Paddock, neither stock nor men did well, succumbing to disease and bad seasons. In 1866 the price for cattle and wool fell to ruinous levels, just as it was time to renegotiate the agreement between the partners in Bowen Downs. By then the station had debts of £14000. For members of the consortium who'd had very little capital to begin with, it was more than they could afford. As Gordon Buchanan later put it:

The men who did the pioneering and bore the heat and burden of the day [Landsborough, Cornish and Buchanan], went out without a penny.

The sleeping partners, city men, managed to hold on and eventually, as shareholders in one of the most prosperous pastoral holdings in Australia, reaped a rich harvest.

It was a terrible blow to the men who had built the station from nothing. Edward Cornish caught 'gulf fever' (a form of dengue fever) soon after and died despite desperate efforts to save his life. Buchanan took almost a decade to recover from the loss of Bowen Downs. He went farming with his brother Andrew on a small selection in the mountainous country along the Bellinger River in New South Wales. When that didn't work out he moved on to a mining venture.

Bad seasons plagued central Queensland and the north-west until the mid-1870s, when Buchanan was offered a job managing Craven station on the rich volcanic plains near Emerald. The job brought him back to the country of far horizons. As the seasons improved he was soon in demand as a pilot and head drover for mobs of cattle and sheep heading for new pastures in western Queensland. In late 1875 he was engaged by a Melbourne investor, Benjamin Crossthwaite, to pilot a mob of cattle to Rocklands station, on the head of the Georgina River, near Camooweal on the Northern Territory–Queensland border.

Once again, the work gave him the opportunity to explore the country farther afield. Buchanan was particularly interested in the country on the Northern Territory side of the border, where land could be leased without having to stock it for three years. In his journeys he may have been accompanied solely by a young Aboriginal man from the Gulf, known only as Jimmy. The two men reputedly could match each other for endurance, especially when it came to going without water. Throughout his life, when other Europeans were desperately thirsty, Buchanan could get by with just a mouthful.

He could also make do with rations that were well past their use-by date. He was once observed sieving weevils out of his flour. When it was suggested the flour was rotten, he simply replied, 'Oh, it's not too bad while these things can find nutriment in it.'

It may have been on one of these exploratory trips that Buchanan had a challenging encounter with the Aborigines of the region. He was fishing when he saw the reflection of a warrior creeping towards him. Buchanan didn't look up and tried to appear calm while he frantically tried to think what to do. Just then, he got a bite. As Buchanan reeled in the fish, the Aborigine hesitated; perhaps realising he might be able to kill two birds with one spear. When he landed the fish, Buchanan finally looked up into his assailant's eyes. He offered the man his catch. It was accepted and the crisis passed.

Buchanan's explorations led him to the Barkly Tableland, which offered superbly grassed country but suffered from the perennial problem of a shortage of water. Men had perished trying to cross it from Queensland to the Overland Telegraph Line (that had been run from Adelaide to Darwin in the early 1870s). Buchanan believed he could get through.

With fellow drover Sam Croker, and either a young Aborigine (probably Jimmy) or a man named Tetley, he left Rocklands on 10 October, 1877, and headed north-west across the border. For the first 200 kilometres they found themselves on wide, grassy, treeless plains with numerous creeks that flowed east towards the Georgina River. Then they came upon a watercourse that is still known as Buchanan's Creek, which took them west for another 50 kilometres before it spread out over a fertile flood plain with abundant birdlife.

Beyond the flood plain was what is now known as Attack Creek (so named after a later incident not involving Buchanan). Then came a 50-kilometre dry stretch. Here the explorers were heartened when, after nightfall, they noticed Aboriginal campfires burning not far away. The next morning they approached an Aboriginal camp. The people they encountered had never seen Europeans or their horses, yet despite their initial nervousness and the language barrier,

Buchanan and the others managed to communicate their need for
water. The Aborigines showed them to their wells and let them and
their horses drink.

The men were soon on their way but only 10 kilometres further
on, to their great satisfaction, they came upon the Overland Telegraph Line. They were near Powell Creek, 180 kilometres north of
present-day Tennant Creek. The telegraph operators in this extremely
isolated location were astounded when the tiny party emerged from
the bush and told them they'd just become the first to successfully
cross the Barkly Tableland. Unfortunately, the biggest surprise was
in store for Buchanan.

He'd just discovered good water supplies spread across rich grazing land and immediately sent a telegram seeking to secure leases
over it. He was the first white man to set on eyes on the place, but
the message came back that it was almost all gone. Speculators had
leased most of the best of it, snatching at blank spaces on the map
from their offices in the cities. The leases didn't have to be stocked
for three years, which meant they cost almost nothing to acquire,
while they could be sold and resold generating profits through pure
speculation. Buchanan eventually managed to lease an area that was
well grassed but poorly watered. He later sold the property which
nevertheless became known as Buchanan Downs.

The trail he blazed across the Barkly eventually became known as
the Barkly Stock Route. It wasn't much used to begin with because
the water sources weren't sufficient for large numbers of stock. Eventually bores were sunk in the early years of the twentieth century,
allowing its full potential to be realised. Until that happened, the preferred route to the Northern Territory was Buchanan's next great
achievement.

At the beginning of 1878 he was asked to take 1200 cattle from
Aramac station, near Bowen Downs in central Queensland, to Glencoe station, just south of present-day Darwin. It was a journey of

2250 kilometres, 1600 of them through trackless wilderness. No one had attempted anything like it before. The explorer Leichhardt had pioneered the route on one of his expeditions in the 1840s. Only two small mobs of cattle and one mob of horses had followed, and that had been years before Buchanan's proposed trip.

Buchanan's droving plant consisted of three drays carrying supplies for twelve months. They were the first vehicles to attempt the route, which meant he would have to make cuttings in riverbanks at suitable crossing points. He had to make sure there were no obstacles the drays couldn't negotiate. So blazing a new stock route meant all but building a road. This had to be done while scouting camps and water sources at intervals of 10 to 20 kilometres, so the cattle could have easy stages to travel each day.

With Kate's brothers, Hugh and Wattie Gordon, plus a cook, a nephew of one of the cattle owners, two other drovers and an Aborigine named Harry, they left Aramac in April 1878. Buchanan followed the track to the Gulf that he'd pioneered in 1864 then turned west, crossing Barkly Creek, Beames Brook and the Gregory River. From there they followed the Nicholson River to Turn Off Lagoon, 100 kilometres east of the Northern Territory border. Now the route turned north-west, passing the last Queensland station, Westmoreland. From this point they were on their own.

Buchanan quickly established the daily routine. Every morning he set off ahead of the drovers and passed the site he'd selected the day before for that night's camp (while leaving clear tracks for the stockmen to follow). He then started scouting for the following night's camp site. Every day he rode between 30 and 50 kilometres, before returning around nightfall to the new camp. Finding the camp in the dark wasn't easy. According to Gordon:

Only once, on a very dark and cloudy night, did he fail to do so, and he was out by himself without food for two days and nights. He passed

within half a mile of the camp, but the cattle being quiet and bells silent
there was nothing to indicate its proximity. Eventually he knew by the
miles travelled that he had overshot his mark; and there was nothing
to do but wait until daylight.

Although the daily distances were kept short for the sake of the cattle, there was still plenty of work for the drovers. An hour before
daylight the horse drover started rounding up the horses that were
to be used for that day's work (horses usually worked one day on and
two off). Gordon described the scene: 'Brought near to be saddled,
their glaring eyes weirdly reflected the glowing camp fire, which fire,
giving confidence to man and beast, was the centre of safety and a
rough comfort.'

While the horses were being readied the cook was preparing
breakfast, which was eaten in the cool air and soft light of dawn.
Then the cattle were roused with a cracking of stockwhips and the
shouts of the drovers. They gradually set off on Buchanan's trail,
grazing slowly towards the next camp.

During the morning the horse drover and cook overtook the cattle with the drays and spare horses, hastening forward to set up that
night's camp. The drovers usually carried their lunches with them.
In Buchanan's case it consisted of nothing more than a pocketful
of dried raisins. Dinner at the night camp usually comprised 'bully'
beef (tinned corned beef so named because it originally came from
Booyoolee station and was initially called Booyoolee beef), damper,
potatoes, rice and dried apples. Occasionally there was fresh beef
when one of the cattle was killed or died as a result of an accident.

After dinner a night watch was set around the cattle to ensure
they didn't stray or worse, rush in a stampede of fear and confu-
sion. Each drover's watch usually lasted two or three hours. Two
men were assigned if the cattle seemed restless or Aboriginal people
were in the vicinity, which was often the case. The average working

day was fifteen or sixteen hours, seven days a week. The men were given a couple of hours off per week to wash their clothes.

Just over the Northern Territory border, at Redbank Creek, the camp experienced its first Aboriginal attack when one of the horses was speared and killed during the night. Sixty kilometres further on, another horse was speared, prompting Buchanan to set a watch on the horses as well as the cattle. During the day, on the Calvert River, Aboriginal warriors threatened the drovers from the cliffs that rose on either side of the river. It was the perfect place to launch their spears and there was little the drovers could do to defend themselves. Fortunately, the Aborigines held back.

At night the shadows around the stock camp were alive. A double watch was set. All night the men stayed on alert. Tree stumps and bushes were mistaken for potential attackers. At one point Buchanan fired into the darkness. He hit nothing but was sure he'd seen someone. Morning revealed footprints that confirmed Aboriginal warriors had been moving around the camp throughout the night.

The pressure on Buchanan was immense. Every decision he made affected the lives of seven other people and over a thousand head of stock. The aggressive nature of the Aboriginal people in the vicinity of the Calvert River may have been due to their experience with the earlier droving journey of Darcy Uhr, around 1872, when he reputedly shot his way through the country. Buchanan had so far managed to avoid any bloodshed on either side, but there was still a long way to go.

Beyond the Calvert the Aborigines finally left the drovers in peace, but at the Robinson River, which they reached where it was tidal, another menace reared its head – saltwater crocodiles (*Crocodylus porosus*). The giant reptiles may not have seen cattle before, but they pounced as soon as the stock came near the water, terribly mauling several. A horse was also speared at Snake Lagoon, but survived. Then peace reigned all the way through to the Macarthur River, 80 kilometres away.

The stock crossed the river above the site of the present-day town of Borroloola which, when established in the 1880s, was destined to become the main port for supplies being sent to the region. On the western bank Buchanan and his men found an area of good grass where the cattle and horses could rest and recover their strength. Then they pressed on to the Limmen River, only to find that, it being the dry season, fires had burnt out almost all the feed in the country ahead. Supplies were also starting to run low.

Buchanan decided to ride with Wattie Gordon to the Katherine Telegraph Station, 500 kilometres away, to secure extra rations. Buchanan hoped that by the time he returned the first rains of the wet season would get the grass growing along the rest of the route. In the meantime the stock at the Limmen River, could graze on the river flats.

Free from the slow-moving cattle, Buchanan and Gordon covered the distance to Katherine in less than a week. Switching between three or four horses, and with his remarkable endurance, Buchanan could cover more than 100 kilometres a day, often riding well into the night when the need was urgent.

While he was away the Aborigines at the Limmen River attacked the stock camp. The nephew of one of the stock owners, W. Travers, was on his own, making damper. He had a loaded revolver in his belt but he never got a chance to use it. When the other men returned to the camp they found him dead, almost decapitated by a blow from an axe, his hands still covered in dough. It wasn't clear if he'd allowed someone into the camp or been surprised by a sudden attack. Everything had been ransacked and most of the remaining supplies were gone.

Travers, who'd been well liked by the other men, was buried in a bush grave marked by his name, and the date was cut on a tree not far from the stock camp. It was another of the many lonely graves scattered throughout the outback.

A couple of days later an attempt was made to rob the grave, but the drovers fired at the Aboriginal robbers, who fled. The stockmen gave chase, tracking the warriors into a mountainous area that was a perfect place for an ambush. Realising they were only lightly armed against a potentially larger force, the drovers decided to retreat.

The date for Buchanan's expected return came and went, leaving Hugh Gordon, the man in charge, with a difficult decision. There weren't enough men to drive the cattle on. Their supplies weren't going to last much longer. He chose to wait a couple more days then abandon the stock and make a dash for the Overland Telegraph, following Buchanan's tracks. As luck had it, Buchanan returned with the supplies and an extra man, the mercurial Sam Croker, who'd turned up when Buchanan was about to make his return journey.

Despite his desire to maintain good relations with the Aborigines, Buchanan allowed a punitive expedition to be mounted. The warriors were tracked to a cave in the mountains and the ringleader was shot dead. Some of the Aboriginal women were then compelled to help recover some of the tools that had been stolen.

The cattle were mustered in preparation for moving on, whereupon it was found that up to twenty-five had been speared. Rather than become embroiled in a cycle of tit for tat, Buchanan decided not to engage in further reprisals. The stock were soon at the Wickham River, where a short stretch of dense scrub made life difficult for the cattle and the drays. Once through, Buchanan set a course across country, heading east to the Hodson River, a tributary of the Roper. He then travelled down through the rocky gorge of what became known as Hell's Gates. After that, the worst was behind them.

Buchanan moved his cattle a short way along the Roper, where open grassy plains provided plenty of feed. By then it was January 1879, nine months since they'd set out and the height of the wet season. As if on cue the heavens opened, and over the next couple of months 2.4 metres of rain was dumped on the region. Further progress was almost impossible. It was only during occasional breaks in the deluge that a few short stages could be managed. The one bright spot was that the delays allowed newborn calves to gain enough strength to travel onward with their mothers (a few could also be carried on the drays). As a consequence, the herd was larger than when it left Aramac.

When the rain finally relented, around March, Buchanan continued up the Roper to the Elsey Telegraph Station. There more rain delayed them for two weeks, during which Hugh Gordon contracted malaria. The telegraph operator treated him with calomel, quinine and Epsom salts. As Gordon recovered, the rain finally stopped and the drovers pushed on to Mataranka and Katherine. They crossed the Katherine River and arrived at Glencoe station in May 1879, thirteen months after leaving Aramac.

Behind them, more stock were already following the new track forged by Buchanan. The rush for leases in the Territory in 1877 had given the leaseholders until 1880 to stock their runs. Since it could take more than a year to drove cattle to the Northern Territory, by mid-1879 time was running out. Consequently, huge numbers of stock were suddenly on the move.

The drovers from Buchanan's overlanding expedition soon disbanded, some to work on the newly formed Northern Territory stations, others to return to Queensland. It's not entirely clear what Buchanan did immediately after the trip, although it's likely he explored new country to the west and south-east of Glencoe, searching for that elusive block of land where he could settle down and make his fortune. Before he could do that, he had to assist in the greatest chapter of the story of stocking the Northern Territory.

Glencoe had been sold to new interests who'd also formed the nearby Daly River station. In July 1881 they asked Buchanan to stock both with another mob of cattle. Of course he'd done it all before, but this time there was one major difference. The owners wanted to move 20 000 head. This was by far the biggest mob of cattle ever droved in Australia. At the time, a manageable mob was considered to be no more than 1250 – a sixteenth of what was proposed. It was an extremely demanding job, particularly for a 55-year-old, but for a man of Buchanan's calibre the challenge was too great to resist.

Soon he was hiring the best head drovers and men he could find. Cattle were mustered from stations around St George, on the New South Wales–Queensland border. Under the care of Wattie Gordon, 16 000 head were soon on their way towards the Gulf. Buchanan set off for Rockhampton where he started buying some of the 700 horses required for the massive operation. While he was there he purchased an additional 4500 head of cattle from Richmond Downs station. There the freshly mustered cattle didn't take well to being yarded. They rushed and destroyed the fences, Buchanan and the men with him barely managing to avoid losing the mob itself. With the yards ruined, three or four men had to watch the flighty herd night and day until finally they headed off for the Gulf.

Both these mighty herds came together at the crossing of the Leichhardt River, near the Gulf of Carpentaria and the tiny settlement of Burketown, late in 1881. With the wet season already beginning some of the stockmen went on strike, possibly reluctant to leave the pleasures of the Burketown pub for the vast unknown. The loss of the men made managing the enormous herd incredibly difficult, but Buchanan eventually convinced some of the men to return to work. As time went on he also picked up new men to supplement his staff.

During gaps in the rains, the ponderous operation started moving forward. It involved some sixty men, with the cattle divided into nine mobs each roughly 2000 head. Each mob travelled a day apart, creating a long train of cattle that extended over 80 to 90 kilometres and took nearly two weeks to pass any given point. One can only imagine what the Aboriginal people in the region made of the enormous cloud of dust that extended from one horizon to the other and remained there day after day as the slowly moving cattle, horses, men and countless drays of the droving plants made their way through their lands.

Not all of them were daunted by what they saw. One night an Aboriginal warrior tried to creep up on a drover named Hedley sleeping in his swag. The drover was inside a box mosquito net provided to protect the men from malaria. When the warrior lifted the net to get a clean strike with his axe, Hedley shot him dead at point-blank range.

At the Calvert River there was more trouble. A handful of cattle were speared and although the attacks made little impression on the mighty herd, they caused restlessness among the cattle and rushes that were potentially far more dangerous. The worst stock loss was at the next river crossing, the Robinson, just east of present-day Borroloola. There the mob under head drover, Jack Farnifull, struck the river where it was brackish. Many of the thirsty cattle rushed and drank the salty water. Some died. Others went mad and ran into the scrub, never to be seen again. Gordon Buchanan referred to it as 'rather a bad smash' and wrote that 'a great number were lost'. At the Robinson and other rivers saltwater crocodiles also attacked, killing some cattle and stampeding many more.

As the mob pushed on, the bulk of the journey passed without major incident. There were only two fatalities among the drovers, when two men came down with an undiagnosed illness. Another drover shot himself in the leg while cleaning his gun. He was carried on one of the drays until he recovered. Towards the end of the journey there was another stock loss when two of the head drovers raced to beat each other to Glencoe. Jack Warby drove his whole mob into the swirling waters of the Katherine River in one huge mass. When the lead cattle took fright and tried to turn back, the press of stock behind them drove seventy under and they drowned.

Meanwhile, with the money he was earning droving other people's cattle, Buchanan could finally afford to take up leases on the country he'd explored west of the Overland Telegraph Line. Even as he was delivering the cattle to Glencoe, he had a mob of his own cattle on the Gulf Track bound for a property he was forming with his brothers-in-law – Wave Hill, in the Victoria River district. Once again he blazed the trail to the property, in the process helping stock one of the largest properties in the world, Victoria River Downs. From there he took 4000 head to the Ord River, in Western Australia, pioneering a 450-kilometre direct route from Katherine. Just as he'd crossed Queensland with a mixture of stock routes and exploring trips, he'd now crossed the Northern Territory (and nearly two-thirds of Australia).

Wave Hill was to be Buchanan's base of operations for more than a decade, despite being extremely remote. Initially his nearest neighbour was 400 kilometres to the east. In every other direction there was nothing. The isolation had countless disadvantages, most of which Buchanan could deal with. However, there was one that he never saw coming.

In 1883, as the station was being established, Buchanan's attorney, William Kilgour, put in place a financial partnership with Buchanan's older brother, William. Kilgour probably did this with the best intentions. William, the oldest of the Buchanan boys, had stayed on the family's original property and managed it while the younger Buchanans had been out seeking their fortunes. He'd only ventured to the Australian goldfields, where he noticed a remarkable similarity to the geology around his own district. He went back and eventually struck it big, making his fortune. William was now doing most of his farming from a desk, but with his backing Buchanan had enough capital to deal with the difficulties of Wave Hill's distance from markets and the frequent spearing of cattle by its indigenous inhabitants. Despite its drawbacks, the quality of its grazing land made it one of the best cattle stations in the world. It still is.

In 1886 Wave Hill had to send cattle prodigious distances, first to Katherine, across to Queensland, then on to markets in Brisbane and Sydney. It was a terribly long way to drove, but apart from the odd gold strike in the Northern Territory and Western Australia, with the subsequent influxes of hungry miners, there was nowhere else they could go.

In 1886 Buchanan contemplated the possibilities of a new stock route that would cut almost 650 kilometres off the trip to Queensland. The direct line from Wave Hill to the Overland Telegraph at Powell Creek was blocked by a belt of almost impenetrable scrub, appropriately called hedgewood. Unfortunately, the hedge was 160 kilometres thick and it had thwarted every attempt by explorers to find a path through it. Typical of the man, Buchanan was returning from Queensland (probably by the Barkly Stock Route) with 100 horses when he decided he'd had enough of the long detour around the hedgewood scrub.

At Powell Creek he met his old exploring mate, Sam Croker, who'd been rounding up stray cattle, and the pair decided to not only pioneer a stock route through the hedgewood, but to do it with stock in tow. They travelled up the Overland Telegraph to a creek just north of Newcastle Waters Telegraph station. There Buchanan left a bucket on top of a tree stump (at what's now known as Bucket Creek) to mark the beginning of the new route.

The drovers travelled up Bucket Creek before turning north-west into the supposedly unknown. In fact, Croker had befriended local Aboriginal people who told him there was water about 80 kilometres ahead. They agreed to show the drovers the way through the hedgewood to the waterhole they called Murranji. It was a long way for horses and cattle to go without a drink. It would be a lot worse if they covered that distance only to find the Aboriginal people were leading them astray. Buchanan and Sam pushed along nervously for two days, keeping the pace steady for the sake of the stock while their thoughts raced ahead to the hoped-for waterhole. At last, Murranji glinted through the scrub. In the middle of the arid hedgewood there was sufficient water for all their stock. The grateful drovers rewarded their guides with 'plenty tucker'.

Now the Aboriginal guides said there was another waterhole about as far again to the west. With an offer of more tucker they agreed to continue guiding the drovers. This time, after they left the belt of hedgewood country, they came to what's now known as Yellow Waterholes. From there, Buchanan knew it was only 50 kilometres west by north to the Armstrong River, a tributary of the Victoria River which formed the stock route from Wave Hill to Katherine.

The Murranji Track was soon to become one of the most famous stock routes in northern Australia, in part because it was a great short cut but also because it could be a white-knuckle experience for drovers. The Murranji and Yellow Waterholes weren't permanent. The long, dry stages between them meant that disaster was ever-present for those who risked the journey. Nevertheless, for decades to come, the Murranji Track and Barkly Stock Route comprised the main route for enormous numbers of stock heading for Queensland from the Golden West. Both owed their genesis to Buchanan and Croker and their ability to enlist the help of Aboriginal guides.

At Wave Hill new gold strikes in the Kimberley provided temporary markets and prompted Buchanan and the Gordon brothers to establish stations and stock routes farther west. Buchanan also experimented with supplying cattle to markets in Singapore. In 1890 he shipped thirty bullocks from Derby, but the returns barely justified the effort. Two years later, a gold strike on the Murchison River in Western Australia, far to the south-west of Wave Hill, prompted Buchanan to attempt the establishment of yet another great stock route. If he succeeded, it would also be the longest, 2600 kilometres across Western Australia then down the coast to the Murchison, practically on Perth's doorstep (only 400 well-watered kilometres to the south).

As his son later put it, 'As leaders of this expedition, the old bri-
gade was chosen.' Buchanan with Hugh and Wattie Gordon again
took to the western track 'behind the hornies [cattle]'. They left in
March 1892 with 1000 bullocks, heading for the coast, 700 kilometres away. They passed the mining town of Halls Creek, near which
Buchanan's son had established Flora Valley station in 1887 (this
was to become the north-western end of the Canning Stock Route,
driven through the Great Sandy Desert twenty years later). They then
had an easy well-grassed trip to the Fitzroy River, which took them
down to the coast. At that point Buchanan became the first and possibly only drover who could claim to have taken stock from one side
of Australia to the other, from the Pacific to the Indian Ocean. Nearly
all the stock routes over that distance had been blazed by him as
well.

From the mouth of the Fitzroy, Buchanan now faced 800 almost-
waterless kilometres as he skirted the Great Sandy Desert. The
Western Australian government had sunk wells 20 to 40 kilometres
apart along some of the route, but many were in disrepair. The men
took buckets and canvas troughs with them to ensure they'd be able
to water their stock. The cattle weren't accustomed to troughs, so
when they reached the first well it took some time before they could
be encouraged to drink. Eventually thirst overcame timidity, after
which the hard part was keeping up with them as the water had to
be drawn from the well by hand.

There were few dangers from Aboriginal attacks on the track south
because a telegraph line followed the coast and the operators had
taken great care to establish good relations with the local population.
The weather was another matter. The cyclone season had passed,
but the men still heard tales of their fury. Gordon Buchanan wrote:

> Such was the force of the wind that cattle and sheep were, in exposed
> parts, driven into the sea and iron telegraph poles bent over or broken.

No one could stand up against it. The tallest local tale is of a stockman who, having to abandon his horse, took refuge behind a stump. Clinging to this in a few hours all the clothes except his belt and boots were blown off and the shifting sand had nearly covered his stump.

At one of the camps the cattle were allowed to spread out and forage during the night, but in the early hours of the morning something spooked them. Several hundred rushed. They bolted due east, into the heart of the Great Sandy Desert. Hugh Gordon was sent to round them up. He tracked the cattle for 60 kilometres, not seeing a single water source along the way. He eventually realised that if he went any further and didn't find water, he'd be beyond the point of no return. The tracks of the cattle still headed straight into the desert. Reluctantly, he turned back. Even so, by the time he made it back to the coast, having covered 120 kilometres without water, he and his horse were in a desperate state. He later learned that if he'd continued for just 30 kilometres more he'd have struck the De Grey River. There he would have found the wayward bullocks as well, happily quenching their considerable thirst.

Buchanan and the stock continued down Ninety Mile Beach before striking inland to the De Grey, where many of the lost stock were recovered in the vicinity of Coppins station. They then passed superb grazing country around the mining town of Marble Bar before tackling the long dry stretch beyond the Fortescue River.

To give themselves the best chance of getting through, canvas waterbags were slung on the horses. They went 80 kilometres without finding a drop of the precious fluid, Buchanan as usual scouting far ahead for any potential source. At last his efforts were rewarded when he found a small soak in a creek bed. When he dug it out, the water barely flowed into it. Still, it was better than nothing. He and the others spent an entire night with buckets and canvas troughs watering the thirsty bullocks. At times when the beasts threatened to rush the water and trample the troughs, Buchanan drove them back by opening an umbrella in their faces. It was an accoutrement he seems to have picked up in his later years for protection from the blazing sun of northern Australia.

The next day the cattle remained at the soak while Buchanan scouted ahead for another source. He found nothing. Meanwhile, the soak had all but run dry. Now he had to choose between a retreat of 80 kilometres to the Fortescue or pushing on and hoping they got through. If they didn't, it would mean the end for the cattle and possibly themselves. Wrote Gordon Buchanan:

> The whole party 'burning their boats' moved off with a grim determination to see it through. This second dry stage was longer and more gruelling than the first, but having a creek to follow the cattle travelled better as they expected water at every bend. Occasionally they lengthened out into a string a mile long, when the leaders would have to be checked to prevent the pace becoming too hot.
>
> Eventually, and just in time, for some of the bullocks were beginning to go mad, a fair-sized waterhole was found in the Ashburton at the junction of a creek. Word was sent back to the drovers, who steadied the mob some distance away, allowing only 50 or 60 to go to water at a time.

From there they had a relatively straightforward trip – through a pass in the Hammersley Range, on to the Gascoyne River and then down to the sheep stations on the Upper Murchison. There they sold all the bullocks to one of the local graziers. The new stock route, a way to the south for cattle from the Kimberley and the Northern Territory, became known as Buchanan's Track. It was the last piece in a jigsaw of stock routes that reached right across the continent, an achievement unparalleled in Australia's history.

Unfortunately, Buchanan's newest triumph did him little personal good. No sooner had he pioneered this new stock route than the West Australian government introduced a duty on cattle crossing the border from the Northern Territory. Wave Hill was on the Northern Territory side and the tax, combined with the length of the stock route, made it too expensive for the man who'd opened the new market for Kimberley cattle to benefit from it.

Worse was to come. In 1894 Wave Hill was deep in debt. Much of the money was owed to Buchanan's wealthy brother. To get it back, William put the station up for auction. Whether he had a right to do so is questionable. Just as suspect was the result of the auction. The successful bidder was William. Buchanan lost his property to a brother who'd never set foot on the place. In the whole time William owned it he never saw it. Two years later, cattle prices rose and a port facility was opened at nearby Wyndham, giving cheaper access to the southern markets. Wave Hill became a goldmine. In 1894 Wave Hill cost William £15 000. It was sold in 1912 for £200 000.

Buchanan and his enduring love Kate lived for a while at their son Gordon's property near Halls Creek. He dabbled in mining and managed Ord River station for a while. In 1896, at the age of seventy, he was contracted by the South Australian government to explore the possibility of a stock route through the Tanami Desert, to cut the corner from the Victoria River district to the Overland Telegraph further south. With a string of camels and an Aboriginal assistant (who was handcuffed to the leading camel to stop him from deserting) they succeeded in crossing the Tanami, but couldn't find enough water or feed for a stock route. He also assisted in the search for missing members of the Calvert Expedition (see Chapter 4).

Despite the succession of disappointments he'd endured trying to gain his own foothold on the land, Buchanan still enjoyed legendary status across the north of Australia. Many of the stations and districts that were now successfully raising cattle owed their genesis to him. In 1896 the *Northern Territory Times* described him thus:

[He is] an unassuming explorer who has a far better claim to renown than most of the crowd who have posed of later years as Australian explorers. He must be now seventy years of age and he is possibly too old to stand many severe bush crises, but in his best day nothing was too rough for him . . . Hundreds of bush yarns are current about 'Old Bluey', as stockmen familiarly call him, but in none of them have we ever traced anything but the most flattering recognition of the good work done by Buchanan in the pioneering days of the Far North.

He was also known among Aboriginal people as Paraway, a corruption of his answer 'Far away' to their questions about where he was going next. It's perhaps fitting that his respect for Aboriginal people, demonstrated particularly in his relations with the inhabitants of Wave Hill, ensured that they were still on their country, working as stockmen, when in the 1960s Wave Hill became the flashpoint that led to the Aboriginal land rights movement. Many of the northern properties have since passed into Aboriginal hands, providing employment in the cattle industry Buchanan pioneered. Many properties still have their sacred sites, places men like Buchanan recognised and took care not to disturb.

In 1899 Buchanan's health started to fail him. He and Kate finally left the Kimberley and moved back to the milder climate of New South Wales. He bought Kenmuir, 10 hectares of land near Tamworth, where he grew lucerne to help make ends meet. It was a humble ending for a man *The Bulletin* described as having helped settle more new country than any other man in Australia. His legacy spanned the continent. One of the greatest bushmen the outback has ever known died on 23 September, 1901.

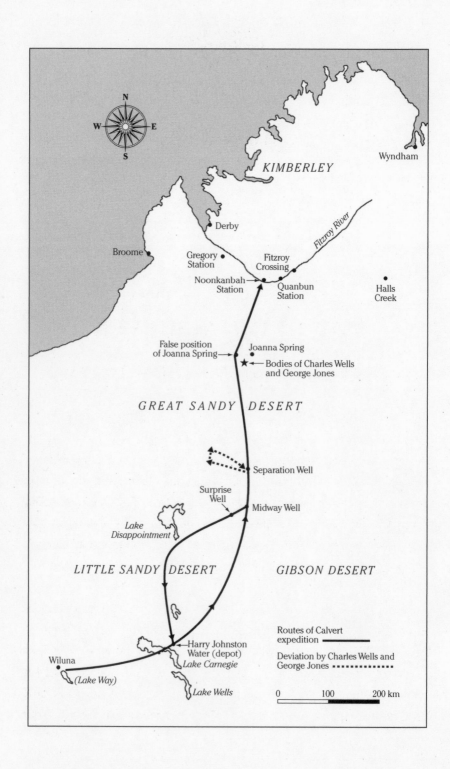

Routes of Calvert expedition ——————

Deviation by Charles Wells and George Jones ••••••••

Dervish Bejah, circa 1950
(National Archives of Australia)

4

THE QUIET ACHIEVER
Dervish Bejah (c. 1862–1957)

The group portrait of the Calvert Scientific Exploring Expedition of 1896–7 is what you'd expect a photograph of Victorian-era explorers to look like, except for one detail. While five of the men are stiffly posed in their best suits, with bowlers, pork-pie hats or boaters, the sixth is a man apart. He wears a turban. His dark skin, neatly shaped beard and direct gaze give him a bearing both exotic and quietly self-confident.

Yet his presence in the official photograph is surprising. His name was Dervish Bejah and his role in the expedition was 'Afghan in charge of camels'. At the time the social rank of camel drivers was considered well below white Europeans, so for expedition leader Lawrence Wells to include Bejah in the photograph suggests he'd already developed a great respect for his 'Afghan'. In fact, if Wells had bothered to ask he'd have found that Bejah was from Balu-chistan, a fiercely independent province in what is now Pakistan. When Bejah was born, probably in 1862, Baluchistan was part of India and when he grew up he joined the Indian army, rising to the rank of sergeant.

By then the value of camels and good cameleers was well recog-nised in Australia. First imported to Tasmania in 1840, camels were soon playing a vital role in exploration of the arid interior of the mainland. Camels were slower than horses but could travel further in a day and carry heavier loads. Bullocks were stronger still, but camels could go further without water, if they were conditioned to it. They could graze a greater range of vegetation.

Camels quickly became a feature of exploring expeditions, but they were also the backbone of the outback's supply networks. They carried drilling equipment into arid areas to sink wells along stock routes for cattle and sheep. They carried the comforts of civilisation to some of the loneliest stations in the outback.

Bejah responded to the demand for cameleers and left his home in India bound for Fremantle, Western Australia, in 1890. He was working in South Australia when Lawrence Wells recruited him (and an assistant, Said Ameer) for an expedition 'Equipped at the request and expense of Albert F. Calvert, Esq., F.R.G.S., London, for the pur-pose of Exploring the remaining blanks of Australia'.

Specifically, the Calvert Expedition was planning to investigate Western Australia's Great Sandy Desert but even as it was being organised, in the autumn of 1896, time was running out. It was imperative that they carry out their work before the terrible heat of summer set in and exploring took second place to survival. It was late May when the seven expedition members – Wells, Bejah, Wells' cousin Charles, naturalist George Keartland, mineralogist/photogra-pher George Jones, cook and assistant James Trainor, and assistant cameleer Said Ameer – assembled in Adelaide and prepared to take ship for Western Australia. There the expedition spent the precious first days of winter haggling over camels.

At Mullewa the local cameleers refused to part with their best animals, fearing what the expedition might do to the creatures on which their livelihoods depended. When the expedition eventually purchased twenty mediocre beasts on 11 June, the cameleers' worst fears were immediately realised. The expedition loaded fourteen beasts each with 227 kilograms of equipment and supplies, enough to last four months. The six riding camels carried loads of 45.5 kilograms in addition to their riders. In total the baggage weighed more than 3.5 tonnes; 575 kilograms for every member of the expedition. If Bejah thought the burdens were too much for the camels to bear, Wells' journal of the expedition makes no mention of it.

It wasn't long after they reached the road to Lake Way, 500 kilometres inland, that Wells started having problems. On 25 June he wrote: 'I find that it will be necessary, owing to heavy loads and condition of the camels, to proceed by short stages until our work of exploring commences, when a depot will be formed, and the poorer animals spelled until their condition improves.'

On 13 July they passed Lake Way, but barely paused. It was already the middle of winter and they'd only reached the edge of the unexplored desert country. They headed north-east into the unknown, a region of thousands of square kilometres that had only been traversed by Warburton in 1873, Forrest in 1874 and Giles in 1876. Wells had also explored the southern section of the desert in 1892.

Towards the end of July they found a chain of excellent waterholes where the men feasted on ducks and Bejah found a tortoise shell, which suggested the water supply was permanent. With just a month of winter remaining, Wells wanted to press on but, near Lake Carnegie, his plans suffered a further setback. Two of the camels ate 'poison weed' (probably sand hill corkbark, or poison pea).

'We noticed one of our best pack camels trembling in the hind quarters,' Wells wrote, 'and thinking he had hurt himself whilst rising (his load being heavy), we removed his pack to another animal. However, shortly after starting, he lay down and would not rise again. Almost immediately afterwards another was affected in the same manner.'

Bejah was left to tend the sick beasts while Wells and the others set off on short exploration sorties in the surrounding country. He gave the animals a mixture of warm water and soap, hoping to purge them of the poisonous vegetation they'd eaten, but they didn't improve. One deteriorated until its hindquarters were almost paralysed. Bejah did everything he could for them, and both managed to cling to life.

The problem for Wells was that he had so much equipment he couldn't afford to lose a single camel. Until they recovered, if they recovered, he was forced to establish his depot at nearby Harry Johnston Water. On 2 August, Wells tried to make the best of it:

> Having found sufficient feed for the camels about here, I have decided to give them all a week's spell, after which it is my intention to start on a flying trip to the Northward . . . into the centre of the Great Sandy Desert, the object being to look for water, so that I may get my party and impedimenta through to the Fitzroy River, and map in, by different routes, as much as possible of the intervening country.

Wells envisaged a north–south journey of more than 800 kilometres. On 10 August he set off with the mineralogist, Jones, Bejah and seven camels loaded with six weeks' supplies including 150 gallons (680 litres) of water in kegs. Charles Wells, the other members of the expedition and thirteen lucky camels (including the two sick ones that were slowly improving) were left at the depot with instructions to move about as the need for good camel feed dictated.

Two days later, the 'flying expedition' got its first impression of what lay ahead when they came across a group of Aboriginal men and women. On 13 August Wells wrote:

> Two of them came to accompany us this morning but on ascertaining the direction we were taking they became greatly alarmed, and wished, evidently, to explain to us that there was no water in that direction. They tried hard to induce me to alter our course; to go first East and then North-West.

When it became clear that Wells had no intention of taking their advice, the locals fled. The wisdom of their action soon became clear. There was no water. Huge red dunes lay at right angles to the course Wells was determined to follow. The desolation was almost total. Wells wrote on 14 August:

> There was nothing to prove that natives had ever been in this country; and the only signs of bird life were in the shape of two (2) crows and an eaglehawk. At 2 p.m. the camels were showing signs of distress, owing to the number of sandridges they had to encounter, and three of the number were carrying 600 pounds [273 kilograms] weight . . . From the tops of the highest sandridges at camp we had, in all directions, a most wretched view, nothing but red sandridges being visible for many miles.

So far, all the Calvert Expedition had discovered was that the Great Sandy Desert was aptly named. As the days passed, Wells and Bejah spent increasing amounts of time searching for camel feed and water. The camels were suffering so much from the torment of their loads, difficult terrain and constant hunger that Bejah was forced to tie them up at night to stop them escaping. He was also fearful that they'd find their way to the various types of 'poison weed' and that in their desperation nothing would stop them eating it. Since they

were unable to forage, Bejah started doing it for them, cutting feed
and carrying it back to them – this while accompanying Wells on
foot after they made their afternoon camp, continuing the search for
water. At times the pair walked 20 kilometres. Day after day, they
found nothing.

At one stop, Bejah noticed 'plenty poison plant at camp'. He
promptly set about pulling up every plant he could find. He then
burned everything he'd gathered.

By 20 August they'd covered 260 kilometres since leaving Harry
Johnston Water. The last 210 kilometres had been through completely
arid terrain. It was a very long way for camels to go without water,
but Wells refused to turn back. He was adamant that he'd find it if he
just kept going. To add to their woes, Wells and Bejah were starting
to suffer from sandy blight, the outback's catch-all expression for a
range of eye infections caused by dry dusty conditions and poor sanitation due to a lack of water. The infection is spread by hand contact
and the irresistible urge to rub the inflammation. Wells attributed the
cause to the glare of the sun on the porcupine grass.

It was at this point that Wells recorded (seemingly with some pride)
that he'd not broached a single keg to give water to the beleaguered
camels. He wrote of their situation:

> As long as I consider the camels can do without water I shall push on;
> but when forced to encroach on the kegs I must go no further, and,
> should the worst confront us, I believe, with the various patches of feed
> I have noted since starting, we can get back with some, if not all, of the
> camels.

Wells now appeared to regard the camels as expendable, despite the
fact that his mountain of equipment was now being supplemented by
botanical and geological specimens. He took a similar attitude when
it came to looking after his eyes. His sandy blight meant he could

barely see to calculate his latitude and longitude, but he refused to 'waste' water bathing them.

Meanwhile, Bejah was doing everything he could for the poor creatures in his care. Every day he gathered whatever feed he could find, ripped up poison plant and scoured the sandhillls for the least hint of water. On August 22, Wells recognised his contribution. Ascending a 100-metre hill that rose above the dunes, he named it Bejah Hill, explaining, 'I have named this hill after the faithful Bejah, who has proved himself a splendid fellow and an excellent camelman.'

Alas, the view showed an endless succession of sandhills to the north-west and north-east. They had reached a region of utter desolation. The camels had gone without water for almost a fortnight. As they continued north-east, Bejah couldn't find them a scrap of food. They were still carrying crushing loads and Wells was driving 30 to 40 kilometres over the endless dunes. It was also growing increasingly hot as the last days of winter ebbed away.

On 24 August Bejah had had enough. Wells recorded, 'Bejah shepherded his camels until midnight, and then tied them up. This morning he would not eat any breakfast; and said, "Camel no eat, me no eat." The poor animals look like starved kangaroo dogs this morning.'

The tactful cameleer hadn't confronted the expedition leader directly, but he'd drawn a pretty clear line in the sand – if Wells didn't care what happened to the camels, he might think differently about human life. Wells makes no reference to what he thought of Bejah's attitude but the route he took that day says a great deal. He altered course 90 degrees from north and north-east to west-north-west. It wasn't a complete about-face, but it was a start.

Wells' journal also recorded that they set off at 3.30 in the morning to make the most of the coolest part of the day. When it was light they took in the view: 'Not a vestige of feed was to be seen here, and not hills of any height to be seen for at least thirty miles [50 kilometres].

Glaring red sand extends in all directions, and the outlook appears most hopeless. Although but 9 a.m., it is intensely hot.'

At 11 a.m. the heat forced them to make camp. There was no feed for the camels. Wells finally broke open the water kegs and gave the camels half the supply. They were 400 kilometres from the depot at Harry Johnston Water and even he admitted, 'I dread the idea of having to return by the route we have come.' Nevertheless, the next day he turned south.

As he and Bejah set off on their continuous search for water, Wells was 8 kilometres from the camp when he noticed a pigeon flying purposefully to the west. It looked like it was heading for water, but he had been disappointed so many times before that he almost ignored the bird. Doggedly he and Bejah followed it over a sand ridge. They saw more pigeons and a clump of green tea-tree. When they noticed an abandoned Aboriginal campfire and a patch of good feed for the camels, their hopes rose. Not long after, they discovered a small hollow filled with damp sand. The two men started digging and were soon rewarded when slightly salty water started seeping into the hole. The water, the first they'd found in fifteen days, was sufficient for the camels to drink all they wanted and even for the men to bathe. Wells named the water Midway Well.

The find reinvigorated Wells, who now started making plans to map the country to the south-west and south on his journey back to the depot. It also allowed him to plan on bringing the whole expedition north with the knowledge that there was at least one source of water along the way.

First though, he had to get back through the dunes and waterless country between Midway Well and the depot. It took them two gruelling weeks, during which they found only one small soak that yielded little for man or beast. On 8 September they at last reached a waterhole in the vicinity of the depot and got their first taste of good, fresh, abundant water in almost a month. Not long after they came upon the expedition's other camels, all fat and healthy. Wrote Wells:

Bejah was so delighted at seeing them that he left the poor brutes he was leading and ran off to the others, talking to and playing with them in a most excited manner. No doubt to him it was the next best thing to meeting a countryman. Continuing on down the creek, we soon saw, in the distance, two figures approaching us. They were my cousin and Said Ameer, coming on their usual morning round to muster their charges. For some time they did not notice our approach, mistaking our camels for theirs. My cousin seemed so overcome by our sudden appearance that he completely lost his voice for the time being, and, giving Mr Jones and myself a hearty grip, he moved on to Bejah, to whom he first spoke. He afterwards told me, when conducting us to his camp, that he had never before experienced the same feeling, and attributed it to the sudden meeting, and his anxiety for our welfare for the past fortnight, as he had expected us back within three weeks.

Bejah's joy may have been prompted by surviving the ordeal and finding all twenty camels still alive. Then he discovered to his dismay that Wells, rather than being chastened by the Great Sandy Desert, was determined to retrace his route north to Midway Well. From there he'd attempt to continue to the Fitzroy River, hoping to find Joanna Spring, first discovered by the Warburton Expedition, along the way.

Wells seemed to have forgotten that there'd been insufficient feed for seven camels and that they'd been driven to exhaustion as they struggled over the immense dunes. He'd forgotten that even in the last days of 'winter' the heat had forced them to set out well before daylight and camp before the ferocious temperatures of the afternoon. Wells hoped rather than knew that he'd find water on the almost 600-kilometre journey beyond Midway Well. He calculated a loading of 2831 kilograms of water and equipment, to be divided among fourteen pack camels. The material left over was buried.

The second journey into the desert was cursed from the start – perhaps literally. At one of their several camps at the depot (they had shifted around to find feed for the camels), they found signs of Aboriginal activity. Wrote Wells:

> A small hole about eighteen (18) inches [45 centimetres] deep was sunk in the ground, and the bottom was lined with gum leaves. Upon these were placed several curious pieces of conglomerated, nodular ironstone, with blood upon them; then on top more gum leaves and pieces of stone. A small pad leads for a few yards to the trunk of a gum tree overhanging the creek; on this there was also blood. Another pad leads in the opposite direction from the hole to a distance of one chain, where a stone was firmly placed in the ground, with smaller ones on either side of it. Perhaps this means a little witchcraft, foreboding us ill-luck for having encroached on the preserves of the natives and eaten their game.

That night dust storms swept the camp. There was thunder and lightning but not a drop of rain. The next day, 15 September, they loaded the camels, forced them to their feet, and marched off into the desert. All too soon they were among the dunes, the camels quickly tiring as they made ascent after ascent. Every day that followed the heat grew worse. The camels deteriorated rapidly.

After only four days, Wells realised the loads were too much for the camels and that they needed more water. Several kegs were opened and the camels drank, reducing the weight they were carrying by 280 kilograms. Over the following days Wells' journal was littered with references to 'wretched sandridge country', 'terrible sandridges', 'awful sandridges' and 'the same horrible outlook'. On 23 September, Wells made what seems a blindingly obvious observation: 'I find that the more foot exercise one takes the more water one consumes.'

They did have a bit of luck when Wells happened on a new water source, Surprise Well, on 28 September. He'd been following the route of his return journey while his cousin and most of the camels made straight for Midway Well. The new source of clean fresh water gave the camels and men a much-needed respite. The camels also made the most of the feed that flourished around the well.

Wells, Bejah and two camels set out from Midway Well on 2 October to scout for water to the north. After two days they noticed very old Aboriginal tracks and followed them to an area of lush vegetation. Searching the area Bejah found another water source, which was eventually named Separation Well. The find, 60 kilometres north of Midway Well, put the expedition almost within striking distance of Joanna Spring, which was still approximately 300 forbidding kilometres further north.

'I can see that there must be no delay,' Wells belatedly wrote, 'owing to the lateness of the season. In so terrible a country as this, where glaring red sandridges all trending almost at right angles to our course, present themselves to the view in every quarter, and where camel feed and water are scarce and the heat of the sand is intense, it is extremely difficult to proceed at this time of the year.'

Given that assessment, what happened next almost defies belief. Separation Well got its name because that's where the expedition split up. On 10 October Charles Wells and George Jones took three camels, 250 litres of water and a month's supplies and set off on a side trip. They planned to travel 160 kilometres to the north-west, then turn back to the north-east until they came upon the tracks of the main expedition some 80 kilometres south of Joanna Spring. They believed that with lighter loads, and by travelling mostly in the same direction as the dunes, they'd be able to travel faster. The reasoning wasn't just flawed, it approached insanity.

It seems the fresh water of the Great Sandy Desert had a remarkable ability to dissolve the realities of the expedition's plight. With his belly well hydrated, Lawrence Wells no longer spoke of the dangers of delay. Instead, re-energised for the work of exploration, he wrote:

> These welcome little spots around the only three wells of value hith-
> erto discovered are, in this wretched country, truly oases, and the only
> places of rest for man and beast. Herbage and bushes suited for camels
> surround each of the waters for short distances, thus enabling the trav-
> eller to refresh his weary 'ships of the desert' with water and food; and
> it is on such occasions as these that one realises the value of water. In
> Australia its absence is frequently the only danger of importance that
> the explorer has to encounter.

Having divided his men and resources, leaving two of them without the skills of an expert cameleer, and deciding to advance into a desert where the heat was becoming more intense by the day, Wells was about to discover that the absence of water wasn't the only 'danger of importance' in the Great Sandy Desert.

On 11 October, the two parties set out. No sooner had they done so than Wells was describing, 'The same disheartening outlook every-where!' On 14 October it was so hot that he was forced to make camp at 9.15 a.m. The camels sought shade rather than forage in what Wells now described as 'this wretched wilderness'.

Despite the heat, he and Bejah searched for water until they could search no more. It was always Bejah who went with Wells. Ameer, Keartland and Trainor stayed in camp. On October 17 the search nearly killed the pair:

> Staggering over hot sand, parched with thirst, I became exhausted, and
> only able to manage a quarter to a half mile at a time, sinking down
> at the top of each sandridge in a half stupor, and falling into a sleep
> each time only to jump again with a start and urge Bejah to rouse him-
> self. The tops of the ridges becoming cooler as the night advanced, we

repeatedly pulled our clothes off and poured the cool sand over our burning skins. On approaching the signal fires from camp we were forced to lie down again and Bejah seemed to collapse. We called for relief and the others were soon around us, tending us both and doing everything to relieve our suffering. Mr Keartland is kindness itself, and Trainor seems unable to do enough for us. As we were unable to move for some hours our start was delayed until morning.

The symptoms Wells describes indicate both men were suffering hyperthermia – extreme heat stress. It's exacerbated by dehydration and if untreated is almost invariably fatal. If the body's internal organs become overheated, they fail. When they fail, you die. (It's what happens when children or pets are left in cars in summer, even for a short time.)

Two days later they were still in the vicinity, trying to get water from a native well they'd found. It gave a scant supply, barely enough for the camels, but they needed all they could get. Wells called the find Sahara Well, and although it yielded less and less as they continually emptied it, they stayed there until 20 October. That night they set off at 8 p.m., Wells having concluded that travel was now only possible at night. Even then, the desert's heat didn't ease until well after midnight.

There wasn't enough water at Sahara Well to fill the kegs, which meant the supply was less than 150 litres for five men and seventeen camels. Feed for the camels was extremely scarce. On 23 October the expedition came upon an Aboriginal group. They were surviving on the supply from a tiny well that yielded only two buckets of water an hour. There was nowhere near enough for five more men and their camel train, and the Aboriginal people became extremely concerned about their water source. Nevertheless, the men set about getting all they could and by working continuously for thirty-six hours, sixty-five buckets of water were collected from what was named Adverse Well.

Wells now estimated that he was 80 kilometres from Joanna Spring. He had three camels that were close to useless; the rest weren't much better. When given water, two camels couldn't drink. Facing the realities of the situation Wells wrote, 'As so much depends on our flight now, a considerable quantity of our goods must be abandoned.' Among the jetsam were rocks Jones had collected 'which are very heavy and, I think, not very valuable'.

The flight began at 11.30 p.m. on 25 October. Keartland counted sixty-five sand ridges in the space of 14 kilometres. Some were 30 metres high. On the summit of one, a camel that had been unable to drink collapsed and died. Wells attributed the death to 'urinic poisoning or inflammation'. Carrying crippling loads through a searing desert with insufficient food or water might have had more to do with it.

After making camp the next day, Bejah had a quiet word with expedition leader Wells. He told him 'six of the camels were very bad, and would neither eat nor chew the cud'. Faced with the fact that the animals were dying, Wells decided to abandon all the collections of Keartland and Jones and take only a small load of water and the barest essentials. Six camels carried the lightened loads. The sickest camels carried nothing. That night, after travelling 16 kilometres, the expedition came upon the best patch of camel feed they'd seen in over a week. Wells paused to allow those animals that could still eat to graze.

On 27 October, Wells touched on his growing concern for his cousin Charles: 'Since my own experience, I am in doubt as to his welfare.'

Two nights later, another camel collapsed. Urged on by Bejah it rose, staggered a short distance, then sank again. Several times he got the forlorn creature to its feet, but finally nothing he did would make it rise. It had to be abandoned. Later that night two more camels lay down, but Bejah and Ameer managed to get them back up and moving again.

On October Wells saw smoke to the east of their camp and headed towards it, hoping it was his cousin. Bejah (probably suffering heat exhaustion) tried to follow, but after 11 kilometres he became too sick to go and turned back to camp. With only a quarter of a litre of cold tea in a small bottle, Wells walked 20 kilometres in the searing heat of mid-afternoon before realising he might not be able to return.

> Retracing my steps as best I could I hardly remember how I got back to camp. Many times, at the semblance of a shade, I sank to the ground with a singing sensation in the ears, going off into a stupid doze only to jump up with a start and push on again . . . On one occasion, when rising from the ground I noticed my own boot tracks and found I was going the wrong way . . . On reaching the last high sandridge, at 7 p.m., I saw Mr Keartland's signal fire. Getting on top of the ridge at another spot I could see the camp fire and hear voices, but was unable, through weakness, to call for assistance. After lying on top of the ridge for some time I set alight to some porcupine [Spinifex] to attract attention, and afterwards got within a quarter mile [400 metres] of the camp, where I was met by Mr Keartland and Said Ameer . . . After almost a whole night's travelling, a twenty-four miles [40 kilometres] walk in such a country and climate is sufficient to kill a salamander.

By Wells' reckoning they were very close to the location of Joanna Spring but couldn't see any sign of it. He was well aware that even a small error in the calculations made by the Warburton Expedition could put it many kilometres away, in any direction. Searching could prove fruitless and potentially lethal, given the expedition's situation. Wells decided there was nothing for it but to attempt the 200 kilometres to the certain water of the Fitzroy River.

October passed into November. They travelled exclusively by night but it was becoming impossible to sleep in the heat that rose with each morning's sun. Wells and Keartland had sandy blight. There was only enough water for the men for five days. For the camels there was none.

Any hope of reaching the Fitzroy depended solely on the ability of the camels to hold out. Wells recorded that during the night he and Bejah rode without shirts and hats, getting badly scratched as they pushed through patches of scrub. The cuts were an acceptable price for keeping cool. On 5 November Wells noted: 'The camels are very bad, many of them making a peculiar noise in the throat, and all of them have their tails matted with a gluey, urinic matter.' He calculated they were 40 kilometres from the Fitzroy.

The following night they pushed on with hopes of reaching the river by dawn. An exhausted Wells turned once again to his camel man. 'Selecting a star about the required bearing I instructed Bejah to steer in that direction for an hour and then call me for another bearing, while I rode in the rear and had a sleep.'

Wells was awake at 3.30 a.m. when a duck flew up from some grass, a sure sign that water was near. Half an hour later, they heard the distant bellowing of a bullock. At first light they discovered they were surrounded by lagoons full of fresh water. Bejah and Said Ameer held the camels back to stop them rushing the water and drinking themselves to death. The frantic beasts were given a bucket of water each, and were then shepherded to some feed near the banks of the Fitzroy. All of them were in terrible condition, two so bad that Bejah doubted they could survive.

Despite their ordeal, Wells gave the animals no rest. He was out of the desert. He had to get to a telegraph station. There was a rescue to organise. It was only after one of the sickest camels collapsed and he insisted it be left behind that it dawned on him the animals needed at least some respite. They could all drink freely, but most barely picked at the feed that was available to them. None could chew their cud. When Wells relented and made camp, Bejah went back for the sick camel. He led it gently into camp during the evening.

ABOVE: Illustration of a wombat *(Vombatus ursinus)*, from David Collins' *Account of the English Colony in NSW*, 1803. Its discoverer was the convict pioneer John Wilson.

BELOW: A water bore on James Tyson's Tinnenburra Station, south-western Queensland, in the 1890s. Tyson's pioneering irrigation methods revealed the potential of country far from river frontages. *(John Oxley Library, State Library of Queensland)*

Top: Droving in the Kimberley, Western Australia, circa 1910. Driving cattle through such narrow gorges exposed cattle and stockmen to ambush from traditional land-owners. *(E. L. Mitchell, National Library of Australia, nla.pic-vn4330803)*

Bottom: Droving a mob of bullocks in the Northern Territory in 1954. The skills of stockmen and their mounts were tested on long, dry stages as they tried to keep cattle moving without putting them under too much stress. *(Neil Murray, National Archives of Australia)*

Top: Members of the Calvert Scientific Expedition of 1896–7. From left, Charles Wells, George Jones, Lawrence Wells, Bejah Dervish and George Keartland. A.T. Magarey, far right, was the agent for the expedition sponsor. *(State Library of South Australia, B9758)*

Bottom: Bejah with some of the camels he was to nurse through horrendous conditions in the Great Sandy Desert in the summer of 1896–7. *(State Library of South Australia, B10486/1)*

ABOVE: The body of George Jones, one of two members of the Calvert Expedition (1896–7) who embarked on an ill-advised side trip and perished after their camels strayed. At the time he and Charles Wells were too weak to go after them. *(State Library of South Australia, B61236)*

MEPHAN. FERGUSONS Pipe Factory "FALKIRK" West Australia

Shewing FIVE MILES of 30 In. Pipes AWAITING DELIVERY

for COOLGARDIE WATER SCHEME 19.10.98

ABOVE: The pipes shown were sufficient for 8 kilometres of the Goldfields Water Scheme's main pipeline, which extended for more than 550 kilometres on its completion in 1903. *(Battye Library, State Library of Western Australia, 013512D)*

Above: A miner 'dry blowing' for gold in the Coolgardie–Kalgoorlie region circa 1896. This was one of several dry-blowing methods made necessary by the lack of water that the Goldfields Water Scheme hoped to address. *(Battye Library, State Library of Western Australia, 0008930D)*

Top: The Couston pipe-joining machine that improved progress on the Coolgardie pipeline but ultimately caused a political scandal that lead to the demise of the scheme's chief engineer, C.Y. O'Connor. *(Battye Library, State Library of Western Australia, 012640D)*

Bottom: After the dust had settled from the political brawls around the Goldfields Water Scheme, the celebrations spilled into the streets of Perth when it finally opened in 1903. *(Battye Library, State Library of Western Australia, 000904D)*

Top: Conditions for workers on the Trans-Australian Railway (built from Port Augusta to Kalgoorlie between 1912 and 1917) were at times extremely primitive. These blacksmiths were at work on the Nullarbor Plain. *(State Library of South Australia, B34931)*

Bottom: The Ooldea Sandhills on the eastern side of the Nullarbor Plain were the major physical hurdle for the Trans-Australian Railway. Picks, shovels and brute physical labour were used to shift thousands of tonnes of sand and earth, often in searing temperatures. *(National Library of Australia, nla.pic-an11193362-15v)*

ABOVE: Work on the Trans-Australian Railway accelerated in 1913 when two Roberts track-laying machines were imported from the United States and commenced operations at both ends of the line. Carriages fed raw materials to the machine on conveyor belts. A steam engine to push it forward onto the newly laid rails can be seen in the distance. *(Battye Library, State Library of Western Australia, 011860D)*

ABOVE: Without camels and cameleers (seen here carrying supplies past the railhead in 1912) the Trans-Australian Railway couldn't have been built. The irony was that it would soon make them redundant. *(State Library of South Australia, B24837)*

The next day Wells had the expedition on the move again. He struck the road from Derby to Fitzroy Crossing. Not long after, he came upon the local mail contractor. In Wells' words, the man was 'camping in the heat of the day'. It was sensible behaviour, even for someone who didn't have a string of desperately sick camels. Wells gave the contractor messages explaining the situation then headed off to Noonkanbah station. He arrived there on 10 November, but when he found he couldn't get any rations, decided to revert to travelling at night and left that evening.

Bejah pointedly walked, gently leading the two sickest camels, until Wells relented and made camp 6 kilometres from Noonkanbah. The next evening he moved on to Quanbun, en route for the Fitzroy Telegraph Station. On 14 November Wells' relentless to-ing and fro-ing killed one of the sickest camels. He wrote, 'He had everything possible done for him by Bejah, but was too far gone to recover.'

On 15 November Wells received a message from Fitzroy Telegraph Station that there was no news of his cousin. There was a message from John Forrest, Premier of Western Australia, expressing both 'congratulation and sympathy'. The explorer-turned-politician knew the Great Sandy Desert well enough to conclude that Wells and his men had done well to survive while Charles Wells and George Jones were dead. Wells lacked Forrest's acuity.

'I feel my cousin's absence most acutely, and cannot think what has happened,' he wrote, 'unless he has found water at or near Joanna Spring, and spelled some time . . . At the present time I feel I can do nothing towards finding them. These camels are almost useless now for day-travelling in the desert.'

That said, he promptly took Bejah and six camels, and embarked on the first of three futile rescue attempts in the Great Sandy Desert. Each time the exhausted camels, the dunes and the heat of high summer drove him back. Nat Buchanan came down from the Kimberley to assist in the third attempt, but when the camels ate poison weed and two died, they barely made it out of the desert with their lives. The wet season north of the desert eventually put an end to Wells' efforts to organise searches. He had to wait until the rains lifted, knowing that when they did he would be recovering bodies, not rescuing men.

They were finally able to move again in mid-March 1897. By then, disjointed information about two white men in the desert was circulating among the northern cattle stations and settlements. One said that desert Aborigines had reported a man with a camel still alive at a well, the other and his camel dead. The survivor was reputed to have killed and eaten an Aborigine. Wells decided to head to Gregory station to investigate. He soon ascertained that the white men seen were probably himself and Buchanan.

Having spent a week following the rumour, Wells, with Bejah, Keartland, Trainor and two Aboriginal guides, headed for the desert. While enjoying the milder weather they managed to reach the much-sought-after Joanna Spring on 9 April, discovering that its location was out by nearly 50 kilometres. The reliable water made the oasis very popular and Wells noticed one Aboriginal man was wearing a piece of cloth he believed belonged to his cousin. He asked the man and the others present if they knew anything about 'Untu white fellow purrunng' (a dead white man).

'Kutharra purrunng,' they said, and held up two fingers. They then tried to convey something of the men's condition, which Wells took to indicate they'd been dead for some time. On 13 April, the expedition came upon another group of Aboriginal people. It was evident they had never seen a living white man. Wrote Wells:

> Bejah and myself showed ourselves, whereupon several women and children, panic-stricken, fled for the next sandridge, and seven men, armed to the teeth with spears, boomerangs and waddies, came out into the open and threw out a challenge, calling 'Yarra, Yarra.' Bejah

suggested going back for Mr Keartland and Trainor, whilst the two boys said, 'Look out boss, him sulky fellow.' Telling Bejah that if we ran away now they would come after us with spears, I began an approach, with Bejah about two chains [200 metres] behind me, and the boys bringing up the rear. Bejah was very excited, calling to me not to get too close to them, as their spears were shipped [in their spear-throwers and ready for immediate use].

Wells was eventually able to make his peaceful intentions clear and his efforts produced more evidence of the missing men. Several items in the warriors' possession – plates, a quart-pot, tomahawk, iron and clothing – appeared to have come from Charles Wells and George Jones. However, when Wells asked about 'purrunng' white men, the natives agreed that they were dead but would not supply any further information.

From the refusal of the Aboriginal people to talk about what had happened, Wells concluded that it was an indication of guilt and that his colleagues had met with 'foul play'. He spent a couple of days trying to track down more natives before heading back to Derby to organise police assistance to arrest the natives in the vicinity of Joanna Spring and compel them to cooperate.

It was the perfect time of year for exploring the Great Sandy Desert when the final search party set off accompanied by Police Sub-Inspector Ord, Trooper Nicholson and two trackers. Bejah once again accompanied Lawrence Wells. The expedition reached the vicinity of Joanna Spring on 24 May where a 'wizard or doctor rejoicing in the name of Yallamerri' was seized. In his possession they found pieces of iron and part of a camel saddle. When asked where he'd got them, Yallamerri said 'purrunng white fellow' and pointed to the south-west. An Aboriginal warrior, Pallarri, was compelled to assist the search as well. At Joanna Spring both men were chained to a tree by their necks. Their legs were handcuffed.

The next day the searchers spelled the camels at Joanna Spring, shooting birds for food and questioning Yallamerri and Pallarri. 'They say that two are dead and that the sun killed them,' wrote Wells, 'but they profess ignorance regarding the locality, and state that the women and children had found the remains and taken the goods.'

On 26 May the searchers headed west, repeatedly questioning the two extremely reluctant men about the dead white men. When they reached a sand dune 20 kilometres from Joanna Spring, the two men refused to give any sensible indication of which direction to go. Ord rode up to Pallarri, lifted him off the ground by his hair and shook him. When Wells asked Pallarri where the white men were, Pallarri laughed at him. Ord told Nicholson to dismount and 'administer a little moral suasion'.

Both Pallarri and Yallamerri were terrified by the trooper. Yallamerri turned to Wells, shouted 'Purrunng white fellow' and pointed to the south. He and Pallarri set off at a trot on the new course. They continued in a straight line until nightfall. The next morning, 27 May, the two Aboriginal men again tried to avoid guiding the search, but again Trooper Nicholson forced them into cooperation. Five kilometres from camp Yallamerri held his hand up and said, 'Purrunng white fellow.' Wrote Wells:

Immediately in front of us was a high point of sandridge with a low saddle to the West. Being on my camel this morning I had a better view, and seeing a rope hanging from a small desert gum tree on the ridge, I drew Sub-Inspector Ord's attention to it. The natives, now at the foot of the ridge, exclaimed in one awed breath 'Wah! Wah!' I could then see my cousin's iron-grey beard and we were at last at the scene of their terrible death, with its horrible surroundings . . .

Dismounting, Mr. Ord and myself went to my cousin, whilst Nicholson and Bejah went where they saw some remnants of the camp equipment and found the body of Mr G. L. Jones, which was partly covered with drift sand. Where Charles Wells lay, half-clothed and dried like a mummy, we found nothing but a rug, a piece of rope hanging from a tree, and some old straps hanging to some burnt bushes, which held the brass eyelets of a fly that had either been rifled by the natives or burnt by a fire which had been within a few feet of his body.

The scene was just 25 kilometres from the real location of Joanna Spring. Fragments of a journal found with the body of George Jones revealed that four days after leaving Separation Well, the pair were so affected by the heat that they both became unwell. They hadn't been able to find water and, belatedly realising the impracticality of their plan, they turned back to Separation Well. They followed the tracks of Lawrence Wells and the others, though they were now two weeks behind. When one of their camels died, they were forced to walk much of the way, which left them exhausted. When the remainder of their camels strayed, they were too weak to round them up. When they ran out of water, they knew they were doomed.

After the expedition Wells was vilified in newspaper reports of the tragedy. History was much kinder on Bejah. His efforts to sustain the camels in his care were regarded as the reason a far worse disaster didn't overtake every member of the expedition. At a reception for the survivors, given at Government House in Adelaide, Wells presented Bejah with the expedition's compass, a memento he treasured for the rest of his life.

*

Bejah returned to Marree (known at the time as Hergott Springs) and resumed his life transporting goods throughout the arid areas of South Australia, New South Wales and Queensland. For years he was a familiar figure on the Oodnadatta, Strzelecki and Birdsville tracks. In 1909 he married a Marree woman, Amelia Shaw, who bore him a son, Abdul Jabbar (who became known as Jack). He continued to work into the 1930s, his strings of camels competing with the encroaching motorised transport that found the rough outback tracks, sand dunes and occasional floods hard-going.

In the late 1930s, when washing machine magnate Alan Simpson funded an expedition led by Dr Cecil Madigan to attempt the first crossing of the Simpson Desert (named in honour of their benefactor), Bejah was the obvious choice of cameleer. In August 1938, Cecil Madigan went to see him.

> I found him the grand old man Larry Wells had always represented him to be, still full of tales of the great adventure of the journey of the Calvert Expedition . . . and proud to tell that Wells had called him his friend. Bejah said with great regret that he was too old to go [he was then seventy-eight], but his son Jack, who was away at the time, would go, and Jack was a good boy on whom I could rely. He had a big round up of camels to show me and there were obviously plenty to choose from. The only uncertain quantity was Jack, whom I did not see till the following February, when I made another trip to Marree for that purpose. Jack Bejah impressed me favourably at once. He was young, solidly built and powerful, and seemed keen on the undertaking. He had his own camel team which he used on stations and fencing jobs in the outback, and could make up the required number from his friends' herds in Marree, where there seemed to be a sort of pool of camels, mostly out of work. Jack was tough, knew camels and the country, and seemed just the man for the job. Indeed, he later thoroughly proved himself to be a worthy son of his father. He was one of the first members appointed to the party, and he could not have been a better choice.

Madigan met Bejah again when the expedition was about to start. Bejah's son had already set out with his camel team but Bejah made a point of going to see Madigan when his train pulled into Marree at six in the morning.

'He was very anxious to impress on me that we should never let the camels loose,' Madigan recalled. '"Always have your camel in your hand" he kept repeating, shaking his hand as though holding a nose-line. It was not clear just how the camels were to get any feed. Bejah had had trouble with the camels getting away in the night during the Calvert Expedition, a thing that could be fatal.' In fact Bejah had seen two men die for just that reason.

Bejah retired around the time of Madigan's expedition, and dedicated himself to growing date palms. He was still living in Marree a decade later when author George Farwell met him while undertaking a journey up the Birdsville Track, researching his book *Land of Mirage*. It fell to Farwell to document the passing of the cameleers. Roads had improved and trucks had become more reliable. Large numbers of unemployed camels had been over-grazing Marree's common. The decision was eventually made to shoot the creatures that had once been the lifeblood of outback transportation. After they were gone many of the 'Afghans' returned to their villages in India and Pakistan. They'd spent their lives being treated as outsiders and felt there was nothing for them in Australia. Bejah regarded it as home.

Farwell found the old cameleer still 'tall and aristocratic' although he was nearly ninety. Bejah took him to the town's mosque, a building made of tin. As they walked, Bejah gestured towards a ragged date grove.

'One time,' he said, 'all big camp here. All Afghan. Here – over that way, out there – all camels and camel camp. One time my people have one hundred strings. That is many thousand camel. And now – now all gone.'

Bejah showed Farwell the mosque, a building whose interior was in stark contrast to the humble exterior. Beautifully embroidered prayer mats lay on the stone floor, images of Mecca and the Muslim judgment day hung on the walls. In the centre of the mosque the

Koran was wrapped in silk. Most impressive of all was Bejah. Farwell wrote of him:

> There was deep reverence in his manner, yet nothing of ritual or dogma. Our whole visit had been easy, almost informal, but I felt that somehow he had drawn strength from these few minutes in this sanctuary . . . There was no bitterness in him. Resignation, yes – disappointment, a sense of nostalgia for days that were past. Bejah Dervish [sic] was a courageous old man, for he had seen his world slowly crumble around him. He continued to stride through the town with measured dignity.

In his acclaimed 1954 film, *The Back of Beyond,* John Heyer also briefly featured Bejah, who was then well into his nineties. The film showed him slightly hunched as he walked to prayer on a treeless bluff outside the town. He was described as the last of the lords of the desert. He was still turbaned, as he was when photographed with the Calvert Expedition nearly sixty years before, but time had turned his beard pure white and his face was deeply lined. The film's narrator translated his prayer – for contemporaries who had perished in the stony desert far from their homelands. Soon the prayer was for him.

Bejah died in Port Augusta Hospital on 6 May, 1957. With him the days of an extraordinary breed of outback pioneers drew to an end. They were men apart, but the end of their era didn't go unnoticed. Bejah's death was reported in newspapers from *The Mail* in Adelaide to *The Times* in London.

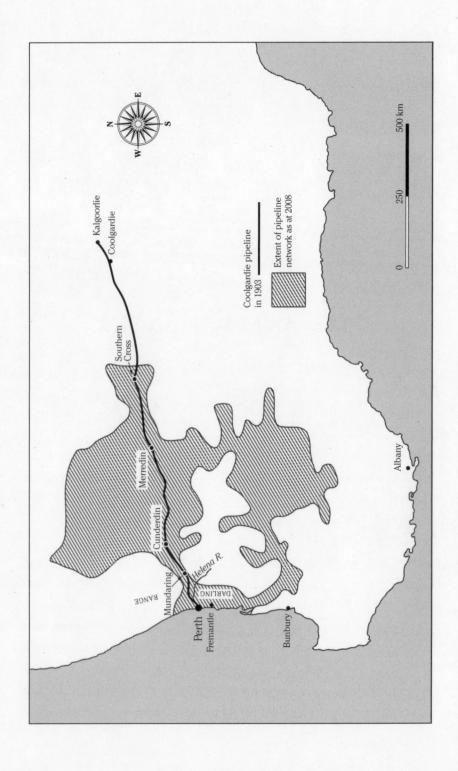

C.Y. O'Connor, circa 1897
(Battye Library, State Library of Western Australia)

5

THE WATER BRINGER

C.Y. O'Connor (1843–1902)

Gold has always been revered among precious metals, but chief among its extraordinary qualities is the power it exerts on the human mind. Through such power it has lured thousands to the furthest corners of the world and transformed societies. Many have died or been ruined for their pursuit of it.

Gold has written many chapters in history. In 1892 it was Western Australia's turn. That was the year prospectors Arthur Bayley and William Ford found gold near where the town of Coolgardie now stands. The find was in semi-desert 200 kilometres east of the nearest settlement (Southern Cross) and 450 kilometres from Perth. Others had found traces of gold in the area at around the same time, but on 17 September Bayley and Ford staked their claim and revealed that in a matter of days they'd mined more than 15 kilograms of gold. The news was electrifying. Thousands rushed to Western Australia by ship, then to the goldfields by wagon, on horseback and even on foot.

The rush became a torrent of humanity in 1893 when Paddy Hannan, Thomas Flanagan and Dan Shea found The Golden Mile, an almost solid lump of gold that made the ground under what was soon the town of Kalgoorlie (40 kilometres north-east of Coolgardie) the richest in the world. It was like a dream come true but for one major problem. There was no water.

Explorer David Carnegie was drawn to the rush in its early days and in *Spinifex and Sand* described 'the selfish striving, each to help himself, the awful sufferings of man and beast, horses and camels mad with thirst, and men cursing the country and themselves, for wasting their lives and strength in it'.

Water was being carted 50 kilometres to the diggings by horse teams or camel caravans. It was sold at up to a shilling for 4 litres ($2 a litre at present values). Basic hygiene became prohibitively expensive and the threat of disease was ever-present. According to Carnegie:

> Enough to drink was all one thought of; two lines of eager men on either side of the track could daily be seen waiting for these water-carts. What a wild rush ensued when they were sighted! In a moment they were surrounded and taken by storm, men swarming on to them like an army of ants.

At the end of 1893, as the heat of summer intensified, the situation grew worse. Even the distant water supplies were failing and notices were posted warning that the track to Coolgardie would soon be closed to avert a catastrophe. It made no difference as people continued to rush to the scene. Soon more than a thousand were toiling in the fierce heat. The lack of water forced the miners to devise a method of separating gold from dirt known as 'dry blowing'. In its simplest form this involved repeatedly pouring dirt from a metal pan held at head height into a pan on the ground. The wind blew the dust away, leaving pebbles, gold nuggets and the heavier grains of gold behind. Wrote Carnegie:

> Desperate hard work this, with the thermometer at 100°F [37.7°C] in the shade, with the 'dishes' so hot that they had often to be put aside to cool, with clouds of choking dust, a burning throat, and water at a shilling to half a crown a gallon! Right enough for the lucky ones 'on gold' and for them not a life of ease! The poor devil with neither money nor luck, who looked into each dishful of dirt for the wherewithal to live, and found it not, was indeed scarcely to be envied.

Even those who struck gold didn't fare particularly well. Of the five men whose finds led to the development of Coolgardie and Kalgoorlie: Bayley used his wealth to buy a farm near Avenel, Victoria, but died in 1896; Flanagan died in 1899, in poor health after having his leg amputated the year before; and Shea died in poverty in Perth in 1908. Only two of the men lived to a ripe old age: Hannan died in Melbourne in 1925; Ford died in 1932.

Despite the terrible conditions, the population in the goldfields continued to grow and by 1895 was 5000. For the next five years it grew by 5000 every year. The number of companies formed to exploit the finds also exploded – more than 800 listed on the London Stock Exchange between 1893 and 1897. The future for the colony of Western Australia, which had become self-governing in 1890, looked bright. First, though, it had to solve the water problem.

The goldfields encompassed a region of more than 100000 square kilometres. Within that area there wasn't a single permanent river. The annual rainfall was less than 27 centimetres. When bores yielded water it was heavily mineralised and the flow was weak. When mines were dug some ground water flowed in, then even that started drying up. The job of finding a solution fell to Western Australia's Department of Public Works, newly established with the arrival of self-government. The department's chief engineer was Charles Yelverton O'Connor.

O'Connor was an Irishman, born in County Meath in 1843. He trained as an engineer before migrating to New Zealand in 1865, where he soon built a reputation for the roads, railways and port facilities he constructed in the rugged west of the North Island. He'd thought he would spend his life there, but in the early 1890s he was passed over for promotion and started looking for work elsewhere. New Zealand's loss was Western Australia's gain. The state's first premier, John Forrest, regarded O'Connor as the perfect man to run his new public works office. So, in 1891, after twenty-five years in New Zealand (where he'd met and married his wife, Susan, and had eight children), O'Connor moved to Perth.

When O'Connor asked Forrest the extent of his responsibilities, the premier replied, 'Everything.' He wasn't joking. O'Connor had to plan and oversee the construction and operation of the government's railways, roads, port facilities, water supplies and much more. His job covered the entire infrastructure needs of the largest state in Australia, which at the time was also one of the least developed. Fortunately, O'Connor soon demonstrated superb organisational abilities and excellent skill in managing his small, hard-pressed staff. He had a brilliant mind and a keen sense of humour. He was fond of recounting the reaction of the premier's wife upon meeting three of his children. She looked at them, then at the balding O'Connor, and blurted, 'Your wife must be very good looking.'

O'Connor's projects not only addressed the problem at hand, they took into account the financial constraints of the fledgling state. Wherever possible they were flexible enough to grow and adapt to the demands of the future. In Fremantle, for example, he devised a plan for a port facility that could be expanded until the port became the gateway to the entire state. In fact, it formed part of an overall development strategy for Western Australia's future.

O'Connor regarded supplying water to the goldfields as the next part of that strategy, a step that presented the greatest challenge of his career. While his staff used all their ingenuity to grapple with the immediate water crisis – building railways and organising trains to bring water from the coast, constructing condensers to purify the mineralised water from the bores, excavating enormous water storages (known as tanks) to capture any rainfall and utilising every conceivable conservation method – O'Connor contemplated the bigger question of establishing a permanent supply.

The more he looked at it, the bigger it got. At first he thought that providing elaborate infrastructure wasn't such a pressing issue since the need for it might evaporate as quickly as water on a claypan (when the gold ran out, fields could be deserted overnight). However, as the mining companies dug deeper, they kept finding more of the precious metal and it began to look more like a long-term proposition. He also realised that much of the land between Perth and the goldfields had good potential for agriculture but for the lack of water, and that townships servicing the railway lines to the goldfields were also inadequately supplied.

Finally, O'Connor reflected on Western Australia's place in a future Australian Commonwealth. In the 1890s the state was cut off from the rest of Australia by trackless desert. From Perth the only way to get to the eastern states was by ship. If the state ever wanted to build a railway line to the east, the steam trains that would use the line would also need water and plenty of it.

Taken altogether, it was clear that the water problem needed a long-term solution rather than a quick fix. It's thought that Forrest asked for a plan early in 1895, but even if he hadn't, the frequent demands for action from goldfields mayors and mine operators ensured the water problem was never far from O'Connor's mind. It's likely that O'Connor had been working on the problem for some time because in August 1895 one of his junior engineers, when writing to a colleague in Victoria about job prospects in the west, mentioned 'an expected large-scale water scheme'.

The particularly dry summer of 1895 brought an acute repeat of the annual water crisis for Coolgardie and Kalgoorlie. In December, Premier Forrest mentioned in parliament that O'Connor's office was working on a solution while directing that immediate steps be taken to address the current shortage. Tanks were to be dug, even at sites O'Connor's field officers believed unsuitable. Drilling operations were to begin, to depths up to 1000 metres, despite advice from O'Connor's geologists that artesian water would not be found.

Such measures did little to alleviate the situation, but they did silence local pundits who were sure there was artesian water under the goldfields and also took the pressure off the government, for that summer at least. In May 1896 the fruitless drilling continued, and *The West Australian* noted: 'The government is determined to spend a sum of money in effectually putting to rest the belief that artesian water may be found under the gold mines of Coolgardie . . . We may be satisfied that the attempt will not be conceded as hopeless until so much money has been poured into the hole that the public conscience will revolt against prosecuting the search further.'

Two months later, in July, the drilling rigs of the Department of Public Works were grinding away at the bedrock beneath Coolgardie when John Forrest introduced the Coolgardie Goldfields Water Supply Loan Bill to the West Australian parliament. In detailing the plan he emphasised the need for a long-term solution to ensure mining could proceed without interruption. He noted that on his visits to the region he'd seen unwashed men, at risk of typhoid, waiting for water deliveries. It had cost him £1 (equivalent to nearly $200 in 2008 values) to water his five horses. He said that many of the miners were sending money out of the colony to their families because conditions on the goldfields were too harsh for their families to join them. He estimated that a reliable supply would cost less than $8 for 1000 litres (in present values). The scheme would cost £2.5 million (approximately $500 million in present values) and take three years to construct.

And the scheme itself? What O'Connor wanted to do was construct a dam on one of the rivers in the Darling Ranges near Perth, pump 23 million litres of water a day to a height of 304 metres to get it over the ranges, and then pipe it 550 kilometres to the goldfields. In essence, he wanted to turn an entire river inland and send it to the parched outback. Even by modern standards the project was immense. Yet for all its size it was remarkably straightforward. There was nothing new in constructing dams, pumping stations or pipelines. It was the number of them O'Connor was proposing to link together that was unique. It would be the biggest water main anyone had constructed anywhere in the world, ever.

Opposition to the idea was almost universal. Representatives from the goldfields, who still believed there was abundant water in artesian wells and mineralised lakes, described it as 'a scheme of madness'. However, in a departmental note written in August 1896 O'Connor reflected, 'The fact that there is no water famine at present existing in Coolgardie has, I believe, had considerable influence on the attitude which certain persons have taken as regards the scheme (the agony stage having been passed for the time being).'

While the honourable members struggled with the idea, others were quick to realise its potential. Shortly after the bill was tabled in parliament, O'Connor received an offer from a British firm to buy the entire supply of water for the first twenty years at the price Forrest had quoted. All they wanted in return was a monopoly on water supplies in the region. Tempting as this early version of a public–private partnership might have been, the offer was declined. Despite vehement objections, the loan bill was passed in September 1896.

While the government set about raising money to build the scheme, preparatory work was already under way. The route for the pipeline was surveyed, mainly along existing railway lines that would make supplying materials easier and keep construction costs down. Maintenance would also be easier once the pipeline was completed. The site for the dam, near Mundaring on the Helena River, was also surveyed.

Before the real work started, O'Connor proposed that the entire plan be submitted to a commission of leading engineers in England. If nothing else, a tick from such a commission might blunt the attacks of his critics. O'Connor left Perth in January 1897 for London. While he was there he attended Queen Victoria's Jubilee and received a CMG, on 23 July, 1897, in part as recognition of the successful completion of his harbour at Fremantle. When O'Connor returned to Western Australia in September, he had with him the interim report of the commissioners. 'The scheme as propounded is quite practicable', the report said, and referred to it as 'this remarkable aqueduct'.

It should have been full steam ahead, but when O'Connor returned to Perth it was to a newly elected parliament. Forrest was still premier, but opposition to the scheme was stronger than ever. In addition, a global economic downturn meant the government was struggling to borrow the money to build the scheme. However, four years after Bayley and Ford's initial find, the member for North East Coolgardie, F.C.B. Vosper, was beginning to realise that none of the quick fixes were working. While not actually supporting O'Connor's scheme, he did concede that, 'As a representative of the goldfields I find myself totally unable to offer any opposition.'

Meanwhile, out on the goldfields, they were still drilling for artesian water. In one of the holes they'd started using an expensive diamond drill to penetrate the bedrock. The continuing failure to find artesian water saw opposition to O'Connor's scheme gradually evaporate. On 25 November, 1897, when the diamond drill had reached a depth of

3002 feet 6 inches (915.2 metres), the government finally called a halt. Government geologist Gibb Maitland couldn't resist an I-told-you-so in the *Annual Report of the Geological Survey*: 'The result of this experiment . . . should tend to modify the opinion of those who incline to the belief that artesian water can be obtained in impermeable rocks "if you only go far enough".'

With the opposition in retreat it was now the difficulty in securing loans that put the brakes on the water scheme. The first loan finally came through in January 1898 but by then they'd had to cut jobs in the Department of Public Works. O'Connor had lost half his staff.

By the middle of 1898 the leader of the opposition, George Leake, was proposing that all the work except building the dam be carried out by private enterprise. O'Connor opposed the idea, in part because it meant his department wouldn't be able to closely control key elements of the scheme, in particular the crucial pipeline. He was happy to order materials from contractors, but refused to trust construction to anyone but his employees.

Finally, in October 1898, John Forrest managed to push through the Coolgardie Goldfields Water Supply Construction Bill, mostly through the sheer force of his personality. O'Connor originally estimated three years to complete the project. Two years had already passed in political and financial wrangling, but now the clock was really ticking.

The government had already called for tenders to manufacture 60 000 steel pipes, 28 feet (8.53 metres) by 30 inches (76 centimetres). In October it took the two lowest quotes, from two Australian suppliers, and split the job between them. One company was G&C Hoskins of Sydney, which was already supplying pipes to the West Australian government for Perth's metropolitan water supply. The other company was Mephan Ferguson of Melbourne. The choice of Mephan Ferguson was yet another of O'Connor's radical leaps of thinking. The company had devised a new method of steel-pipe fabrication that employed a locking-bar mechanism down its length instead of rivets or welding. It was in use in very few applications, but O'Connor believed it would make laying the world's longest pipeline more efficient and, most importantly, it would have fewer leaks. The lack of rivets would also allow water to flow in the pipes with less friction. In late 1898 both firms signed contracts to produce the new pipes.

To make the pipes, the government had to order 70000 tonnes of steel. In the mid-1890s, when O'Connor had begun initial costing, there was a glut of steel production and prices were low. But by 1898 a strike in England and a tightening of supply meant much higher prices, if a supplier could be found. Eventually mills in Germany and the United States took orders for half each and by March 1899 the first steel for the pipeline was being unloaded at O'Connor's port in Fremantle (where he had his home and office).

The scheme's next obstacle was one that measured 9000 square metres. Out at the dam site on the Helena River, O'Connor's principal assistant on the water scheme, Thomas Hodgson, discovered that what they'd thought was bedrock was actually a massive boulder. It had to be removed before construction could begin. Worse, it was sitting on a fault line filled with debris. That too had to be excavated for nearly 30 metres below the riverbed. There was nothing for it but to start breaking rock and digging.

O'Connor went out to the site repeatedly during December 1899 to check on progress and advise his staff. They rounded up extra drills and installed electric lights so a second shift could work into the night. By the end of the month, O'Connor himself determined that they had excavated far enough. He gave the order to start pouring concrete, while devising a conveyor system to help safely deliver material to the bottom of the shaft.

Out on the goldfields, an economic downturn saw town officials transform their opposition to the scheme into a clamour for construction to be accelerated when they realised that it could provide work for unemployed miners. A royal commission also belatedly arrived at the conclusion that 'the future prosperity of the Eastern Goldfields is bound up in the question of permanent water supply and we strongly recommend the completion at as early a date as possible of the Coolgardie Water Scheme'.

In Perth, pipe manufacturing was gathering momentum: the two companies were turning out up to 800 pipes a week between them. By the beginning of 1900 the first shipment was ready. Orders for pumps were being placed. Soil along the route was being tested to ensure it wouldn't corrode the pipes in areas where they would be buried to protect them from the outback's extremes – out in the open the pipes would be heated to as much as 60°C.

Among the countless details requiring his attention (not to mention his responsibility for supervising other projects across the state), O'Connor now turned his attention to the best way of joining and caulking 60 000 pipes. He settled on a method whereby a metal ring was wrapped around the joint, and the small gap between the two pipes was packed with hemp and molten lead. As the lead cooled it was hammered into the joint to make the seal. This complicated, crucial procedure, carried out in extremes of heat and cold 60 000 times for 550 kilometres, had the potential to take a very long time.

Once again, the problem presented by the water scheme inspired the solution. Engineering contractor Thomas Couston was working on other projects in Western Australia when he realised that a machine he'd devised might be able to mechanise the caulking process. In 1899 he showed it to senior engineer Thomas Hodgson, who liked what he saw and encouraged Couston to develop it further. In April 1900, Couston was able to demonstrate that machine-caulked joints were far better than those done manually, although the area around the locking bars still had to be hand-finished. The machine could also do the joints faster and at a cost saving. The Western Australian government was so impressed that it didn't just buy the machine, it bought the patent as well. Couston was hired to supervise its use and train its operators. The first machines went to work in March 1901.

By then, the political landscape of the state had changed dramatically. It had become part of the Commonwealth of Australia when the states federated in January 1901. John Forrest had been elected to federal parliament as the first member for the Western Australian seat of Swan. His departure created a power vacuum in state politics and, following the state elections of 1901, four governments formed, collapsed and reformed. In such a climate the staunchest opponents of the water scheme seized the opportunity to renew their attacks. With Forrest gone, they turned their attention to O'Connor.

The purchase of the caulking machines was the principal target, particularly as the teething problems seemed never-ending. Couston was discovering that working for the government was nothing like working as a contractor – he couldn't hire and fire, and purchasing even the smallest item involved endless red tape. Some departments even randomly refused to approve purchases in the misguided belief that it was an effective way to cut costs. By January 1902, 20000 pipes had been laid and jointed. The work had taken two years. The process was gaining speed as the caulking crews grew more experienced, but there were still 40000 pipes to join. When Couston suggested to O'Connor that doing the work under contract might be more efficient, the beleaguered engineer was under so much pressure that he considered it. Couston estimated he could complete the work by 30 September, 1902, at a price favourable to the government. O'Connor sent a memorandum to his new Minister for Public Works, Cornthwaite Rason, recommending Couston's offer provided that his employees received equivalent conditions to government workers and that certain quality assurances were met.

What O'Connor needed was a quick decision. What he got was a prolonged political and bureaucratic nightmare. Rason decided to refer the matter to Cabinet. They didn't want to take the decision either, so the matter went to parliament. Rason tabled Couston's proposal on 21 January. The next day he moved that parliament accept it. Instead they deferred the debate. While the decision stalled, the enemies of the scheme moved in.

On 24 January correspondence between Forrest and Leake (now Western Australia's premier) regarding delays on the scheme was made public. The appropriately named Leake's letter highlighted the fact that the scheme was supposed to have been finished in three years, while ignoring its opponents' time-wasting tactics. Leake next demanded information from the Department of Public Works on the cause of the delays. With typical efficiency an officer of the department, E.E. Salter, had a response for him on 25 January, a Saturday. Salter pointed out that much of the responsibility rested with the indecision of politicians and the calls for go-slows when funds were running short.

The following morning *The Sunday Times* didn't let the facts get in the way of a good story. It launched a scathing attack on the scheme and O'Connor. It described him as 'that man whose whole career in the service of this state is fraught with sinister conundrums and peccant marvels'. On 29 January the attack returned to the parliament. John Glowery of South Province and F.T. Crowder of East Province used parliamentary privilege to slur O'Connor, but when the government was challenged to defend its senior officer, the Minister for Lands Adam Jameson responded: 'I cannot but think that many mistakes may have been made in the execution of the scheme . . . The present Government have absolutely nothing to do with these mistakes . . . Therefore it was not incumbent on me to jump up for the purpose of refuting Mr Crowder's statements.'

When the discussion resumed on 3 February, Leake said most of his government had opposed the water scheme 'tooth and nail'. He went on, 'We do not wish to have the mistakes of other people thrown on our shoulders. We do not want to be saddled with other

people's blunders.' He proposed that a parliamentary select committee look into the scheme and Couston's contract, followed by a royal
commission.

The select committee started its hearings the following day. It was
comprised of Charles Harper, W.J. George, J.L. Nanson, Rason and
Henry Daglish. None were engineers, goldfields representatives or
qualified to assess Couston's contract. Most, if not all, were opponents
of the water scheme. The politicians took evidence on everything
from the effectiveness of locking-bar pipes to the administration of
the Department of Public Works. The one person it didn't call was
O'Connor, the man whose reputation was being shredded in parliament, the press and the inquiry. O'Connor was in South Australia,
sent there for three weeks by his government (he left on 23 January) to serve on a commission advising South Australia on plans for
Adelaide's harbour works. The media and some politicians stooped
to the suggestion that he'd fled the state.

On 9 February *The Sunday Times* was at it again with an article
titled 'Corruption by Contract':

> It is an open rumour everywhere that this shire engineer from New
> Zealand [O'Connor] has absolutely flourished on 'palm grease' since
> the first day when the harbour works and the Coolgardie Water Scheme
> were agreed upon . . . Apart from any distinct charge of corruption this
> man has exhibited such gross blundering or something worse in his
> management of great public works that it is no exaggeration to say that
> he has robbed the taxpayers of this state out of millions of money.

Meanwhile, the select committee was coming up short on evidence.
The best they had was a suggestion that O'Connor's senior engineer
on the project, Thomas Hodgson, had been involved in speculative
land deals associated with the pipeline. In this he was not alone.
Anyone in Perth with a bit of spare cash had long ago calculated

what formerly parched land would be worth once the pipeline began to flow. Speculation was rife. The more troubling aspect of Hodgson's activities was that he'd borrowed from Couston to finance some of his deals. The arrangement had the potential for a conflict of interest, but when the select committee reported on 17 February all it could conclude was that most matters, including Hodgson's land deals, required 'closer inquiry'. Significantly, the inquiry found no evidence of wrong-doing on the part of O'Connor. As for the question of Couston's contract to joint the pipeline, the reason for the inquiry in the first place, it was all but forgotten.

The following day, the last before parliament rose, Leake's government pushed through all the readings of a bill to set up a royal commission. During the debate, Crowder commented: 'If a Royal Commission be appointed to inquire into the methods of the Works Department I shall do my best to prove to the Commission that a terrible waste of money is going on.'

The political slanging match even managed to drown out the annual desperate cries from the goldfields for water. It was high summer once more, and a particularly dry one, which meant the demands for immediate action were in full flower. The pleading fell on deaf ears as the West Australian parliament continued to demonstrate that it couldn't even decide how to join two pipes together.

By then, O'Connor was back from his trip to Adelaide. The effect of the personal and professional attacks was evident to everyone who knew him. When he got off the boat from Adelaide, his family could see he was depressed. When he asked about the latest newspaper reports, they tried to change the subject. Colleagues thought he looked constantly worried. His sense of humour was long gone. Some reports suggested he had begun to drink heavily.

On 26 February the royal commission was appointed. Before it met, O'Connor had his staff go through the recent parliamentary debates and highlight every comment regarding the pipeline project. He then dictated a response to every criticism. On 2 March, a Sunday, he called unexpectedly at the home of an acquaintance, barrister Matthew Moss, a former mayor and MP. He discussed the attacks that had been made on him. O'Connor was worried about his legal position regarding the allegations of corruption. Moss dismissed his concerns and told him not to pay much attention to the push and shove of gutter politics.

At least the pipeline was going well. The reservoir had long since been completed, and the pumping stations were coming on line. The most difficult sections of pipe, through the Darling Ranges, were complete, and the pace of caulking was accelerating in the remaining, easier sections. On Saturday 8 March a 10-kilometre stretch of pipe was tested. It worked perfectly. A grand total of one leak was found. Water would soon be flowing to the first main town, Cunderdin.

On Monday 10 March, O'Connor rose early for his customary horse ride along the beach near his home. His daughter Bridget normally rode with him, but that morning she was unwell and didn't go. Before setting out, O'Connor wrote a short note:

> The position has become impossible. Anxious important work to do and three commissions of enquiry to attend to. We may not have done as well as possible in the past but we will necessarily be too hampered to do well in the imminent future. I feel that my brain is suffering and I am in great fear of what effect all this worry may have upon me – I have lost control of my thoughts. The Coolgardie scheme is all right and I could finish it if I got a chance and protection from misrepresentation but there's no hope for that now and it's better that it should be given to some entirely new man to do who will be untrammelled by prior responsibility.
>
> 10/3/02

In the pale morning light a groom helped O'Connor mount his horse and watched as he cantered down the street in the direction of the sea. When O'Connor got there, he then turned south along the beach, heading towards Robb Jetty. A short time later his body was found, floating in the water. He had died from a single gunshot to the head, fired at point-blank range. The inquiry into his death returned a verdict of suicide. Among his papers there was further evidence of his state of mind. The brilliant engineer had attempted to do some simple mathematical calculations and failed.

The royal commission met between March and July. After it concluded, its interim report suggested calling tenders for the caulking work. In the end, Couston never got his contract. Instead, departmental labour caulked the line, mostly using Couston's machine. Hodgson was highly criticised and resigned. The report found nothing against the late chief engineer.

The final verdict on Charles Yelverton O'Connor's life and work came nine months later. The pipeline had been completed under the new chief engineer, William Reynoldson, and towards the end of January 1903 the politicians started assembling for the opening ceremonies. At the reservoir near Perth, on 22 January, Lady Forrest turned on Pumping Station No. 1. The pipeline's water flow was more than matched by a torrent of self-congratulation among the scheme's supporters and detractors. One of them, MP and editor of *The West Australian* John Hackett, gave credit where it was due. In his newspaper the following day he wrote:

> Two men and two men only were responsible for the Coolgardie Water Scheme, Sir John Forrest and Mr C.Y. O'Connor, the man who had given his life for it . . . Though many had derided the idea of the pumping scheme, though many had opposed it, now that the scheme had achieved success a great number of men claimed the idea as theirs, all of them seemingly thinking of the idea at the same moment.

On 24 January the dignitaries gathered in Coolgardie's exhibition grounds. With the temperature a scorching 41°C, John Forrest turned a valve that sent a fountain of pure fresh water spurting into the air, much to the delight of the assembled citizens. The ceremony was repeated at Kalgoorlie later that afternoon. The scheme was declared a complete success. Amid the endless toasts, future prime minister George Reid commented that he'd never heard so much talk about water and seen so little drunk.

The scheme on completion cost £2.66 million. It had gone £166000 over budget in part due to new federal government duties that weren't part of the original 1895 costings, and had taken four years and two months to build. A year after the pipeline opened, consumption of water amounted to only a quarter of what it could supply. It was found that even with an abundance of water, average daily consumption levels of households in Coolgardie and Kalgoorlie were only a third of those in Perth. The old habits of water conservation were hard to break. Leaks on what was now known as the Goldfields Water Scheme were only a quarter of what O'Connor had expected.

Gradually, the land from Mundaring to Kalgoorlie was populated and the wool and wheat belt of the Golden West began expanding north and south of the pipeline. Today, the network of mains and pipelines amounts to 8000 kilometres, supplying water to over 100000 people in 110 towns and localities over an area of 100000 square kilometres.

O'Connor is a revered figure in Western Australia. There are memorials in Coolgardie, Kalgoorlie and Fremantle. The beach where he died has been renamed C.Y. O'Connor Beach. A sculpture marks the location of his death. O'Connor's life has been fictionalised in Robert Drewe's award-winning novel *The Drowner*. Drewe acknowledges that O'Connor was one of his childhood heroes. His pipeline is still regarded as one of the most important pieces of infrastructure ever built in Australia.

One of O'Connor's colleagues from his days in New Zealand wrote after his death: '[He] personally combined gentleness and amiability with force and vigour and intellectual activity to an extraordinary degree . . . Professionally, he possessed in a high degree all the qualities of a pioneer engineer.'

To the people of the outback who benefited from his genius he was the water bringer – Aquarius down-under. Folklore has it that for years after the scheme's completion, the women of the towns that benefited from O'Connor's clean, fresh water thanked God for him every time they turned on a tap.

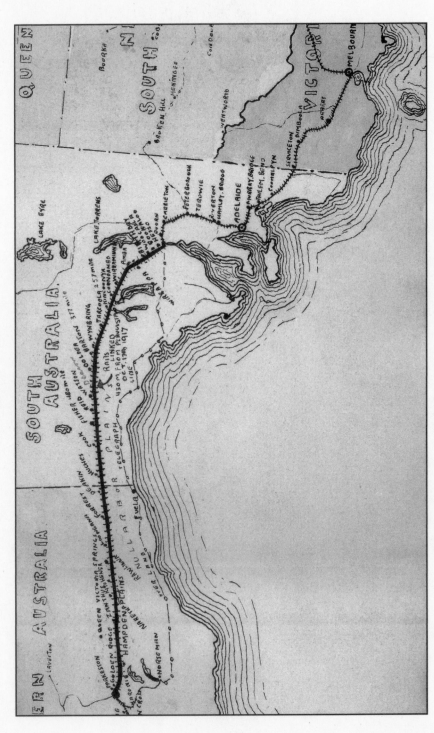

ABOVE: A hand-drawn map showing the route of the first passenger journey from Port Augusta to Kalgoorlie
(*State Library of South Australia B4102/1B*)

Henry Deane, circa 1890.
Photo by John Hubert Newman
(National Library of Australia, [nla.pic-an] 24082144)

6

A BOND OF IRON

The Trans-Australian Railway

(1912–1917)

On 1 January, 1912, on the corner of Market Street and Flinders Lane, Melbourne, an engineer seven years past retirement age opened the doors to the office space that was to become the headquarters of Australia's greatest work of nation-building since Federation. Henry Deane was sixty-five years old, a former chief engineer for the New South Wales government railways (where the retirement age was fifty-eight) with an illustrious career that encompassed projects around the world. Now, in his twilight years, he was about to embark on a project that eclipsed them all – construction of a railway that would link Western Australia with the rest of the continent.

Deane's flowing grey beard and gaunt features testified to decades of tireless service. He was meticulous in his planning and organisation, innovative in his ideas and always prepared to embrace the latest developments in technology. He had suggested electrification of the railways from Sydney to the Blue Mountains and to the proposed national capital at Canberra. He'd even suggested a tunnel under Sydney Harbour, a crossing that would have the advantage of not disrupting shipping. It was an idea so far ahead of its time that it wouldn't be realised until almost a century later.

Deane had been involved in the planning of the trans-Australian railway since 1903, when state railway engineers were first called together by the Federal Department of Home Affairs to consider the reports and surveys of men like Western Australia's chief engineer, Charles Yelverton O'Connor, who had examined the feasibility of the line in the days after Western Australia made the line a condition of joining the Commonwealth.

The trans-Australian had been a long-held dream in the west. In 1892 O'Connor had said the new port at Fremantle was a vital prerequisite for the larger work ahead: 'I looked upon it that the people of the other colonies would never by mad enough to support a trans-continental railway approaching Perth or Fremantle unless they had a perfect assurance that the harbour there would be of the first class.'

The water pipeline from Perth to Coolgardie and Kalgoorlie was also regarded as vital for steam trains setting off into the arid expanse of central Australia. More water sources would need to be found along the 1700-kilometre line, but the Coolgardie supply would be crucial during and after construction.

The work done by Western Australia reflected its keenly felt isolation. It was looked upon as a neighbouring island of Australia, cut off by oceans of sand and wilderness. The actual sea voyage from Perth to Adelaide was 1600 ship-breaking kilometres across the Great Australian Bight, most of them through the Roaring Forties. At the time

of the railway proposal, there was no road of any kind from Kalgoorlie in the west to Tarcoola in the east. The only white people to have
crossed it were explorers. In 1841 Eyre was the first to travel across
the Nullarbor, in 133 days. In 1870 future politician John Forrest did
it in 142 days. Now it was planned to build a train line that would
drastically reduce the trip to a mere three days.

Supporters of the line saw it as the first physical connection
between Western Australia and the rest of the country, a 'bond of
iron' that would connect Western Australia to the Federation with
something more tangible than sentiment. Unfortunately, after all the
talk of forging a nation, it soon became evident that the new federal
parliament had other agendas. In fact, they were too many to count
as every decision was stricken with jealousy and self-interest, and
every state's representative fought for a share of any spoils on offer.

There was nothing in the trans-Australian railway for the eastern
states, which had the overwhelming majority of Australia's population and votes in parliament. As the months after Federation turned
to years, even South Australia revealed its reluctance to support a
link with Western Australia, as Adelaide's merchants feared the line
would pass north of their city, sidelining them.

However, the case for the railway was far from lost, particularly while the formidable John Forrest was in parliament. In 1901
O'Connor had conducted a preliminary survey at his behest. Forrest
was also behind other studies done in 1901. None of them found
any physical obstacles to constructing the line. A 1903 conference
chaired by Henry Deane confirmed the findings. The project was feasible. All it required was the political will.

For the next three years the will was sadly lacking as attempts
to fund the work to survey the route (let alone build the line) were
repeatedly defeated in federal parliament. When the matter came up
again in 1907, fortunately some politicians were starting to realise
they were supposed to be governing for all Australians. Queensland

Senator Tom Dawson had nothing to gain when he called on parliament to break out of its 'parochial stupor'. When South Australian interests were appeased with the promise of a trans-continental railway from Adelaide to Darwin (this promise took another 100 years to be honoured), the vote was passed.

In mid-1908 survey parties set out from South Australia (led by J.T. Furner) and Western Australia (led by R.J. Anketell). Both parties used camels for transport because previous studies had revealed the 1700-kilometre route from Kalgoorlie to Port Augusta didn't have a single permanent water course. Furner wrote of the country he saw: 'No life of any kind exists, excepting a few reptiles and insects.' Another member of his expedition considered the region to be 'the most desolate belt of country in Australia'.

While the survey was being carried out, John Forrest had Henry Deane appointed consulting engineer in chief for the trans-Australian railway (he could only be employed as a consultant because he was supposed to be retired). Deane immediately set out to meet with the surveyors in the field. A photograph shows him – a frail-looking white-haired figure at a camp site in the bush – enduring the discomforts while gaining first-hand knowledge of the challenges ahead. To some extent he was in his element. Deane's great passion was eucalypts and he was such an authority that *Eucalyptus deanei* (commonly called mountain blue gum, or Deane's gum) is named in his honour.

His botanical experience helped him understand the four distinct terrains that the railway line would traverse. Heading east from Kalgoorlie, there was a 270-kilometre belt of granite country. It ended abruptly at the 700-kilometre-wide limestone plains of the Nullarbor. The porous limestone beneath it didn't hold water close enough to the surface to support a single tree, and Deane observed: 'A trip along this line can be confidently recommended to those critics who complain of the "eternal gum tree" in Australian landscapes.' On the far side of the Nullarbor, nearly 100 kilometres of shifting sandhills presented the most challenging terrain for railway building, while the final 650 kilometres of arid undulating country that extended to Port Augusta presented no particular difficulties except that it was as dry as the preceding 1000 kilometres. The highest point on the line was 150 kilometres from Kalgoorlie, at 415 metres. The lowest point was Port Augusta, at sea level.

The survey was completed in mid-1909, concluding that if the line was designed to carry a passenger train daily and a freight train every second day, it would cost just under £4 400 000 to build.

Now it was simply a matter of starting work, but for the next two years nothing happened. The Western Australians, led by John Forrest, continued to campaign for the line. At one point Forrest actually threatened to dissolve the west's participation in the federation, destroying the Commonwealth. What was more remarkable was that he was the Commonwealth's Minister for Defence at the time. The Western Australian parliament also threatened to secede, although it took no action.

In the end, it was someone outside the nation's self-interested politics who got things moving. In May 1911 Lord Kitchener, British Chief of the Imperial General Staff and arguably the most powerful man in the world at the time, arrived with a Royal Navy squadron and dropped anchor in Sydney Harbour. After conducting a review of Australia's ability to defend itself, he compiled a long list of criticisms for the nation's politicians. With regard to the trans-Australia railway he reported:

> Unless this line is built Australia will be helpless before any aggressor who is able to mount an attack in which intelligence and outflank are the order of the day. The country could be seized in twenty different places without one Australian defender appearing on the scene.

Shocked into action at this prospect, the federal parliament introduced legislation to build the trans-Australian railway within months
of Kitchener's report. In September 1911 the Minister for Home
Affairs, the flamboyant expatriate American King O'Malley, con-
jured extraordinary visions of central Australia's future if parliament
passed the Kalgoorlie to Port August Railway Act:

> Before many years have rolled by, the country [along the line] will hold a
> very large population. Larger than ever crowded within the gate of Ath-
> ens, when her fighting men under Miltiades won liberty for humanity
> on the field of Marathon, larger than that of Sparta when she 'bossed'
> Greece and sent forth her sons, quickened by the encouragement of
> their mothers' benediction to return with their shields, or on them;
> larger indeed, than that which crowded on the seven hills of Rome
> when, under her mighty rulers, she commenced that sovereign sway
> that afterwards embraced the whole world.

One comparison he didn't make was that after the legislation was
passed (in December 1911), actually building the line would require
a Herculean effort. The ageing Henry Deane, an unlikely Hercules,
was the Commonwealth Railway's first staff member. For a short
period at the beginning of 1912 he was the only employee, with not
a metre of railway line, a locomotive or carriage under his management. His new organisation started with nothing, but its first job was
to build the longest railway in the country.

Jobs for senior positions were advertised in the government
gazette, clerical staff hired, and tender documents drawn up. By February, key appointments were being made. Among them was Captain
F.W. Saunders, supervising engineer for construction at the eastern
end. The supervising engineer at the western end was a character
named Henry Chinn. He was considered unsuitable for the position by most of the railway men Deane was recruiting (there were

several superior applicants), but the Minister for Home Affairs, King O'Malley, overruled Deane and personally appointed his favourite.

At the same time, federal parliament received an unexpected lesson in the benefits of nation building. In February 1912 the board of the country's biggest mining company, BHP, met to consider building a steel mill in Newcastle, New South Wales. The mill would process iron ore from new BHP leases at Iron Knob and Iron Monarch in South Australia (both ore deposits had close to 70 per cent iron). The BHP board noted that tenders for rails were about to be called for the trans-Australian. The timing couldn't be better. The decision was made to build the mill and supply rails for the trans-Australian. Suddenly, two states that had resisted the project vehemently (New South Wales and South Australia) gained handsomely.

Sourcing the railway's other big construction requirement, 2 300 000 sleepers, was a different matter. South Australia made steel sleepers. New South Wales specialised in concrete. Western Australia was the source for wooden sleepers: jarrah sleepers from private companies; karri sleepers from the government mills. Deane, an engineer, believed termite-resistant jarrah was the best choice. O'Malley, a politician, preferred karri treated with arsenic. His choice was influenced by his Labor leanings and the better conditions for workers at the Western Australian government mills. Thus the trans-Australian's first battle line – between private enterprise and government employment – was drawn, even though the contract was so big that no single supplier could meet the entire order.

Sleepers weren't the only distraction. In July the federal opposition placed O'Malley's hand-picked supervising engineer in its sights. Henry Chinn was described as a 'flatulent ink waster' when it was found his engineering qualifications were suspect. He'd been sacked from most of his previous jobs or forced to resign. Worst of all, he'd helped Labor politicians expose Liberal failings when the Liberals were in government, which was why he'd been favoured by O'Malley.

Away from the political slanging matches, in July 1912 construction began on the trans-Australian railway. At the eastern end, sidings and workshops were built and the scene was set for the turning of the first sod. Locals noted that in the sandy soil of Port Augusta, finding a sod to turn wouldn't be easy. On 14 September, 1912, Prime Minister Fisher, John Forrest, South Australia's premier and governor, and other dignitaries gathered for the ceremony at a cutting just outside Port Augusta. King O'Malley was there, giant opal pin in his cravat, evocations of glory on his lips. He wasn't as forthcoming about the backroom deal he'd done with the Western Australian government to supply karri sleepers.

In the west, Chinn was chafing at the slow progress. He thought himself a man of action, but his requests for funds, clerical staff and office supplies were rebuffed or ignored by Henry Deane, who had already realised that the trans-Australian faced challenges unique among railways elsewhere in the world and directed tendering and recruitment from his headquarters in Melbourne.

Signs of activity might have been few at Kalgoorlie and Port Augusta, but elsewhere the nation's resources were being marshalled for the effort ahead. There were no towns, roads and infrastructure to support construction. Everything – labour, equipment, materials, food, water, medical facilities, accommodation – had to be brought in. At the stage when construction of the trans-Australian extended hundreds of kilometres into the wilderness, there would be only one supply line – the railway itself. Deane's plan was to use newly completed line to support construction of the next section. The trans-Australian would have to lift itself by its bootstraps.

One of the most important orders placed during 1912 was for two American-made Roberts track-laying machines. They cost £2400 each. The American King O'Malley fully supported the purchase. A feature of the mechanised devices was that they ran on the rails they'd just laid. Their conveyor belts extended beyond the end of the line to deliver sleepers, rails, fishplates and dogspikes to teams of navvies who then laid them. When everything was in place, the track-layer advanced onto the newly completed line. Up to 100 kilometres ahead of the track-layers, advance teams cleared and levelled the terrain along the pegged and surveyed route, supplied by camel trains carrying water, food, tools and fresh labour.

In such an operation, every small detail had to be taken into account. If anything failed, ran out or was neglected, disaster loomed. In November, an outbreak of typhoid at Port Augusta made that abundantly clear. There was a shortage of water for sanitation in the town and it resulted in thirty employees on the trans-Australian being taken ill. Three died before the outbreak was contained. Soon, thousands of men would be hundreds of kilometres from civilisation, utterly dependent on supply trains for everything they needed.

Over in the west, the government was having supply problems of its own. Rains in Western Australia's south-west curtailed timber operations at the state government mills. Soon the government was begging for more time to deliver its sleepers. They wouldn't start arriving until November 1913. Other suppliers who'd been given smaller orders and could supply the shortfall started lining up for a slice of the action.

In December 1912 the continuing attacks on Henry Chinn prompted the prime minister to call a royal commission to look into the charge that he was unfit for his job. Not surprisingly, the Labor-appointed investigation into one of its own found no case to answer. Chinn kept his job. Unfortunately for him, 1913 was an election year.

Deane continued marshalling the equipment and material for the work ahead. Steam locomotives were working on the short sections of track already laid. A standard gauge of 4 feet 8 inches (1.4 metres) was chosen over the protests of South Australians, whose railways were based on broad gauge (1.6 metres). Carriages were being built to provide mobile services for everything from works departments to medical services, post and paymasters. At both ends of the line materials stockpiles were growing.

Deane and his engineers were also contemplating the hardest question: steam locomotives or internal combustion? At the time no steam train could travel 1700 kilometres without replenishing its water and coal at least two or three times along the way. In 1913 no diesel train was operating over anything like the distance of the trans-Australian (some were in service doing short-haul work in Queensland and Victoria). If Deane chose steam, it meant drilling for water, constructing large catchments, lining them and covering them to stop seepage and evaporation. Diesel meant chancing an innovation that might turn the trans-Australian into an extremely elongated white elephant. Deane sought information on the available options from locomotive manufacturers all over the world, but as construction progressed he couldn't delay making a decision for long.

In June 1913 Australia went to the polls. The stench of the Chinn affair contributed to a groundswell of opinion against the Labor government and allowed a coalition of liberals led by Joseph Cook to seize power by just one seat. The new home affairs minister, Willie Kelly, was member for the Sydney harbourside seat of Wentworth – as far from the trans-Australian (physically, intellectually and politically) as it was possible to get.

By then the ground had only been prepared for 30 kilometres ahead of a short section of line at the western end and for only 20 kilometres in the east. Further afield water drillers had been finding good flows at many locations, but tests revealed the water to be heavily mineralised. If it wasn't purified – which involved condensers, fuel and trained operators – the water would destroy the boilers and tubes of the steam trains so quickly the line wouldn't be viable. Unfortunately, the hope of finding a suitable diesel locomotive for the trans-Australian was no more promising.

In the same month that the new government won power, the

Roberts track-layers arrived aboard ship from America. The first was landed at Port Augusta, and the work of assembling it began. It would be a couple of months before it would be operational. Ahead of it, the pace of pegging and levelling increased.

On 12 August, 1913, the new government sacked its old enemy Henry Chinn. In his place a solid railway man, John Darbyshire, was appointed supervising engineer of the western section. Henry Deane now had two good men running the day-to-day operations at both ends of the line. Unfortunately, Chinn didn't go quietly. He made a series of allegations of mismanagement on the trans-Australian that gave the Labor opposition, which controlled the Senate, cause to launch an inquiry. When construction of the trans-Australian should have been getting down to business, Henry Deane spent eleven days being grilled by politicians determined to embarrass the government in any way it could. Chinn's allegations appeared credible when considered alongside progress on the trans-Australian. In September 1913 only 15 kilometres of track had been laid from Kalgoorlie. At Port Augusta 25 kilometres had been laid. It wasn't much to show after nearly two years of work.

Yet appearances were deceiving. Deane's meticulous preparations for the work ahead were almost complete. On 8 October, 1913, the trans-Australian witnessed its first major development (at least from the point of view of its constructors). On the eastern end of the line, the first of the enormous Roberts track-laying machines began operating. An article in John Flynn's *Inlander* magazine described how it worked:

It operates at the head of a train, with the engine pushing from the rear from time to time. Every truck in this train is loaded with sleepers and rails, and is fitted with a 'gutter' on either side: these gutters meet to form a continuous channel from the far end right past the track-layer, and out in advance over the prepared earthwork. The floor of the gutter is provided with frequent rollers slightly above the general level, and these are kept turning by a small stationary engine on the track-layer. In operating this huge machine, for the whole train constitutes one machine, rails from the trucks are merely dropped into the gutter alongside the flat truck and the revolving rollers carry them steadily forward to be received by the platelayers, who are busy in front. In the same way sleepers are deposited in the other gutter, and they advance automatically, being carried somewhat further forward. The gang must work to time, or the heavy supplies will be emptied upon them! So a highly trained party toils away, spreading sleepers in neat array as fast as they come along: fitting rails pair by pair to the last couple, on which the monster is standing: deftly adjusting fish plates: screwing up the bolts: and driving sufficient dogspikes in some of the sleepers. Then the whole train moves forward to the new terminus one length ahead, the process is repeated by perspiring men, and on the railway creeps – a stride every four minutes or less.

While the crews were gaining experience with the new machine, they managed to lay a kilometre per day. The following month the track-layer at the western end started operation. Behind both track-layers, small armies were soon busy keeping up with their insatiable appetites for construction materials. Huge stockpiles of rails, sleepers, spikes and fishplates were on hand to keep the machines at both ends moving. Behind the stockpiles, trains were constantly shuttling more material forward. Day after day the track-layers crawled forward into the trackless heart of Australia.

Not to be outdone, the federal politicians continued their inexorable harassment of the trans-Australian's chief engineer. When Henry Deane finally admitted that the time was not yet ripe for diesel locomotives, the need to order steam locomotives was urgent. He went to his minister seeking approval to place an order. Kelly agreed, but when the House of Representatives learned of the decision, in October 1913, it launched an inquiry into the way the decision was made.

While Deane was facing that inquiry, the Labor-controlled Senate brought down a finding from its previous inquiry, in favour of Chinn and critical of Deane – this despite the revelation that Deane had refused to consider Chinn's proposed route for the line because it bypassed Kalgoorlie, the line's western destination.

Deane wasn't the only one feeling the heat. At the end of 1913 the trans-Australian had a total of 787 staff working on both ends of the line in temperatures in the mid-forties. It was the first summer of concerted track-laying and the teams were discovering just what could and couldn't be done in such extreme conditions. Dust covered them from head to foot. Flies descended on them in multitudes and swarmed over their food. When the men stopped for breaks, they often did so without any provision for shade. The hard work and even tougher work environment quickly weeded out anyone who wasn't up to the task. Those who stuck it out were soon recognised as a breed apart.

The hardest job continued to be Henry Deane's. To add to his many problems, at the beginning of 1914 the Cook government announced a royal commission into the contract for railway sleepers. The Liberals were, after all, pro-private enterprise, and the previous government had awarded the bulk of the contract to Western Australia's government mills. The commission was the last thing Deane needed as the mighty track-layers lumbered forward.

While Deane's reputation was being savaged, the government did little to defend him. By February 1914 the 67-year-old had had enough. On 5 February he wrote to his minister, Willie Kelly, in terms that have more than a few echoes of C.Y. O'Connor's final letter (see Chapter 5):

My work during the past two years has been of a very strenuous character, and, except for a few days at Christmas, I have scarcely taken a holiday beyond the statutory ones. During the last six or eight months the strain has been excessive, so much so that there has been a risk of breakdown, and I have come to the conclusion that, from considerations of health, it is necessary that I should have some permanent relaxation from these most arduous duties.

The government accepted the great engineer's resignation 'with regret'. While Deane worked out his notice, he was made the scapegoat when yet another scandal erupted, this time over the hasty letting of an earth-moving contract. Henry Teesdale-Smith had just finished an excavation job for the South Australian government, and had men and equipment on site near Port Augusta. When Deane realised that his presence was an opportunity too good to miss, he sought approval from his minister to give Teesdale-Smith a contract for crucial earthworks out on the trans-Australian line.

When the details became public, all hell broke loose. Senator Hugh de Largie, who had led the Senate inquiry into the Chinn affair, pursued Deane mercilessly over 'the smellful job with which, I think, he can be charged'. Under the protection of parliamentary privilege he stated that a man of his character wasn't entitled to a pension from the taxpayers of Australia. To add to Deane's woes, two days after he'd resigned Prime Minister Cook cancelled the contract for karri sleepers.

Two weeks after his resignation, R.W. Hawthorne, Leslie & Company, a major British locomotive manufacturer, sent Deane the specifications for the Paragon diesel locomotive. The manufacturer claimed that it could travel the length of the trans-Australian railway while hauling a 300-tonne express. It was the answer to Deane's prayers, but by then he was in no position to champion diesel locomotives, in particular ones that were unproven.

Meanwhile, the federal government's interference in the sleeper contract went from bad to worse. When Prime Minister Cook and

Home Affairs Minister Kelly made overtures to the private mills of Western Australia for jarrah sleepers, the premier closed most of the jarrah forests of the south-west. On 26 February the federal and state governments held crisis talks on the matter. They ended in deadlock.

In the midst of all this, the government was advertising for the position of chief engineer. The position was the stuff of headlines around the country. Despite the controversies there were plenty of applicants, including one from a hopeful Henry Chinn. His papers were marked 'unsuitable'.

On 1 April, 1914, the Cook government announced that the new engineer-in-chief would be Norris Bell, head of the Queensland government railways. Bell, a Scot, had built lines from the arid inland to the sweltering tropics, but nothing could prepare him for the political jungle warfare surrounding the trans-Australian. What he inherited from Deane was an organisation teetering on the brink of chaos. An admirable total of 250 kilometres of track had been laid, but progress was threatened by the deadlock over sleepers. After experiencing a summer on the trans-Australian, the labour force on the western section had gone on strike for more pay. Locomotives were on order but in short supply. The Labor-controlled Senate had announced an inquiry into the Teesdale-Smith affair.

Bell evaluated the situation and realised there was only one safe place to lay the blame. He wrote a report that deposited the responsibility for every shortcoming in the trans-Australian's progress at the door of now-retired Henry Deane. When Deane requested a copy, he was told it was out of print.

The trans-Australian certainly had its shortcomings, but out on the line it was the workforce that suffered for all the politics and mismanagement. Three weeks into Bell's tenure a letter to *The Age* of 22 April, 1914, revealed:

One gang of over 40 men were left without bread and groceries for nearly ten days, 83 miles [140 kilometres] from the nearest town . . . During the past few weeks a large number of employees have been put on. With the usual blundering shortsightedness, that draws high salaries on this job, no tents or tent poles were available, and nearly 100 men are now living like dingoes under the shelter of the scanty saltbush, or coiled up in concrete pipes and other places to escape the elements. Some of these men have been sleeping on the ground and without tents for over three weeks, waiting for the Department to unwind its red tape. Just before the holidays the riding ganger at the head of the road sent for 60 men. When the men got on the works it was discovered that there were no shovels for them, and many of them had to tramp off the job. Some of the men were charged for riding back on the construction train to Port Augusta . . . A deliberate attempt is being made to goad the employees into reprisals and to strangle the day-labour system.

At the eye of the storm Bell started to impose his own ideas on the trans-Australian. He would have nothing to do with fancy locomotives – steam was the way to go, despite the increasingly obvious problems with boilers and boiler tubes. He pushed through Deane's plan to upgrade rail orders to heavier ones able to carry more traffic, and his plan to ballast the whole track (for which the government allocated an additional £700 000). In 1914 the number of employees on the line rose to 1850.

Then, in August 1914, everything changed. World War I was declared and Australia joined the fight. A month later, the Cook government was ousted in federal parliament's first double dissolution, Labor's Andrew Fisher became prime minister and William Archibald home affairs minister. The strategic importance of the trans-Australian was emphasised on 1 November when HMAS *Sydney*, patrolling the Indian Ocean approaches to Australia (from its base at Fremantle Harbour), sank the German cruiser *Emden*. As Lord Kitchener had foreseen, even when Australia's sea routes were threatened, the trans-Australian (built far enough inland that it couldn't be shelled by enemy warships) would still allow equipment and personnel to be moved as needed for national defence. Accordingly, the war made work on the trans-Australian a high priority. By year's end 450 kilometres of track had been laid. Three months later, despite the crippling heat of another central Australian summer, the tally had reached 720 kilometres. The progress was all the more impressive because it was achieved during an outbreak of typhoid. The Reverend Stewart wrote in the *Inlander* magazine:

> There is always a fly in the ointment. In this case it is literally not a fly but myriads of them. They swarm everywhere practically all the year round. Innumerable methods are tried to rid the place of them, but all to no purpose. Small tents may of course be rendered fly-proof, but in the large tents – words fail to describe it! It is a time-honoured saying that you can pick an East-Wester because all the time he is eating he is waving one hand before his face and over his food.

Under such conditions the risks of disease were ever-present. In January 1915, new cases of typhoid appeared among workers on the eastern section of the line. Soon, scores of men were afflicted. As the situation deteriorated work was shut down and the ailing men were brought back to the hospital at Port Augusta. At the epidemic's height, 120 men overwhelmed the hospital. Some were accommodated in tents, others in a carriage shed Bell had converted to medical use. Out on the line hygiene inspectors strove to improve sanitation in rail camps spread across hundreds of kilometres. It took two months to get the situation under control. By then, twelve men had died.

Their places were soon filled. As the Anzacs were storming the beaches of Gallipoli in April 1915, the ranks on the trans-Australian swelled to over 3200. At times the track-layers were advancing up to a mile (1.6 kilometres) a day. The progress was so rapid it necessitated regular camp moves for the crews working at the railhead. Once the track-layers were 60 kilometres beyond the main railhead camp, a day was taken to pack everything – from personal belongings and tents to workshop tools, materials stockpiles and even small buildings. It was then loaded onto the supply trains and moved to a new camp at the railhead where everything was reconstructed. Deane's strategy of lifting the trans-Australian by its bootstraps was an extraordinary undertaking, but it worked.

May 1915 saw completed sections of line put to commercial use. Sandalwood cutters shipped timber on the western end. Sheep, cattle and salt were transported on the eastern end. At the same time parliament voted the remaining funds, £1500000, to complete the project. The total was £5900000, £2000000 over original budget estimates due to the decision to build with heavier rails and rising prices as a consequence of World War I.

The vote still brought out critics. Senator Stewart from Queensland believed: 'Members of Parliament, if they had their choice, would certainly take the sea route in preference to the land route, because a journey occupying two or three days over the desert will be a severe trial upon any man's endurance, whereas the journey round by steamer is one of the most pleasant sea trips I know of anywhere.' Senator O'Keefe from Tasmania, who knew the Great Australian Bight's atrocious seas a little better, interjected: 'Sometimes.'

Supply trains were now travelling 8000 kilometres a month (twice the distance they covered in normal operations elsewhere) as they brought supplies to the men at the railhead. When the water trains didn't arrive, thirsty men downed tools. In the heat of the outback it was a sensible move which probably saved many from death by heat exhaustion.

Throughout 1915 the press sniped at Bell about every perceived failing in the railway's construction. The politicians, chastened by

the war's mounting casualties and the heavy weight of their responsibilities, were notably silent. However, late in the year, trouble was
brewing.

Dudley Gilchrist was an accounts clerk working in the trans-
Australian's Melbourne head office. It wasn't a difficult job, but it
did require attention to detail which, apparently, was beyond Gilchrist. When his boss, J.P. Monro, rebuked him for his sloppiness,
Gilchrist took exception and requested a transfer to Kalgoorlie. For
a city man it was like asking to be sent to a desert Siberia and he
soon regretted his decision. From his new posting he wrote to Norris Bell complaining about Monro. Bell supported Monro. On 15 July,
1915, Gilchrist took annual leave and returned to Melbourne, travelling with another clerk, Dane Carrington, who'd been dismissed
from the trans-Australian staff because of poor performance. When
they arrived in Melbourne, both men went to see the former supervising engineer Henry Chinn.

After talking to Chinn, Gilchrist sought an interview with Bell. He
requested a transfer back to Melbourne because he was getting married – his father was building a house for him in Melbourne and he
couldn't afford to raise a family in Kalgoorlie on his current income.
Bell refused to have him back, whereupon Gilchrist applied for leave
without pay, which was granted. On 10 August he joined the AIF.

On 25 August Henry Chinn accompanied Gilchrist on a visit to
a Melbourne justice of the peace. There Gilchrist made a statutory
declaration listing eighteen instances of mismanagement by his superiors and charging that 'an appalling state of affairs' existed on the
trans-Australian. The charges included wasting money, putting only
two dogspikes into fishplates on a line that was now carrying heavy
rail traffic, rails laid on the wrong angle for 300 kilometres, no ballasting on the western end of the line, trains being operated without
brakes, police failing to suppress gambling, and bridges having to be
rebuilt because of errors in construction.

Gilchrist took his freshly signed statutory declaration to the former minister of home affairs, now a backbencher in the Fisher government, King O'Malley. The young clerk was either a disgruntled employee trying to exact revenge or a courageous whistle-blower keeping the trans-Australian administration honest. O'Malley decided he was the latter and referred him to the Labor party's chief head-kicker in the Senate, Hugh de Largie, the man responsible for hounding the venerable Henry Deane from office. Now it was Bell's turn. Soon the allegations of Sergeant Gilchrist, as he described himself, were published in newspapers across the country.

Home Affairs Minister Archibald did a reasonable job refuting the allegations, some of which while true were neither new nor critical. For example, dogspikes had been rationed due to shortages, and trains operated without brakes on flat sections where they didn't need them. The story subsided and Gilchrist seemed to sink into oblivion. But the trans-Australian hadn't seen the last of him.

In December 1915 the western end of the line reached the Nullarbor. From there, almost nothing stood between the track-layer and South Australia. Just beyond Nurina, the machine started laying what would become the longest straight section of railway anywhere in the world – 478 kilometres. As the days grew hotter, the work continued. Temperatures regularly soared as high as 46°C. On one day the temperature was recorded at 55°C. In the middle of the day work only stopped when the rails became too hot to touch. Track-laying crews were now provided with canvas awnings where they could shelter from the intensity of the sun. In some locations, they climbed down into cool subterranean caverns to escape the fury of the climate.

Work was eventually scheduled for the early hours of the morning and the late afternoon. A quota was devised. When the track-layers had put down a mile (1.6 kilometres) they could knock off for the day. The arrangement was seen as wasteful by journalists who visited the railhead and saw the expensive track-laying equipment idle.

It was regarded as sensible by anyone engaged in the sheer hard work of laying a mile of track a day in the heat of a central Australian summer.

Over on the eastern section of the line, the conditions were even tougher. There the track-layers and excavators were still negotiating the first 650 kilometres of undulating arid scrub country, making cuttings and building banks. Ahead of them, still waiting to be dealt with, was the greatest challenge of the line's construction, the Barton Sandhills.

Before they reached the hills, politics intervened once more, though this time in even more bizarre ways than ever before. First, a Cabinet reshuffle saw King O'Malley return to the home affairs ministry. Then, on 15 December, 'Sergeant' Gilchrist wrote to him detailing his latest predicament. Gilchrist was in a military prison, having been arrested for being absent without leave. Shortly after writing to O'Malley, Gilchrist was moved to a military hospital. From there, on 18 January, 1916, he was discharged from the army as medically unfit. Whereupon O'Malley reappointed him to the trans-Australian's western section on the grounds that he was a 'returned soldier'.

For a federal government minister to become involved in the appointment of a junior accounts clerk is extraordinary, but it was only the beginning. When the western section's supervising engineer, John Darbyshire, refused to reappoint Gilchrist, O'Malley sacked him. Next, the western section's clerks threatened to resign if Darbyshire wasn't reinstated. O'Malley accused them of declaring war on the Commonwealth and instead appointed one of Darbyshire's deputies, H.E. Marnie, as the new supervising engineer. Marnie also refused to reinstate Gilchrist. So O'Malley sacked Marnie.

The trans-Australian may have been plagued with accusations of mismanagement, but the men laying the rails through the middle of Australia had hammered out powerful loyalties on the anvil of the outback. The workers threatened a general strike if Darbyshire and Marnie weren't reinstated. O'Malley responded by threatening to shut down all construction on the trans-Australian – all this in time of war for the sake of an accountant?

When O'Malley looked to his fellow politicians for support, it dawned on him that he'd gone too far. As a face-saving measure, he suggested calling yet another inquiry, this time into Gilchrist's allegations. By then the workforce on the trans-Australian had had a gutful of the delays and distractions of government inquiries. For perhaps the first time in history, the workers went on strike in support of their bosses. O'Malley was humiliated and forced to reinstate Darbyshire and Marnie. The workers got back on the job. After all the bad publicity, Fisher's government was compelled to hold a royal commission into the management of the trans-Australian, but when Justice Eagleson examined Gilchrist's allegations the government was soon wishing he hadn't.

Meanwhile, out in central Australia, in April 1916 the excavation crews on the eastern section reached the Barton Sandhills. At only 80 kilometres wide, this was the smallest area of distinct terrain of the four on the route, but soon hundreds of men, camels and horses were swarming over the sandhills, moving thousands of cubic metres of sand and soil. They made full use of one of Henry Deane's innovations, the Tumbling Tommy. It was described in the *Inlander*:

One mechanical servant that worked wonders on this railway was the 'Tumbling Tommy', a small scoup [sic] drawn by one horse and controlled by the driver. Along the whole line about 290 of these useful inventions were employed, and in the main party there were 120. Scoups could be employed only on shallow cuttings, but these were the rule, so they were 'spoiled' i.e., the earth was picked up by the scoup, run out a short distance, and there tossed aside. Thus 60 scoupers could work on the section. The other 60 would be sent ahead where a bank was required, and they merely reversed the process by scouping up material at the side, and dumping it where required to form a moderately elevated track.

To ensure everything would be ready before the track-layer arrived, the excavation crews worked up to 160 kilometres ahead of construction. On one 40-kilometre stretch they moved a million cubic metres of material, more than the total excavated over the next 500 kilometres. Dust storms made the work even harder, tearing through camps, hurling loose equipment and belongings out into the desert while men sheltered wherever they could, blinded by the driving sand. Storms shifted entire sandhills, which lay parallel to the route of the line. One blew for twelve hours and dumped 1500 tonnes of sand back onto the route that had just been cleared. When the dust settled, men, horses and camels went back to work while the engineers re-did their sums on just how wide the cuttings through the sandhills would have to be. They eventually stabilised some dunes by facing them with stone.

In May 1916, 1250 kilometres of track had been laid and 450 kilometres remained. The workforce numbered 3395. Among the supply trains running up and down the line were the first 'tea and sugar' trains, which supplied the new depots that were springing up along the line (many named after federal politicians) to maintain the trans-Australian's operations.

The men on the line were the broadest cross-section of humanity imaginable. There were men on the run, employed on a 'no-questions-asked' basis. Police worked constantly to stop alcohol and gambling on trains and in the camps, but many trains travelled with carriages filled with drunk and comatose workers. At one camp a constable who was thought too hard on the two-up school had his tent set ablaze.

Men worked in the wilderness for up to six months at a time, the most skilled earning some of the highest wages in the country. Some

blew their entire pay at the first pub in Kalgoorlie or Port Augusta
that they came to. Yet an extraordinary code of honour existed on
the trans-Australian. When a pay train crashed on the line, £6000
was scattered throughout the wreckage. After extracting the two men
who were injured, the rescue crew worked by lamplight to recover
the money. They accounted for all but 30 shillings.

On 15 September, 1916, Justice Eagleson published the findings of
his royal commission into Dudley Gilchrist's allegations. They were
a significant milestone on King O'Malley's road to political oblivion.
Said Eagleson:

> Out of all the witnesses called, there were only three whose testimony I
> found it impossible to accept, unless and until it has been corroborated.
> These were Henry Chinn, Dane Carrington and Dudley Lynton Gilchrist.
> Chinn's statements on oath put beyond question what was evident from
> his demeanour in the box – his bias was so pronounced as to render his
> evidence worthless. Dane Carrington gave evidence in a manner which
> convinced me that he was not endeavouring to tell the truth, but to mis-
> lead me. His demeanour left a decidedly bad impression on my mind
> concerning his truthfulness. In the case of Dudley Lynton Gilchrist, I
> am satisfied that during the investigation, more especially while giving
> evidence in Kalgoorlie, he has repeatedly committed wilful and corrupt
> perjury of a very flagrant character.

It was also revealed that Gilchrist was not and never had been a sergeant in the Australian army.

At the end of 1916, there remained only 200 kilometres between
the track-layer 850 kilometres from Kalgoorlie at one end and 650
kilometres from Port Augusta at the other. It was at that point, as
the heat of summer rose once more, that the one thing Henry Deane
had worked to avoid took place. Norris Bell ran out of rails. World
War I was biting deep into stocks of iron all around the world and the

trans-Australian was just one victim of the shortages. At the western end of the line track-laying ceased.

While work slowed to a crawl on the eastern section, South Australia launched a royal commission into the effect of the trans-Australian on the Aboriginal population. The line had acted like a magnet to a people who'd never seen anything like the twin ribbons of steel snaking across the landscape, carrying puffing monsters at extraordinary speeds. The camps were bursting with an abundance of food and materials the desert people had never dreamed of. The curious were drawn from hundreds of kilometres. All too soon they became fringe-dwellers around the camps, exposed to the best and worst of people from all over the world. Many were ruthlessly exploited and callously cast aside. Evidence of their plight was provided by the maverick Daisy Bates, a prim Englishwoman who made the study of Aboriginal people her life's work and considered herself Kabbarli (mother) of a dying race. Bates eventually set up a camp at Ooldea, a freshwater soak on the eastern side of the Nullarbor that had been maintained by Aboriginal people for generations. It had never been known to fail. After it was tapped by the engineers of the trans-Australian it went dry within a few years.

Every water scheme, no matter how bizarre, was given consideration by the management of the trans-Australian. The Commonwealth Engineer for Radio-Telegraphy, Mr Balsillie, came up with a scheme to increase rainfall using specially designed rain-making kites. After a trial increased rainfall at Bookaloo by 60–70 per cent (his claim) or 50 per cent (according to the government), he was funded to set up and run 'rain-stimulating' plants that would supplement the water supplies along the line.

By May 1917, rail stockpiles had been rebuilt to levels sufficient to allow track-laying at the western end to recommence. By then much of the preparatory work between the two railheads was complete and the workforce was reduced to 2383. The track-laying machines lumbered across the Nullarbor, rapidly closing the gap between the two ends.

There were just 40 kilometres left when Australia was gripped by extraordinary industrial unrest. Workers who'd spent two and a half years making sacrifices for the war effort could bear no more. Many had paid a terrible price as loved ones and friends were slaughtered on distant battlefields for a cause they no longer understood or cared about. When maritime workers went on strike, Western Australia found itself cut off from essential supplies from the east, and shortages of staples rapidly ensued. In the west, many eyes turned to the work in progress far out on the Nullarbor Plain.

There, the workers were also on strike. This time the dispute was over bad language. When a railway ganger at Ooldea had given his workers a tongue lashing, they'd downed tools. In federal parliament the minister in the newly formed portfolio of Works and Railways, W.A. Watt, was asked just what you could say to make a navvy blush. Watt responded that he'd asked for the words to be submitted to him by mail because if they were telegraphed 'it might fuse the wires and the PMG might refuse to transmit'. His answer provoked laughter throughout the chamber.

Work was soon resumed and the gap between the track-layers rapidly shrank. On 3 October the supervisor on the track-layer at the eastern end of the line climbed as high onto the machine as he could get. He scanned the horizon of the Nullarbor with a spyglass. Then he shouted and pointed. He could see the western track-layer.

Work progressed with a new-found enthusiasm as the great machines crept across the plain in clear sight of each other. At night crews from both machines walked out along the prepared earthworks to mingle with each other. When the machines were 5 kilometres apart, each crew could hear the ringing hammers and chugging engines of the other track-layer as it advanced towards their own.

On 17 October, 995.2 kilometres east of Kalgoorlie, just west of

Ooldea in South Australia, the 1700 kilometres of trackless wilderness between Kalgoorlie and Port Augusta was reduced to just a few metres. An official ceremony had been planned for the joining of the line, but the logistics of getting dignitaries into the middle of Australia proved too much for a nation at war. The *Inlander* quipped that it was when the potentates realised there would be no multitudes to hang on their every phrase that the event was cancelled.

As photographs and news reports revealed, hundreds of railway workers – the people whose toil had pioneered the first great work of Federation through one of Australia's last great wildernesses – were present at the joining of the rails. Several had been present at the turning of the first sod, among them Captain Saunders, supervising engineer for the construction of the eastern section. John Darbyshire, supervising engineer for the western section, was also present as the honour of laying the last two rails was given to the men of the west. A journalist from the *Kalgoorlie Miner* described the scene:

> The West Australian track-layer delivered the last three lengths of rails into the required position, the South Australian track-layer coming close up. The last pair of rails were about three feet [1 metre] too long, so the surplus was taken off by the proper mechanical appliances. The joints were made, the fish-plates fastened, the dog spikes driven home, and that was all . . . The West Australian and South Australian workers had gathered around. When the linking up had finished, both crowds silently dispersed. Not a speech was made or a cheer raised. One wag had chalked on the flange of one of the connecting rails the words 'What we have not been looking for', as if to indicate that he and his mates were very sorry to be thrown out of a good job.

To Captain Saunders went the honour of sending the historic communication: 'Rails linked today, Wednesday, one forty-five pm, South Australian time, at six-twenty-one miles fifty-eight chains fifty-point-

five links. Saunders.' An ailing John Forrest, at the time the federal
treasurer, responded: 'I rejoice to see this day. Western Australia is
from today in reality a part of the Australian Federation.'

The rails may have been joined but much remained to be done. There
were earthworks to be completed, ballasting was still far behind the
track-laying and such mundane tasks as driving the correct number
of dogspikes into every fishplate were still awaiting supplies.

None of that stopped the first express running on 22 October, 1917,
the same day the Australian Light Horse covered itself in glory in the
charge at Beersheba. The train was loaded with VIPs for the first
official crossing of Australia by rail. One of the politicians, when told
he was traversing the longest straight section of track in the world,
commented that it was the straightest he'd been in his life. The train
arrived in Kalgoorlie on 24 October, 42 hours and 48 minutes after
leaving Port Augusta.

Despite the gloom cast across the whole enterprise by the car-
nage on the battlefields of France, the politicians got to make their
speeches when the governor-general travelled aboard the trans-
Australian a week later. When the vice-regal entourage rolled into
Perth, the lord mayor asserted that the state was now 'the gateway to
and from the Old World' and no longer 'the backdoor of Australia'.

One voice that wasn't heard was that of the man who had done so
much to realise the vision of the trans-Australian, Henry Deane. He
wasn't invited to participate in any of the official functions, nor was
he recognised in any monuments or speeches. He quietly tended his
garden in Melbourne and studied his eucalypts. In November 1917
he published a small booklet refuting many of the charges Norris
Bell had made in his 1916 report on the state of the trans-Australian. It was barely noticed. The poem that opens this book points
out that those who build the road may never enjoy travelling it. The
Inlander noted the plight of a group of navvies trying to get back to
Kalgoorlie:

On Monday last at 2 a.m., 30 men left the 603 mile camp for Kalgoorlie in open trucks. Owing to engine troubles they did not reach Kalgoorlie until 3 o'clock on Thursday morning, the trip occupying three days and nights. Not anticipating such a protracted trip, very few of the men had brought sufficient food. They were stranded at Rawlinna cold and hungry when the first train from the East dashed past and the contrast between the condition of the men who had built the line and the . . . well, the rest can be guessed.

The trans-Australian soon became synonymous with luxury, comfort and innovation. It was the first Australian train with showers, the first with a piano in the lounge and one of the first to have air-conditioning (introduced in 1936). The actual completion of the line took considerably longer. Ballasting was finished in 1939, twenty-five years after it was started. Diesel-electric replaced steam in 1951, forty years after Henry Deane first explored the idea. The completion of the standard gauge line that allowed trains to run straight through between Sydney and Perth took until 1969. The standard gauge line to Adelaide took until 1974. The promised line from Adelaide to Darwin was fulfilled in 2003.

The trans-Australian is now regarded as one of the great railway journeys of the world. Few who travel it know the names of John Forrest, Henry Deane and C.Y. O'Connor, the great nation builders who laid the foundations of its construction. The names of the outback pioneers who actually built it are long since forgotten. Yet their monument remains. Two ribbons of steel stretch from horizon to horizon across the emptiness of central Australia. They remain the first great work of Federation and the bond of iron that unifies a nation.

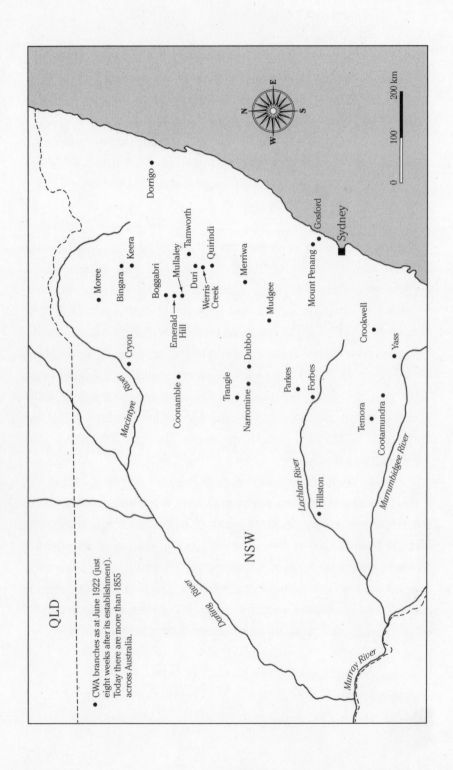

QLD

NSW

• CWA branches as at June 1922 (just eight weeks after its establishment). Today there are more than 1855 across Australia.

Darling River

Macintyre River

Lachlan River

Murrumbidgee River

Murray River

Moree •

Bingara •

Keera •

Cryon •

Coonamble •

Trangie •

Boggabri •

Emerald Hill

Mullaley •

Duri •

Werris Creek •

Tamworth •

Quirindi •

Dorrigo •

Merriwa •

Mudgee •

Narromine •

Dubbo •

Parkes •

Forbes •

Hillston •

Temora •

Cootamundra •

Crookwell •

Yass •

Mount Penang •

Gosford •

Sydney ■

N
W · E
S

0   100   200 km

Grace Munro, date unknown
*(Photo courtesy the Country
Women's Association)*

Florence Gordon, date unknown
(Photo courtesy Helen Townsend)

7

NO PLACE FOR A WOMAN

The Country Women's Association

(1922–)

In 1892 the celebrated exchange between poets Henry Lawson and Banjo Paterson in *The Bulletin* debated the merits of life in the outback. Where Paterson romanticised 'the sunlit plains extended', Lawson saw 'the sun-dried shepherd'. While Paterson equated the wide open spaces with freedom, Lawson looked inside the lonely humpies and what he saw haunted him. He had a particular empathy for conditions of women when he wrote in *Up the Country:*

Land where gaunt and haggard women live alone and work like men,
Till their husbands, gone a-droving, will return to them again –
Homes of men! if home had ever such a God-forgotten place,

Where the wild selector's children fly before a stranger's face.

Home of tragedy applauded by the dingoes' dismal yell,

Heaven of the shanty-keeper – fitting fiend for such a hell –

Paterson responded with *An Answer to Various Bards:*

Now, for instance, Mr Lawson – well, of course, we almost cried

At the sorrowful description how his "little 'Arvie" died,

And we lachrymosed in silence when "His Father's mate" was slain;

Then he went and killed the father, and we had to weep again.

The truth lay somewhere between the clever rhymes of the poets. While the outback had a compelling beauty it could also be remorselessly hard. According to Lawson it was hardest of all on the women. Lawson's best-known short story was *The Drover's Wife,* about a woman alone battling a snake that had crawled into her shanty. He captured the realities for many country women when he wrote:

She is used to being left alone. She once lived like this for eighteen months. As a girl she built the usual castles in the air; but all her girlish hopes and aspirations have long been dead . . . The last two children were born in the bush – one while her husband was bringing a drunken doctor, by force, to attend to her . . . One of the children died while she was here alone. She rode nineteen miles for assistance, carrying the dead child.

The work of fiction went to the truth of the outback. In many areas it lacked basic services – no doctors, nurses, schools or communications. In the early twentieth century the superintendent of the Australian Inland Mission, John Flynn, considered what was available for expectant mothers and those raising families and concluded, 'It's no place for a woman.' Statistics from the time supported his view. In World War I the number of Australians killed in battle was 54 000. During the same period infant deaths in Australia numbered 74 000. The mortality rate was five times higher than today, and highest of all in the outback.

For the most part, outback women endured these conditions in silence. In some circumstances their status was little better than slaves – husbands regarded their wives and the children they bore as a source of free labour. Then, in the early 1920s, the *Sydney Stock and Station Journal* started running letters under the heading 'Making Bush Life Attractive'. It was started in part to arrest the drift from the bush to the cities, which was largely attributed to the almost total lack of services outback. The column was intended to give country women a forum for ideas but it soon became clear that many regarded making bush life attractive an impossible dream.

One writer, Helen Souter, listed problems as basic as doing the laundry. She wrote: 'Tubs, with the water laid on, and runways to take the finished water away could easily be installed – carrying buckets of water as [sic] a back-breaking job – but I'm afraid the thought that "Mother always managed", plus the initial expense, keeps many from the conveniences. Do they ever think how worn out mother was after washing day and its many burdensome jobs?'

On telephones she wrote: 'The knowledge that one was within call of another human being would lessen the loneliness and sense of distance and isolation.' On doctors:

Could not some scheme be devised whereby the doctor could make his calls outback, in urgent cases, and not bankrupt his patient's folk with the mileage rate he charges? Of course we all know that it costs a lot of money to educate the doctor, to keep his car going, and his house and family in the way in which they must live, but from his bills we sometimes wonder if he wants to get it all back from one patient.

Souter also addressed the costs of rail travel: 'At the end of a long dry summer, after fighting bush fires, hay-making, harvesting and all the summer jobs that must be done, a little time away from the heat, the dust, the flies and the worry would work wonders for our country folk and send them out again with renewed vigor to tackle the same old round for another year . . . Starving stock is shifted for little or nothing. Our men and women, and coming men and women, are much more important.'

She concluded with the difficulties in educating children: 'We are ready to pay our share and do our share in getting the school. Can't the Dept. send us teachers? In the city the schools are free to all. Here in the back country they are limited to the children old enough to ride or drive a long distance.'

The desperate situation was palpable in an anonymous letter, 'The Cry of the Bush Mothers':

> Men of the bush are too busy to realise that their womenfolk are fading fast. Look at the bush cemeteries and the wayside graves that speak of all the suffering and loneliness one has gone through . . . Of country women a large number have been city girls with every comfort. I once visited one who had not seen a soul for two years and had come to the country with her husband and baby. She burst into tears and said, 'I don't know what to say, I feel I cannot let you go.' Her health was dreadful and her home consisted of two rooms, earth floor and a verandah. They had left the city for a good position in the country, and had drifted out back to an out station, and that was the woman's home. There are women whose nerves have gone, and it is time men woke up and saw that a woman had at least a comfortable home . . . I have lived nearly forty years in the Bush, and if I penned the lives and tragedies of bush life, I know one would hardly believe them.

As the editor of the *Stock and Station Journal's* 'Home Page', Florence Gordon (writing under the pseudonym 'Urbania'), read the letters she became increasingly depressed. Nowhere was there a voice like Banjo Paterson spruiking the virtues of the bush. Women describing the realities were unanimous about how unrelentingly hard and lonely it was. They'd been enduring terrible lives since the first days of European settlement and there seemed little that could be done about it.

Then in 1921 Gordon met the man who'd originated the idea for the 'Making Bush Life Attractive' column. He was a New South Wales politician, Dr Richard Arthur, a city dweller who'd nevertheless been championing bush causes since his first speech in parliament in 1904. Arthur had been trying to organise what he called A Bushwoman's Conference, a forum to identify problems and seek solutions. He'd written an article for the *Farmer and Settler* outlining his proposal, but nothing came of it. He showed a copy of the article to Gordon. She liked the idea and took it to her editor.

There are few publications more conservative than *The Sydney Stock and Station Journal.* Its articles and columns deal with topics like 'Biters and Barkers', 'The Butter Trouble' and 'The Frozen Meat Trade'. Nevertheless, as Florence recalled, the editor, Mr Milligan, 'gave permission for an attempt to be made to organise a conference and arranged that it should be held in the Country Club'.

On 6 September, 1921, Arthur launched the proposal with a letter in the column 'Making Bush Life Attractive'. He wrote:

Let the women readers of the Journal in every district get in touch with one another, and then appoint their representatives to come to Sydney. My idea is that the women to be chosen should be those who cannot afford to come to Sydney unless the way is made easy for them. It is not the wife of the well-to-do pastoralist that is wanted. Her lot falls in comparatively pleasant places. The women who have struggled with poverty and debt, and monotonous unending toil are those we wish to welcome, and to whom the change would be a delightful respite from their daily round.

Gordon's 'Home Page' became the catalyst for the conference. Every edition of the Journal it appeared in carried details of developments and encouraged women to form Unions of Help that would send representatives to the conference. Women wrote to the 'Home Page' suggesting issues that should be addressed. Most reflected the deficiencies in even the basics of life. As the tone of the 'Home Page' shifted, Gordon's own articles reflected her awareness of a number of issues that affected women in the city as much as the country. In her review of 1921, the veil of conservatism couldn't hide her grassroots feminism when she wrote:

Every woman who proves her capacity to be economically independent blazes the important fact that every woman in the home, or out of it, has a right to be economically independent . . . Women have been altogether too slow to perceive, too patient to press their claims, that the work they do in the home entitles them to the financial reward earned by their work. Is not the failure on the part of parents to recognise the financial value of the work done at home by their daughters and sons, one of the reasons for the drift of young people from the country to the cities?

We, of the Home Page, have tried this year to do something to let light into women's home conditions by forming the Countrywomen's Union of Help. Without cooperation between women, irrespective of age, position or creed, how are we to work to get the BETTER HOMES that is the great objective of the Union of Help? A single woman reasonably claiming that her house should be fly-screened, a sink and taps in her kitchen, that the power her husband uses for his farm machinery be also connected to drive her washing-machine and wringer, her mangle and vacuum cleaner – would probably be regarded by her husband as a tiresome grumbler. But if a hundred husbands in a district found that all the wives were claiming the same things, then each house would have them in a very short time.

It was a long way from modern feminism's demand for equal rights, but in 1921 demanding financial independence and electricity was every bit as incendiary. However, her activism went well beyond penning stirring words. Gordon worked tirelessly to organise support for the forthcoming conference. She enlisted Dame Margaret Davidson, wife of the governor of New South Wales, as patron. She approached a range of people to present papers and lectures at the conference. She pressed the railways to make cheap fares available to allow women to attend.

The conference was originally set down for 21 February, but when it was realised that date would involve many women having to make two trips to Sydney (the Agricultural Society's Sydney Easter Show was a major event on the rural calendar), it was decided to move the conference so it would coincide with the show, in mid-April.

The publicity for the conference also attracted the interest of Grace Munro, wife of a prominent northern New South Wales grazier. Munro (a distant relative of Nat Buchanan's wife, Kate) may have been the kind of pastoralist's wife Richard Arthur didn't want at the conference, but her experience of the bush was every bit as painful. In 1911 she'd had to rush one of her children to Sydney for an emergency appendectomy. While she was away, her youngest child had been taken ill and died.

In February 1922 Munro contacted Gordon and offered to help in any way she could. Up to that point Gordon had been the self-appointed honorary organiser. Now she and Munro set up a small committee consisting of Munro as president, with Gordon, Mrs Sturt from Queensland and Mrs Masey from the Women's Reform League as committee members. Soon after, another fifteen women and men were enlisted. The committee included Helen Souter, who had crystallised many of the issues in her letter to the *Stock and Station Journal* some months before.

Grace Munro's biographical notes in the Jessie Street Library of Australian Women describe her as tall and thin, forceful, energetic and even dominating. If so, she was just what the conference needed. Gordon had been making slow progress forming Unions of Help, from whom delegates were supposed to come, so Munro undertook a trip to northern New South Wales, where she knew just about everybody, to round up support. Other committee women did the same in their regions.

As she travelled her region, Munro already had in mind two basic objectives for the conference. First, she wanted a rest room in every country town, a place where women coming in from the country could go to take a break from their shopping, breastfeed or leave their children in safe hands while they conducted their business in town. Second, she wanted to revive a plan for a rest house or camp at Manly 'where outback mothers could find simple accommodation and some one to take charge of their children for a few hours while they were away on pleasure or business'.

Both objectives bear an uncanny resemblance to the hopes expressed in the anonymous letter that was published in the journal under the title 'The Cry of the Bush Mothers'. They also mirrored the rest rooms that were being set up by the Women's Section of the Victorian Farmer's Union, whose representatives wrote to Florence Gordon when they heard about the forthcoming conference. They provided details of how they were operating and said they would be sending delegates as well.

In February and March 1922 the *Stock and Station Journal* started running advertisements for 'An Open Conference of Country Women'. Its object was to improve the conditions of women on the land and its planned addresses were to cover such diverse topics as 'Infant Management', 'Comfort in the Country Home', practical house building, citizenship, 'The Case for the Woman on the Land', 'Man's Part to the Woman on the Land', 'The Insect Menace to Rural Life' and 'Scientific Diet in Relation to Rural Life'. The speakers included Florence Taylor, Australia's first female architect, and Dr Margaret Harper, physician-in-charge of Tresillian, formerly the Royal Society for the Welfare of Mothers and Babies. What wasn't mentioned was an agenda item that some on the organising committee saw as being the most important of all – creating an organisation that would go much further than a three-day talk-fest. It would be formed specifically to promote the interests of outback women.

As the opening day of the conference approached (18 April, 1922), the organisers nervously waited to see if their planning was going to succeed. Munro used her formidable skills to convince the management of the Union Paramount Picture Company to screen advertisements for the conference in city and country picture theatres. She had large advertising signs made up and displayed at the Easter Show. At the Sydney Showgrounds two committee women, Miss Fourdinier and Mrs Masey, handed out thousands of flyers and talked to hundreds of women about the conference, whipping up interest. Gordon sent a barrage of press releases to every media outlet she could think of and arranged interviews with herself or other members of the organising committee. Still the question remained: would they come?

As Florence recalled:

The question haunted us sleeping and waking. Would that large and dignified room hold a sprinkling of bored women, or would it be alive with the interest that such a conference could arouse? The day came. Long before the appointed time the room was full and continued getting fuller every minute. Extra seats had to be brought in. Animation and interest enlivened all the sessions. That visitors remained as long as they did was significant of the fact that the Conference arranged mainly by women living in the city, had met the wants of their country sisters.

One excited visitor observed that history was being made. Margaret Davidson was accompanied by the wife of the governor of Victoria, the Countess of Stradbroke, giving the attending media a diamond-studded vice-regal photo opportunity. Several publications covered the morning, afternoon and evening sessions extensively. As news of the success of the conference spread, some speakers (in particular male politicians) who had declined invitations to address it suddenly found time in their busy schedules and insisted on being given the opportunity to talk.

Despite their interruptions, numerous practical resolutions were passed. They included calling on the minister for railways to provide special carriages for women and children on all trains and second-class sleeping berths on long-distance trains. The conference called on the minister for health to make greater provision for maternity cases by establishing new maternity wards in country hospitals.

Another suggestion came from Mr F.W. Allen, in a speech he gave on behalf of his wife, who hadn't been able to attend. Gordon reported that, 'While paying a grateful tribute to the Educational Department, he suggested what he considered a better plan, namely, that the Department provide teachers to travel a radius every week, so that all the children within that radius get two or three days tuition every week.' Allen made the suggestion on 19 April, 1922. The New South Wales Department of Education didn't manage to provide such a service until 1956, as part of its School of the Air program (see Chapter 11).

According to the *Stock and Station Journal*'s report, when Mr A.B. Piddington gave his speech on 'Man's Part to the Woman on the

Land', one conference attendee, Mrs Laver, 'took exception to his remarks, which, in her opinion, savoured too much of pity, which the country woman resented. She spoke with spirit and humour. Mr Rieseigh, who said he sometimes found himself introduced as Mrs Rieseigh's husband, answered Mr Piddington on behalf of the man on the land, and pointed out some of the burdens he had to carry.'

On the third day, Thursday 20 April, a day Florence described as 'an heroic example of feminine endurance', the unstated agenda of the organising committee came to the fore. Between sessions, discussions on forming a permanent organisation for women began. Early in the afternoon Grace Munro put forward a motion: 'That the name of the Association be The Country Women's Association, and that girls be admitted as associate members.' They got no further before the meeting was interrupted by a politician. Wrote Gordon:

Into the middle of this Sir Joseph Carruthers [former New South Wales premier and instigator of the Million Farms campaign, which proposed to deal with the drift from the country by establishing a million farms with a million migrant families] asked to speak. Milk and school books seemed to be the hope he held out to bushwomen. By that time the Conference was beginning to feel that it had had enough of baby-foods and books – probably it would have preferred to hear of a plan to provide a weekly jazz for the young people of the bush. However, they managed to despatch Sir Joseph with a pretty vote of thanks, and gleefully hied themselves off to lunch. Refreshed, they returned to the task of the organisation, till the afternoon's programme began. Then once more the great task was tackled.

An interim committee of the Country Women's Association (CWA) was formed with Grace Munro as president. Three vice-presidents were elected. Florence Gordon was made honorary secretary. Five other women were appointed to an executive committee, but one of them had to tender her resignation after it was decided that membership of the CWA would be restricted to women from the country. Women from the County of Cumberland (the district encompassing Sydney) could only join if they were engaged in primary production.

The conference closed with votes of thanks for the organisers (in particular Gordon and Munro) and for the editor of the *Stock and Station Journal* and the secretary of the company that owned it. Both men, Mr Milligan and Mr Palmer, had given considerable editorial support and personal time to the conference. They'd even carried in extra chairs when the conference overflowed.

The following day the new CWA committee didn't waste a moment in rolling up its sleeves and getting to work. A delegation called on the minister for railways to present the resolution on rail travel. Next they went to see the minister for health regarding improvements to maternity services throughout the state of New South Wales. Being politicians, the two ministers gave the women a sympathetic hearing, and did nothing. They expected a few flattering words would work their charm and that would be the end of it.

Big mistake. Within a month, Gordon was reporting the formation of branches at Dubbo, Mudgee and Gosford. In her capacity as honorary secretary she gave an address to a meeting of the Shire Councils Association and received pledges of support and names of women to write to in districts across the state. On 9 and 13 June she reported branches being organised at Crookwell (it was actually the first branch formed, started the day after the conference), Bingara, Boggabri, Coonamble, Cootamundra, Cryon, Dorrigo, Duri, Emerald Hill, Erodgere, Forbes, Hillston, Keera, Merriwa, Moree, Mullaley, Mount Penang, Narromine, Parkes, Quirindi, Tamworth, Temora, Trangie, Yass and Werris Creek. She started publishing suggestions on fundraising, organisation and issues the CWA should address in her *Stock and Station Journal* 'Home Page'. Packages containing details of the organisation and its aims were sent to local government,

Red Cross branches and agricultural bureaux. On 13 June, 1922, the 'Home Page' of the *Stock and Station Journal* carried the first 'Country Women's Association' column. Not long after, Queensland started organising branches as well.

Grace Munro proved herself a dynamic, highly motivated founding president when it came to establishing branches, haranguing all levels of government and producing results. By 1923 there were 68 branches in New South Wales and Queensland, and 17 of them had established rest rooms. In 1924 there were 120 branches and 21 rest rooms plus the first baby health centre in the country, in Moree, which Munro helped found. Munro also oversaw the establishment of Keera House at Dee Why, a beachside suburb of Sydney. It was the first holiday home of many set up to support country families. Also in 1924 the CWA was founded in Western Australia. That year ill health forced Grace Munro to resign as president, but she continued to be active in the association for decades to come.

By 1928 the CWA was the largest women's organisation in New South Wales. The same year the Women's Section of the Victorian Farmer's Union reconstituted as the CWA of Victoria. The next year South Australia's CWA was formed, while Queensland expanded its branches to encompass the Northern Territory as well (its autonomous CWA was established in 1961). Tasmania formed its CWA in 1936. The CWA of Australia brought together all the state bodies in 1945.

During the war, the CWA was such a widespread organisation it was able to make a substantial contribution to the Australian war effort. Rest rooms and other CWA facilities in Western Australia were used as listening posts providing early warning of Japanese attacks. Across the country, branches formed sewing circles to manufacture camouflage nets, sheepskin vests for aviators and woollen garments for soldiers and sailors. The organisation supported women who were left to work their farms while their husbands were in the armed forces. Large donations were made to the Red Cross, aid packages were organised and sent to England during and after the war, branches provided food and entertainment at training camps, and rest rooms provided refreshments and facilities for soldiers in transit.

As the organisation grew, it also became a formidable lobby group – widespread, organised and articulate. Politicians who thought they could dismiss the CWA as mere scone-baking whingers found to their cost that its members had long memories and plenty of power when it came to the ballot box. The CWA is generally regarded as a conservative organisation, but as early as 1936 it was calling for equal pay for women (as Florence Gordon had suggested as far back as 1922). Its charter includes supporting rural women in setting up income-generating schemes and helping them raise their standard of living through education, training and community development.

These days that might appear to be a tame agenda, but throughout its history the CWA has fought for a better deal for all women – house-wives and professionals. And while its primary objective is to help rural women, an inevitable consequence is that in the process it has substantially improved rural communities in general. In the 1980s the national organisation put out a booklet listing the organisation's notable resolutions from 1961 to 1984 – they covered improvements in housing, health facilities, conditions for Aborigines, employment programs, communications, environment, women's rights and much more. No one and nothing was forgotten.

It could be argued that the CWA's greatest achievements have been the things it has done almost entirely on its own. In many cases, when knocking on politicians' doors hasn't got a result, the CWA has solved the problem itself (then, as a courtesy, sent the politicians an invitation to the launch of yet another CWA initiative). The energy of country women when it comes to fundraising is legendary and in addition to the rest rooms and health facilities detailed previously, the organisation has also funded or supported bush nursing, the Royal Flying Doctor Service, children's health schemes, bush book clubs and the School of the Air. The next four chapters of this book detail some of the most significant initiatives in outback Australia, but it's worth noting that every one of them had CWA support. Not one of them had initial support from government.

Today the CWA is the largest women's organisation in the country, with more than 44 000 members and 1855 branches, plus hundreds of rest rooms, baby health centres, holiday homes, hospitals and hostels. In recent years the CWA has seen a decline in membership and many of its facilities have (often belatedly) been taken over by government. In many cases, rural women have found other platforms where their voices can be heard, including state and federal parliaments. Falling membership may also be attributed to the CWA having achieved many of its original goals. Despite this, the association continues to fund and advocate projects and services to make life in the outback something to enjoy rather than endure. It may even have settled Lawson and Paterson's old argument, as expressed in Paterson's *Answer to Various Bards:*

> If it ain't all "golden sunshine" where the "wattle branches wave"
> Well, it ain't all damp and dismal, and it ain't all "lonely grave".

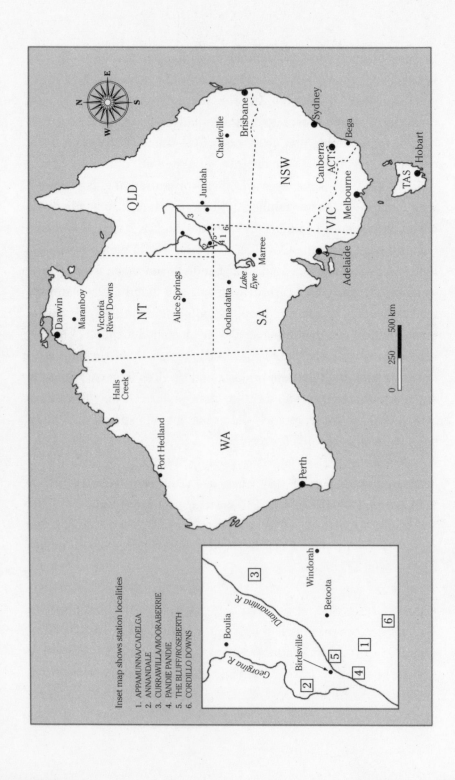

Inset map shows station localities

1. APPAMUNNA/CADELGA
2. ANNANDALE
3. CURRAWILLA/MOORABERRIE
4. PANDIE PANDIE
5. THE BLUFF/ROSEBERTH
6. CORDILLO DOWNS

Grace Francis, circa 1950s from
The Diary of Grace Francis
(State Library of New South Wales)

8

BUSH NURSE

Grace Francis (1892–1959)

As farmers, miners, cameleers and railway workers gradually spread settlement (albeit sparsely) across outback Australia, men and women were forced to adopt a rugged pioneering attitude in response to the lack of even the most basic services. When it came to health, you either got better or you didn't. Another suggestion was to find the nearest sensible woman.

Such stoicism belied a litany of avoidable tragedies, and heart-rending tales were a regular feature of the Australian Inland Mission's *Inlander* magazine. In one of its earliest editions, published in 1914, it told of a twelve-month-old's death while her parents struggled to get her to a doctor. They'd left their property, 100 kilometres from Marree, not long after she took ill. Travelling at night by horse and cart they lost the road. By the time they relocated it several hours had passed. They then had an accident, but managed to press on, only to see the train they needed to catch leave Marree just before they reached it. They waited two days for the next one. It was six hours late. The child died of convulsions ninety minutes before she reached the doctor.

The man behind the *Inlander,* the Australian Inland Mission's Reverend John Flynn, made a habit of publishing such stories with the hope of stimulating action to provide some form of medical service to central Australia. The area encompassing large parts of South Australia, Queensland, the Northern Territory and Western Australia was the size of Europe, but it didn't have a single doctor, hospital or medical facility worthy of the name. Although the AIM's first priority was to bring God to the remotest corners of the outback, Flynn believed healing the body went hand in hand with healing the soul. He also had a personal motivation. In 1883, when Flynn was three years old, his mother died in childbirth. Growing up without her gave him first-hand knowledge of the impact of many of the tragedies he was recording.

When his advocacy got no response from governments, he took it upon himself and the AIM to tackle the problem. Flynn's first plan was to establish 'nursing homes' (forerunners of today's medical centres) throughout the outback. The idea wasn't entirely new. There was already a nurse based at Oodnadatta, funded from the estate of a Scottish woman, Henrietta Smith, whose son had died a lonely death in central Australia. Smith hoped her contribution might save the lives of others and her Smith of Dunesk Mission was a fitting memorial to the young man she'd lost.

The Smith of Dunesk nurses were working from a bush hut when, in 1911, Flynn convinced the AIM to take the service under its wing. The organisation raised enough funds to construct a building for the nursing home, the first in Australia. It took four years before the next home, at Port Hedland in Western Australia's Pilbara, opened in

1915. Maranboy and Halls Creek (both in the Northern Territory) followed in 1917. Beltana in South Australia was established in 1919. A nursing home in Alice Springs operated from a tent until it got a proper building in 1920. In 1923 two homes were established, at Birdsville in Queensland and Victoria River Downs station in the Northern Territory. All the homes were set up with AIM funds and contributions from local communities. Government support for the nursing homes was conspicuous by its absence.

The AIM had far more success recruiting bush nurses (at the time almost exclusively female) to go outback than it did getting doctors to do the same (at the time the profession was predominantly male). Experience soon showed that the challenges for a bush nurse were more bearable if they worked in pairs, even if only one of them was fully trained.

The sacrifices and struggle the bush nurses faced might be difficult to imagine, but we're fortunate that one of the first among them found time to keep a diary of her experiences. The diary of Sister Grace Francis, written between 1923 and 1925, covers the establishment and subsequent day-to-day operations of the nursing home at Birdsville, the remote township near the borders of Queensland, the Northern Territory and South Australia in a region known as Heartbreak Corner.

The name was painfully appropriate. In 1921 the town was resisting the establishment of an AIM nursing home because it was trying to attract the services of a doctor instead. Then one of the women in the town, Mary Smith, gave birth to twins, a boy and girl. They were the first white children born at Birdsville and at first they both seemed healthy. Soon though, both babies fell ill. They declined rapidly, but with the nearest medical facility more than 500 kilometres away on some of the roughest bush tracks in the country, there was nothing that could be done. There were no phones or radios with which to call for help. Within a month of their birth, both babies died.

Only a few months later, in January 1922, Birdsville's constable John Gurn was called out to Annandale station, 90 kilometres north-east of Birdsville in the dunes of the Simpson Desert. He rode there on horseback in temperatures up to 48.9°C. When he got there he was met by the distraught manager and his wife. They took him into the homestead. There, dead from fever, were their two sons, aged two and eight.

The deaths of four children in less than twelve months swept aside resistance to the establishment of a nursing home. Under such circumstances any medical facility was better than nothing. In his search for a nursing sister to establish the new service, John Flynn recognised that Birdsville, remote and isolated even by outback standards, needed a woman of special qualities. He couldn't have chosen better than Grace Francis.

She was born in the country town of Bega, nestled in the lush green hills of the New South Wales far south coast, in 1892. She started her training as a nurse in 1909 and was highly experienced by the time she joined the Australian army during World War I. During her war service she was posted to Europe where she saw and tended the worst injuries human beings can inflict on each other during two years in England and France.

Birdsville was a totally different proposition. The proposed 'hospital' was to be set up in the derelict Royal Hotel, a stone-and-mud building leased by the AIM as a cheaper alternative to constructing a new building. As was the case with many of John Flynn's plans, it was big on ideas but its success would depend on the resourcefulness of the people on the ground. To that end Grace recruited a trusted friend, Sister Catherine Boyd, to accompany her.

Grace also recognised that she was entering uncharted territory and that her story was worth documenting. On 7 September, 1923, her diary begins with their departure from Brisbane. Ahead lay a 1600-kilometre journey from one side of Queensland to the other. The first leg was by train to Charleville. Then they switched to trucks.

Grace Francis was a highly experienced nurse, but her diary makes it clear she had scant experience of the outback. On 11 September, as she and Catherine Boyd were approaching Windorah, they visited a boundary rider's hut and she wrote, 'There were seven altogether in this family and though to us it seemed a desolate life, they all seemed bright and contented.' What Grace didn't realise was that where she was going was far more desolate.

At Windorah on 14 September, while waiting for the car that was to take them the remaining 400 kilometres to Birdsville, the nurses dealt with their first life-threatening case: 'The Police Sergeant asked us to go and see his sick child today. The little chap (four years) looks very ill.'

The next day the boy, Freddie Stokes, was worse, with a temperature of 38.9°C. Grace suspected he had typhoid and advised the parents to take the boy to the hospital at Jundah, 100 kilometres north-east. They left the following morning. Grace went with them, as the boy had deteriorated even further, and they arrived at Jundah around 2 p.m. When the boy was admitted to hospital, the doctor confirmed Grace's diagnosis. The news was extremely upsetting for Freddie's parents, who were well aware that typhoid in the outback was virtually a death sentence. They were about to discover that professional medical care, promptly delivered, could make all the difference.

When young Freddie's condition stabilised, Grace and the Stokes left Jundah (Freddie remained in hospital) to return to Windorah. Grace was glad to be on her way. 'Jundah did not impress me at all and I don't want to ever see it again. In addition to the usual two or three hotels, Jundah supports a hospital, police station, Post Office, several stores and a supply of goats.'

She still didn't know that, compared to Birdsville, Jundah was the

'big smoke'. Back at Windorah, the car still hadn't turned up and
the nurses contemplated making the journey by horse-drawn coach.
They were spared that adventure when, on 18 September, Lou Reese,
owner of Appamunna station, and Mr Brooks from Birdsville arrived
with the car.

They got on their way a couple of days later, stopping for lunch
at the JC Hotel (now a ruin 100 kilometres from Windorah) which
Grace referred to as 'a lonely desolate place among the sandhills'.
It was a taste of things to come. They stopped at Morny station
for the night, then at Currawilla and Mooraberrie the next day. At
each of these giant properties they marvelled at the bush hospitality
extended to them, little realising how rare it was for any of them to
have visitors.

Beyond the flyspeck town of Betoota, the nurses got their first
impressions of Heartbreak Corner. Grace wrote:

> The roads were exceedingly bad. Such sandhills and gibbers, the
> roughest road I have ever travelled. The country seemed to get more
> bare and timberless as we travelled on to Cadelgo. Just through the
> border fence into South Australia [we] passed a house occupied by one
> man who seemed very lonely and isolated. We had lunch on the bank
> of a creek and the flies were so bad I'm afraid we did not enjoy food
> much . . . There are hundreds of kangaroos and emus running along
> with the car. We struck a very difficult crossing at a creek just through
> the fence. Mr Brooks had a job to find a suitable crossing but eventu-
> ally chanced one and there was a drop of two or three feet but 'Marie'
> got over it alright. The road was either rocky or sandy for the next 20
> miles or so. We crossed wide spans of country covered with huge boul-
> ders which seems impossible to travel over. The clear skyline at sunset
> unbroken by timber was indeed very beautiful but oh! the monotony
> of those stones.

That night they slept soundly at Appamunna, a homestead made
of cane grass. They were the first female guests the place had ever
received.

Late in the afternoon on 23 September they arrived in Birdsville.
Grace didn't record her immediate reaction to the township but she
was pleasantly surprised by the hospital, 'a comfortable looking building'. The townsfolk had cleaned the place out and whitewashed the
interior. The roof had several gaping holes, but the six-room building
was in better shape than they expected.

The one thing the new 'hospital' lacked was furniture and medical supplies. They were somewhere on the Birdsville Track, being
transported by camel train from the nearest railhead at Marree, 500
kilometres south. Having only what they'd brought with them, the
two nurses spent their first night at the hotel. That night they experienced their first dust storm and the place 'rattled like a match box'.

The following night there was a function to welcome the new nurses.
Grace was surprised that nine women were there, and learned that
more were scattered throughout the district. It was intended that the
hospital would not only provide medical services but also become a
social hub for the community, and the idea was taken to heart that
first night. There was dancing until 12.30.

The nurses spent the first week meeting people, sweeping the sand
from the dust storms out of the hospital and wondering when they'd
hear anything of their baggage. By 1 October, they grew tired of waiting for it to arrive. Neither woman was the kind who would let the
grass grow under their feet, although this was unlikely to happen in
a town where the annual rainfall was less than 150 millimetres. They
accepted an invitation from the Birdsville school's only teacher, Jack
Griffin, to visit its twenty-eight pupils.

Grace judged the teacher to be 'a lonely, homesick young man'. She
noted that most of the children were suffering from 'sandy blight',
the range of eye infections common in dusty outback locations. Some

children could barely see, consequently their schoolwork was suffering, and Griffin had taken to washing their eyes with a simple saline solution. Until the medical supplies arrived, the nurses could do no better. The one bright spot in their visit was the excitement that resulted when they offered to give the schoolgirls some sewing lessons.

On 4 October there was news of the furniture and medical supplies. They hadn't left Marree. It was hoped one of the Ghans would start out with them that week on a journey that usually took twenty-four days. Despite this setback, Grace and Catherine were undaunted. The teetotal women had had enough of the pub, so they commandeered two camp stretchers and mattresses and moved into their hospital. They made what used to be the bar their bedroom and improvised tables using wooden crates. One of the townspeople gave them the key to an old piano which meant Grace could enjoy one of her favourite pastimes, playing hymns.

The diary entry for 12 October reveals that the novelty of the dust storms, and the subsequent shovelling of sand from the hospital, must have passed. 'ANOTHER DUST-STORM,' Grace's diary noted with exasperation. A week later they had a succession of days when the temperature rose to 40°C. On the fourth day Grace went for a long walk to shake off the feeling of dizziness she felt in the heat, but it only made her feel worse.

Through it all, the nurses still managed to provide basic medical services. They were trained to perform an extraordinary range of procedures, including dentistry, but when it came to one extraction, for a Mrs McAuley, their lack of equipment let them down. Wrote Grace: 'Could not manage to extract as she pulled away and only having her sitting on a box without support for the head it was a difficult job. I hate to let her go with the tooth not out. She has suffered great pain.' (The tooth finally succumbed on 5 December. It came out in three pieces, 'very difficult and very painful'.)

While the medical service was rudimentary at best, the locals were still grateful. When Grace extracted a tooth for a cameleer, Roy Khan, he returned with a box of apples for the nurses and a donation for the hospital. He may also have been the source of a rumour that the camel train with their loading was now only 160 kilometres away.

The nurses also provided a focus for the spiritual needs of the town, at least for its Presbyterians. On 25 October they held their first song service. Grace gave a short sermon for the dozen attendees. Three days later the nurses held their first Sunday school class, for seven children.

There was more 'bush medicine' that day. 'This morning a patient (Mr. West, drover) came in with an abscess on his face and as I only had scissors had to open it with them. It was very superficial and was very easy, the pus just poured out and gave him such relief that when we arranged two boxes and got him lying down and a good hot foment on the face, he went to sleep for an hour or so.'

All through November and into December there was still no sign of their camel train, which Grace noted with frustrated regularity. It didn't stop them settling into the community, though, and they were soon entertaining visitors on a regular basis. A constant stream of people from all over the district brought gifts of fruit, vegetables and meat. The nurses also ran their Sunday school classes, hymn sessions and sewing classes. In the evenings they played ping-pong.

As Christmas approached it became clear that most of the district's children had never experienced a proper Christmas party. The nurses began sending letters to the AIM's network of supporters calling for gifts and Christmas decorations. They recruited a volunteer Santa and foraged for the ingredients for a fruit cake. This while experiencing weather nothing like a traditional European Christmas. On 10 December Grace noted that it was so hot that sleep was impossible. She'd long since stopped diarising temperatures of 40°C. They were commonplace.

On the day of the Christmas party, Christmas Eve, the nurses
were putting presents for the town's children under a locally pro-
cured bushy tree when the best present they could have hoped for
came loping into town up the Birdsville Track. A string of seventy-five
camels was laden with all the nursing home's furniture and supplies.
The camel train's arrival coincided perfectly with the guests for the
Christmas party, a substantial part of the local community. To add
to the chaos, a freak rainstorm threatened to soak the loading as
the townsfolk busied themselves piling everything into their hospital.
After that it was the kind of day Birdsville had never seen, as Grace
recorded:

> Sixty-four turned up at the Xmas tree and we started at 8.45 p.m. It
> looked very nice and the wee folk were so excited about it all not having
> seen one before. When Santa Claus made his appearance the shouting
> was loud and we soon distributed the toys and gave Santa Claus three
> cheers and bade him goodbye. The supper was served to the children,
> meantime the men had a hat trimming competition which was won
> by Mr Crabb of Pandi Pandi, and he was presented with a toy dog.
> At 10 p.m. the children being tired, and ready for bed, we closed our
> entertainment with the national anthem and three cheers for the good
> folk who sent Santa Claus and the Xmas tree along. They are all satis-
> fied that it is the best Xmas yet in Birdsville. A beast was killed in the
> township and Xmas meat distributed.

The New Year, 1924, was so hot that the nurses found it hard to enjoy
the chicken Mrs McAuley sent as thanks for her dental work. Matters
weren't helped as the work of unpacking and properly organising
the hospital had finally begun. Both women found it easier to get a
decent night's rest when they hit upon the idea of taking their beds
outside and sleeping under the stars.

On 11 January Grace noted: 'Extracted a tooth from the black gin

Bulka (she was very good).' At times Flynn's Inland Mission has been accused of discriminating against Aboriginal people in the provision of medical services. However, this reference in Francis' diary (one of several) reveals that she treated anyone who came to the hospital's door. She also referred to visits made to Aboriginal camps around Birdsville and the surrounding stations.

Between the medical work, conducting classes, keeping the hospital clean and sharing kitchen duties, the nurses' daily workload was substantial. The hot weather made it harder still, but the nurses discovered that January was the month for moonlight swimming in the billabongs of the Diamantina River. Grace counted twenty-eight in the river one evening. On 19 January she made a passing reference to a temperature of 42.2°C. In February, though, the heat started getting her down. She wrote, 'The heat is very trying today and we did not venture out at all. On the whole spent a very miserable homesick day.' Again, on 9 February: 'Heat almost unbearable, did a little sewing as well as other usual duties.' On 13 February: 'Spent a very miserable day. The heat is very trying and other things.'

Grace was also a keen tennis player, but she'd found that one of the many things the town lacked was a tennis court. Despite the continuing high temperatures the nurses got involved in establishing one. It was no easy task, either physically or politically. When the local council offered to provide wire netting to use as an improvised net, several of the locals took umbrage at being fobbed off with second best. Grace noted that there was 'quite an undercurrent of ill feeling'. It was so intense that she and those who wanted to accept what was on offer deferred to the real-net-or-nothing faction. It wasn't until things cooled down (on all fronts) that the 'tennis club' was established. There were similar squabbles between the Catholics and Protestants. Once again Grace avoided getting involved, believing it was to be expected of 'a handful of people like this living so long and so close to each other'.

In March, the Diamantina came down in flood. Heavy rains had fallen far to the north and while it was still hot and dry in Birdsville the river rose every day. It prompted Grace to turn her thoughts to the town's sanitation. Everyone drew supplies from a nearby billabong that the river's flow hadn't yet reached. Grace noted a dead horse in the channel that linked the two and suggested something should be done about it. All the men were sure the flood wouldn't rise that high, and did nothing, so Grace and four of the town's women set about dealing with the horse themselves. It was too big for them to move so they gathered firewood and piled it around the carcass. When they set the pyre ablaze the problem was reduced to ash. The next day Francis was vindicated: 'The water is running into the town hole so we are pleased we burnt the horse.'

Water was a constant problem throughout the nurses' assignment in Birdsville. All of it had to be carried from the billabong. Some of the men in the town gave them a hand, but the needs of even a small hospital were so insatiable that the two women were often reduced to half a bucket a day for their personal needs. The lack of water also made growing fresh vegetables difficult. When they succeeded, wandering livestock often made short work of the potential harvest.

Another frustration was the unreliable mail service. The nurses understood that letters from home, news of the outside world and correspondence regarding the hospital's administrative matters were all susceptible to the vagaries of flood, dust storms and mechanical breakdown but that didn't make it any easier. At times it drove Grace to distraction. In mid-March 1924 the mail from Windorah didn't arrive for a month. When the mail man did arrive, on 29 March, there were no letters for either of the nurses 'to our disgust. It will be another fortnight before we can expect him back again.'

The arrival of the Windorah mail man also gave Grace Francis her first chance to send dressings to a man in Betoota who'd accidentally shot himself in the foot six weeks earlier. By the time he got them the wounds had probably healed. On another occasion, when the long-looked for mail arrived, she couldn't resist a sarcastic 'Windorah mail in for a wonder.'

In mid-1924 the hospital proved its worth in the best possible way. A heavily pregnant Mrs Morton, from Roseberth station, came into town on 18 May to spend the last days before the birth in the capable hands of the bush nurses. Three days later there was a horse racing carnival, but the nurses had more pressing matters to attend to. Grace's diary records, 'Baby born at 6.30 p.m. (a son).' Mother and child were both well, helped by a standard of medical attention that had never existed in that part of the outback before.

On 23 May Grace recorded, 'Baby very cross all night,' but three days later wrote, 'Baby Morton very good and is sleeping all night thank goodness.' On 2 June Mrs Morton and her son, Lyle, were discharged. Grace wrote that both were 'very well'. Lyle remained so, and grew up to eventually marry bush nurse Phyllis Beech. He and his descendants are still living in the Birdsville community.

Gunshot wounds were among the injuries the bush nurses had to deal with on a remarkably regular basis. On 5 March, 1924, the overseer of the Rabbit Fence was in town and reported that a man had accidentally shot himself in the foot. Grace sent dressings and advice on what to do, but did not 'think it necessary to go as the wound is through and through'. On another occasion a stockman, Les McAuley, also managed to shoot himself through the foot. Again the wound was 'through and through', but he insisted the bullet was still in him because a search had failed to find it. Grace couldn't find it in the wound. Two days later they tracked the slug down. It was in the shoe McAuley had been wearing when the gun went off. It had been left at Roseberth station after they'd pulled it off to assess the injury.

It was now winter in the remote outback town and the cooler months lent themselves to a better quality of life. In mid-June Grace went on a short break to one of the stations, riding to The Bluff. After a week's stay she swapped with Catherine, who also spent a week enjoying the station's hospitality. In July, Grace recorded 'a day of days':

Went for a ride on Mr Fay's camels. Left at 9 a.m. and only went as far as the river and back and quite far enough. I say I was bluffed at getting on but it was not nearly so difficult as I thought it would be, we took a snap of each other which we are hoping will be good. [Schoolteacher] Jack G's camel was very quick at getting up, I was riding "Girbe", Boyd "Jennie" and J.G. "General Joffre". We were glad to get home again. After dinner and a short rest we went over to the tennis court and all took afternoon tea. The court was good oh and we had a good afternoon's sport, the first real tennis we have had. Most of the members are beginners but the majority have a good style and we ought to have some good players in the future months.

Also that month she accepted an invitation to Appamunna station, where she described a glorious day walking with the daughters of the owners in the sandhills near the homestead.

Weaving through Grace's diary are glimpses of the life surrounding the town. It was still a time when drovers passed through with mobs of up to 1000 cattle kicking up columns of dust as they strung out along the grassy edges of the Diamantina River. There were doggers and fencers, slow-moving camel trains and an indigenous population occupying the fringes of a land that was once theirs alone. She saw horses being broken in the middle of town and met people who had lived their lives in remoteness and isolation but wouldn't trade places with anyone.

The nurses' first anniversary in Birdsville, on 23 September, was marked by an enormous dust storm that blew all day. There was another storm a week later and the old-timers told the bush nurses it had been the dustiest year they could remember. It was little

consolation for the women who had spent much of their time shovelling the dust out of the hospital. In her diary Francis frequently refers
to it being 'inches deep' throughout the rooms. To anyone who hasn't
experienced a Birdsville dust storm it sounds like an exaggeration.
It isn't.

Not long after, the bush nurses faced their first crisis. What started
as a normal bout of winter colds soon spread to most of the town's
children. Then several started showing symptoms that were more
serious. One boy, Norman Hagan, was brought in 'suffering with a
bad cold and earache. The child looks ill and has an inflamed swell-
ing on his forehead which might be serious.' Grace's concerns grew
the following day. She visited the Hagan home three times. Two days
later she was again a frequent visitor but now she was most worried
about one of the Hagan girls, Mary, who was showing symptoms of
bronchial pneumonia.

On 2 October: 'Mary Hagan still very ill and I am most anxious
about her.' The next day, another dust storm caused the child great
difficulty in breathing. With Grace giving her constant care, the little
one struggled on and even improved slightly. By that stage Grace was
visiting several children every day to apply 'mustard poultices'. Three
days later she started to get on top of the situation. She recorded that
Mary Hagan had started feeling a little better. Then she wrote that
the danger had passed and the child was on the road to recovery. On
7 October she wrote, with just a hint of triumph, 'Mary Hagan better.' She'd faced the sort of illness that had taken the lives of many
outback children in similar circumstances. So far, the bush nurses
hadn't lost a single patient.

At the beginning of December, Grace counted the number of people
they'd treated in their first fourteen months at the Birdsville hospital.
It was more than 2000. Their second Christmas in Birdsville was
even bigger than the first. The people of the town now treasured
the women who'd cared for them, healed them and in some cases

probably saved their lives. The whole community got behind the
efforts of the bush nurses. Grace wrote of the second party:

> A number of men came along to help generally and we got the tree
> erected in the yard. By 8 p.m. all had arrived, the tree looked nice
> decorated with balloons, flags and toys. [It] delighted the children very
> much. Santa Claus was announced at 8.15 p.m. and soon we were
> helping him to give the toys out. The adults were each given a balloon.
> Mr. Griffin carried on the competition of tailing the donkey while we got
> supper ready and it caused quite a lot of amusement. Supper at 10 p.m.
> took up a lot of time but I think everybody enjoyed it. The cake which
> was sent by Miss Cairns, Brisbane, was much admired by the young
> folk. After supper we had a short musical programme in which every-
> body contributed. The children sang two songs and two of them gave a
> recitation each. We broke up at mid-night. Mr. and Mrs. Brook and Co.
> stayed and helped us wash up. We felt very tired but very pleased with
> the result of our work. Mr. Griffin and Mr. Reese were two of our main
> supporters and helped with everything.

Christmas marked the beginning of the annual exodus of everyone
who didn't need to be in Birdsville or the outback during the hot-
test months of the year. There was no such opportunity for the bush
nurses. They stayed to continue the medical service for the few folk
who remained. The bush nurses spent Christmas Day thinking of
home folk, far away. On 28 December their Sunday school had only
two attendees.

In January the bush nurses experienced their first real heatwave.
It started on New Year's Day and continued for day after day with
temperatures of 43°C. The bush nurses declined invitations to visit
stations around the district because they could only think of staying
cool. They swam whenever they got the chance. It got so hot that the
men drank the hotel dry. The teetotaller Grace gleefully recorded:

'They are serving fruit salts, which is most amusing and much better than strong stuff, still it brings in one shilling per glass which is profiteering pure and simply.' It wasn't until 26 January that she could write, 'The Ghan with loading from the store in today, and much to the men's delight the beer long-looked-for.'

Alcohol was a constant issue in the town. The bush nurses frequently saw its effects and in June 1924 Grace noted one straightforward cure: 'Mr Lee rode in today and is going out with W. James the Marree mailman. He is addicted to drink and likes to get away from town.' A few days later, on their way back from a picnic at the river, the women saw a horse without a rider, then a man lying on the ground. Grace wrote: '[He was] the worse of drink, but I think the horse must have thrown him as we found horse whip etc. scattered around. We caught the horse and brought it to town, he staggered after us.' The following day, 'Met the man whom we rescued yesterday and he was most ashamed.'

In February many of Birdsville's families had returned to town, and school had restarted, when there was a heatwave that was even hotter than the one in January. Even the locals took it seriously, as Grace recorded:

17th: 'Very hot day. The school had to be closed on account of excessive heat temperature (118) [47.8°C] an almost unbearable HOT northerly wind blowing; the only way to rest is by means of wrapping one's body in a wet sheet. Boyd and I find this a wonderful invention and comply freely with the scheme. The temperature tonight was 114 deg. [45.6°C] with that raging hot north wind preventing the whole of Birdsville from the slightest rest.

The next day the temperature reached 46.7°C; the day after, 46.1°C. Swimming in the deep, brown waters of the Diamantina was now 'corker'. Meat sent in from one of the stations was ruined when 'the sun smiled on it with vengeance'. A couple of weeks later the bush nurses got letters from family in Brisbane describing the 'terrible heatwave' they'd experienced. It had reached 40.6, 'so we were not the only people enjoying the heat'. In reality, Grace's diary hadn't mentioned such mild temperatures for months.

Saving lives was the most important role for the bush nurses, but in March 1925 they were called upon to fill another function – caring for the dying. Early in the month a mailman told Grace of a man out in the bush named Long who was suffering from 'Berri Berri' but refused the offer of a ride into the hospital for treatment. 'Expect he will come in one of these days,' Grace wrote, 'these bushmen are ridiculously averse to women.'

She'd already seen some of the lonely camps out in the bush on her trips around the district, and had visited one old hermit, Harry Marshall, some months before. His home was made of boxes and he lived on what he got from a small vegetable patch. To Grace he looked frail, old and dirty, but she had to admit he was happy with his life.

By mid-March news came in that Long's condition had worsened, and on 12 March Grace wrote:

Mr Long who is camped 18 miles [29 kilometres] from here was admitted into the ward this afternoon suffering advanced heart disease. He has been ill for some time and was treating himself for Berri Berri, but has had an acute heart all the time. He died at 11 p.m. after a struggle for eight hours. I had to let him have his mattress on the ground, he just begged to have it there as the wire mattress was too soft for him. These poor old bushmen are so used to the ground for sleeping that they are uncomfortable on a bed. He managed to sign his will before he died. It was a happy release for him from the pain and breathlessness.

13th: The funeral took place this morning at 11 a.m. The policeman brought his car, in which the body was carried in the back, Sister

and I in the front. I read the burial service. Could not procure timber
to make a coffin so the body was sewn up in cloth and then in white
calico. I have written to his wife who lives in Adelaide.

Not long after, the bush nurses learned they would be relieved in September. They also took delivery of a package of goods they'd ordered
in Brisbane before they'd left in September 1923. It had taken eighteen months to be delivered. Even telegraphic communication was
slow – a wire sent to them on 11 February was relayed via Boulia
(380 kilometres north) and arrived by mail coach on 7 March.

Such experiences highlighted the problems of communication in
the outback, especially in an emergency. The point was emphasised
again just a month later. On 8 April Ray Kidman (a member of the
Kidman cattle family) and three other men were driving up the Birdsville Track when they took a wrong turn. They soon found themselves
in danger of running out of fuel and water. Unable to call for help,
they went two days without food, only managing to shoot a couple
of galahs to get a meal. They eventually found the track and reached
Birdsville with less than a litre of fuel remaining. Had they not located
the right road, they could easily have perished, as happened to five
members of the Page family as recently as the 1960s.

There was another emergency four days later, at Cordillo Downs,
240 kilometres south-east of Birdsville. A young man had suffered a
head injury that had left him unconscious. One of the managers had
made a trip into Birdsville to fetch Grace Francis. The trip back to
Cordillo took two days of hard driving, frustrating breakdowns and
bush camping. At the stops Grace made herself useful by boiling the
billy while the men dealt with whatever mechanical problem had
arisen. She observed:

It's marvellous the places a car can get one, an odd heavy pull over
sandhills and then numerous gutters, a couple of smooth runs over a

clay pan covered with cane grass from 8 to 10 ft [3 metres] high but very dead and dry . . . Reached Cadelgo at about 5.45 a.m. It was a beautiful sight watching the day break over the sandhills . . . The run to Cordillo 70 miles [120 kilometres] was through beautiful country and the grass astounded we drought-blind B'Ville-ites.

At Cordillo the young man had recovered consciousness and was just able to speak. When Grace assessed him she found he had severe pain, an irregular pulse and couldn't bear being moved but she came to the conclusion that his skull hadn't been fractured. She provided him with some pain relief and kept him quiet. She then spent that night and the next day taking care of him. Only when his pulse had returned to normal did she consider it safe to leave him.

On the way back to Birdsville she was met with kindness at every tiny outstation along the way. At Cadelgo the cook cleaned a special knife and fork for her and all the station hands sat around after dinner spinning yarns. Grace maintained that she'd never felt more at home in her life. The vehicle she was travelling in finally succumbed to the hard driving at The Bluff and she ended up completing the two-day return journey in a horse-drawn buggy.

Her mercy dash to Cordillo highlighted one of the greatest obstacles to providing medical services in the outback – communication. It had taken two days to call for medical attention and another two for Grace to reach the patient. Her experience was typical of all the bush nurses across central Australia and the significance of the problem wasn't lost on the AIM's John Flynn.

Once again, it was his organisation, rather than the government, that was searching for a solution. In August, Flynn and radio expert George Towns called at the hospital as part of their early experiments in using radio transmitters in the outback. While Towns set up the equipment, Flynn reviewed the hospital's performance in its first two years. He was moved to tears by what the bush nurses had achieved.

ABOVE: A 1930s poster by James Northfield promoting the Trans-Australian Railway.
(Courtesy of the James Northfield Heritage Art Trust)

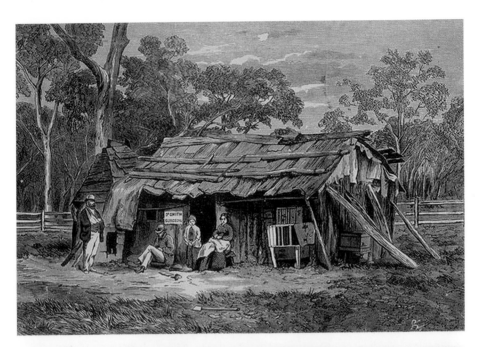

TOP: This Samuel Calvert engraving of a surgeon's bush hut illustrates why the outback was often considered 'no place for a woman'. The founding principle of the Country Women's Association was to improve conditions for women, but the advantages soon extended to their families in particular and the outback in general. *(National Library of Australia, nla.pic-an10280447)*

BOTTOM: The Conference of Bush Women held in Sydney in April 1922 at which the Country Womens' Association was founded. It was initially a New South Wales organisation but rapidly expanded to become the largest women's organisation in the country. *(State Library of New South Wales, Sydney Mail, April 26, 1922, page 8)*

ABOVE: 'Sister Mulvay in the hole in the wall hospital store' at the Royal Hotel, Birdsville. The photograph was taken by schoolteacher Cliff Everitt in 1926 and reveals the primitive conditions in which bush nurses delivered medical care to the outback. *(State Library of Queensland neg. no. 108391)*

ABOVE: The crowd at the opening of the Birdsville tennis season on Easter Saturday, 1927. Bush nurses not only provided medical services, they also helped the development of social activities. Sisters Francis and Boyd had been involved in establishing the tennis court in 1924. The struggle to get a proper net (right of picture), instead of chicken wire, appears to have been successful. *(State Library of Queensland neg. no. 109953r)*

ABOVE: *Victory*, the first aircraft used to provide flying-doctor services in outback Australia, shown with pilot Arthur Affleck, Rev. J.A. Barber and Dr J.A. Spalding. This photograph was taken in 1927 during Barber's reconnaissance trip prior to the establishment of the service in 1928. *(National Library of Australia, nla.pic-an24171724)*

ABOVE: A young girl being loaded onto one of the early aircraft of the Flying Doctor Service in 1938. Such aircraft were able to carry a patient, doctor and pilot only.
(John Flynn, National Library of Australia, nla.pic-an24721288)

ABOVE: A Flying Doctor De Havilland Dragon swoops low over a homestead in the Northern Territory in 1948. As the service grew, stations built airstrips and learned to keep people and stock under control during take-offs and landings. At times aircraft reportedly flew low, cut their engines and called out for directions. *(J. Fitzpatrick, National Archive of Australia)*

ABOVE: The Flying Doctor Service's Dr Jean White and pilot Doug Tennant survived this crash of their De Havilland Fox Moth on Cape York in 1939. They were found four days later. *(John Flynn, National Library of Australia, nla.pic-an24132635)*

ABOVE: The first pedal wireless being operated by its inventor, Alf Traeger, on 17 November, 1928. It was the first of many Traeger radios that would transform communication in the outback. *(John Flynn, National Library of Australia, nla.pic-an24631139)*

ABOVE: A rare image of Alf Traeger operating his prototype hand-cranked wireless. One hand is cranking the generator while the other is tapping out morse code. The photo was almost certainly taken on a field trip to Cloncurry with John Flynn in 1927. The vehicle is a Dodge tourer, one of at least two vehicles used by the Australian Inland Mission at the time (the other vehicle was Flynn's famous Dodge Buckboard). *(John Flynn, National Library of Australia, nla.pic-an24331282)*

LEFT: Mrs Gertrude Rothery sends the first morse code message from Augustus Downs, north-west Queensland, on 18 June, 1929. It marked the beginning of the end of the isolation felt by many in outback Australia. *(State Library of Queensland neg. no. 166304)*

ABOVE: In the Tennant Creek area, Barry Cole, son of a bore-drilling contractor, participates in a School of the Air lesson while his mother, Alia, looks on. The family's Traeger radio meant youngsters like Barry could continue his lessons even as his family shifted across the outback. *(J. Fitzpatrick, National Archives of Australia)*

ABOVE: R.M. Williams was no stranger to hard work and could turn his hand to almost anything. Here, in the Great Depression in the 1930s, he earned a living digging wells by hand. *(Newspix)*

ABOVE LEFT: The greater bilby (*Macrotis lagotis*) is almost extinct in Queensland, its range reduced by 95 per cent. The bilby is now the focus of a major rescue effort that has seen part of the outback returned to its original condition in the hope that it will once more support bilbies. *(Martin Harvey/ANTPhoto.com)*

ABOVE RIGHT: The bilby fence in Currawinya National Park (in mulga country on the Queensland side of the New South Wales border) encloses an area of 25 square kilometres. Feral predators have been eradicated, providing the bilby population with ideal habitat. The fence was built in part with donations from ordinary Australians through the Save the Bilby campaign. *(Courtesy Michelle Havenstein)*

In particular there was a reduction of 'sandy blight' among the children, which had led to an improvement in their schoolwork. Then there was the successful delivery of baby Lyle Morton, whom John Flynn christened while he was there. Lyle had become the first surviving European child born in Birdsville.

On the evening of 13 August, Towns got the radio working and Francis's diary records what has since become a significant moment in history. 'We gathered a few of the neighbours and Mr Towns gave us a "listening in treat" [a concert broadcast from Melbourne] and it seemed very real when the paper report was read out. The concert ended in the National Anthem which also for the moment turned the old store room into a concert hall.'

The following day: 'After tea Mr Towns was able after a lot of trouble to locate Barcaldine [in central Queensland] in the air. He was trying for Brisbane but failed. Later in the evening he was able to get a man from Adelaide and gave three wires from here, two from Mr Flynn and one from us to Chelmer [Grace's family], these to be transmitted to Brisbane. I suppose they will receive them tomorrow. Mr Towns and Mr Flynn were very much happier for having got this much done and no doubt it is a wonderful thing.'

With the benefit of hindsight it was the beginning of all that and more, but in 1925 the radio's promise was all too brief. The next morning everything was packed in Flynn's car and the two men prepared to leave. Grace in particular felt the pain of their going. 'We feel very sad at thoughts of losing our good friends,' she wrote. 'Mr Towns on his way in to afternoon tea stopped at the piano in the kitchen and played "Auld Lang Syne" which brought a lump to our throats.'

A week later another priest, Reverend Cohen, and his colleague called at the hospital. The two men stayed for nearly a week, touring the region with Grace as their guide. Their presence proved a mixed blessing. The second-last entry in her diary was written just after they left and touches on the feelings of loneliness and isolation that never completely left her during two years in Birdsville, even in the midst of the hospitality and warmth of the local population. She wrote: 'We have enjoyed having visitors but oh! the awful blank when they go.'

When the nurses finally left the town, people came in from all over the district, making their way over the rough bush tracks to express their thanks for what the pair had done. Lou Reese wrote in a letter to John Flynn: 'If ever angels came on earth, I would say these are two.'

Grace Francis and Catherine Boyd were among the pioneers of outback medical services (Grace also helped set up the Birdsville branch of the CWA). After 1925 both women continued to work as bush nurses. Francis helped establish nursing services at Victoria River Downs, in the Northern Territory, in the 1930s. At the time it was the most remote station in the fledgling network of nursing homes being set up using Alf Traeger's innovative wireless sets. She was also involved with the Bush Children's Health Scheme.

During World War II she was Commandant of the Volunteer Aid Detachment and trained 500 volunteers. She was awarded an MBE in 1950 for services to nursing. She died on 10 September, 1959, after a long illness, aged sixty-seven. By then she'd lived to see, and had helped bring about, a revolution in outback health care. In 1963 two cottages were built in Birdsville as retirement homes for elderly bush men. One was named Francis Cottage.

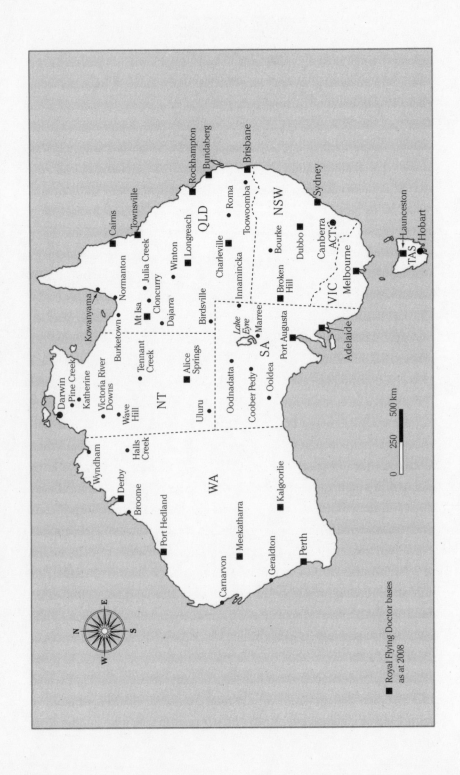

Royal Flying Doctor bases
as at 2008

John Flynn, date unknown
(John Oxley Library, State Library of Queensland)

9

NO BETTER SOUND
John Flynn (1880–1951)

In 1917 a seriously injured young stockman named Jimmy Darcy was brought in to the former gold-rush town of Halls Creek in Western Australia's Kimberley region. He was in agony, having suffered severe abdominal injuries after a fall from a horse while mustering on Ruby Plains station, 75 kilometres south of the town. His mates had carried him in a horse and cart on a journey that had lasted more than sixteen hours. At times they'd had to stop to give the patient a brief respite from his excruciating pain as he was jolted over the rough bush track. Then they'd pressed on, eventually reaching Halls Creek at 2 a.m.

There was no doctor in the town, so they took Darcy to the post office. There the postmaster (who was also the resident magistrate, warden, commissioner of roads, chairman of the licensing board, protector of Aborigines and registrar of births, deaths and marriages) knew some first aid. Postmaster Tuckett quickly realised Darcy needed more than he could do for him, so he telegraphed Wyndham (380 kilometres north) and Derby (550 kilometres west). In both towns the doctors were away.

Tuckett didn't give up. He remembered the doctor who had taught him first aid back in Perth. John Holland, who at the time was pioneering the development of the St John's Ambulance Service, was 1760 kilometres south as the crow flies. Eventually, Tuckett telegraphed Holland and described Jimmy's condition. Jimmy's pain and injuries were located mainly around his pelvis. He was unable to urinate.

Holland diagnosed a ruptured bladder. If it was left untreated, Jimmy's chances were slim. By the time a doctor got to the tiny outback location, assuming they could find a doctor, Darcy would probably be dead. Holland told Tuckett that he would have to perform a perineal cystotomy – make an incision in Darcy's abdomen, locate the bladder and insert a tube to help it drain. Not surprisingly, Tuckett wasn't keen on the idea, as an article in the AIM magazine the *Inlander* explained:

> Operate! Yes, he must. No instruments! Yes, he had at least both penknife and razor. No drugs! Yes, he had permanganate of potash. Couldn't! Yes, he could try. Kill the man! Well if he didn't hurry his patient would die first.

Thus began one of the most extraordinary operations ever performed in outback Australia. In Perth, Holland visualised the patient lying before him, then 'talked' Tuckett through each step of the procedure – except, of course, that all the communication was in morse code, relayed from telegraph station to telegraph station up the coast of Western Australia, then inland to the tiny post office. The first telegram ran to 270 words. It was followed by many more – 4000 words in all. Further complicating matters was the fact that the operation, and a subsequent suprapubic cystotomy, were done without anaesthetic. Tuckett had given Darcy all the morphine there was when he'd first arrived.

Thanks to the skills of Holland and Tuckett, the operations were successful, and Darcy's pain subsided. However, he wasn't out of danger and couldn't be moved. Holland decided to undertake the journey to Halls Creek to personally attend the patient. It took him twelve days. Holland had to sign on as a cattleman to be allowed aboard the SS *Moira*, bound from Perth to Derby. From there he travelled by car and horse, along the way crossing several crocodile-infested rivers. As he pressed on, he heard on the bush telegraph that Darcy's condition was deteriorating. Nearing Halls Creek he was driven through the night in a Model-T Ford on roads that barely answered to the name. When he finally arrived in Halls Creek, it was to be met with the news that Darcy had died just hours before.

Holland's post-mortem revealed that Darcy had not died from post-surgical complications – the incisions were clear of infection and there was no evidence of blood-poisoning. It turned out that Darcy also had malaria, and in his weakened condition an attack had been too much for him.

On his return to Perth, John Holland reputedly met John Flynn. After describing his epic journey, he said to the outback missionary, 'Next time I go to Halls Creek, I'll fly.'

The following year, John Flynn published the details of Jimmy Darcy's death in the *Inlander* as yet another example of the risks of living with a dismal lack of medical services in the outback. By then he'd established what was then called a nursing home (in effect a medical centre staffed by highly trained nurses) in Halls Creek, but a greater vision was already growing in his mind.

The article on Jimmy Darcy preceded another by a young trainee aviator from Victoria named Clifford Peel. The article was titled

'Aeroplanes for Inland'. In it Peel outlined the use of planes to transport doctors to medical emergencies wherever they occurred. The
fledgling pilot dealt with issues of safety, infrastructure, efficiency,
logistics and cost. He noted that most aviation accidents were cur-
rently due to 'stunting' and that in commercial operations the number
would be much lower. As for infrastructure, aviation had distinct
advantages over ground transport. He wrote that 'roads must first
be made and then kept in repair, whilst the air needs no such preparation . . . Landing grounds may present some difficulties in certain
regions, but these will be found where needed. From Oodnadatta,
Alice Springs is about three and a half hours trip [by air]. Overland it
takes nine DAYS – long ones, too.'

Peel proposed a network of three bases located at Oodnadatta
in South Australia, Charleville in Queensland and Katherine in the
Northern Territory. Each of them was already at a railhead, which
made setting up and supplying the bases easier and more affordable.
From their bases aircraft with a range of 1000 kilometres could service almost all of central Australia. According to Clifford, 'In the not
very distant future, if our church folk only realise the need, I can see
a missionary doctor administering to the needs of men and women
scattered between Wyndham and Cloncurry, Darwin to Hergott [now
known as Marree].'

The main stumbling block was cost. Clifford estimated the service he proposed would require four aircraft at a total cost of £10 000
(at present values approximately $950 000), three hangars would
cost £1800 ($175 000) and running costs would be 8 pence per mile
($1.50 a kilometre). As to whether it was worth it, he wrote: 'The
credit side of the ledger I leave for those interested in the development of our hinterland to compute. Sufficient to say that the heroes of
the Inland are laying the foundation stones of our Australian nation.
We will do our share proportionately as the sense of our brotherhood
with our fellows directs our thoughts and actions.'

The article was signed 'J. Clifford Peel, LIEUT, Australian Flying Corps, AIF, At Sea, 20/11/17'. Peel had written to the *Inlander* while en route for Europe and World War I. After completing his pilot training in England, Peel was posted to France on 7 September, 1918. On the morning of 19 September the 24-year-old took off on a reconnaissance flight. He never returned. Nothing was ever learned of his fate.

Australian aviation will really never know what it lost when Peel was killed. He certainly had the vision to identify the need for outback aviation and the acumen to suggest it could be more cost effective than road or rail. Indeed, it was no accident that by 1920 Australia's first airlines, Western Australian Airways and the Queensland and Northern Territory Aerial Service (Qantas), were established in the bush. Airlines couldn't compete with established train and road services operating between major towns and cities, but in the outback the competition was virtually nonexistent.

Fortunately, Peel's idea for an aerial medical service didn't die with him. After the Inland Mission's superintendent, John Flynn, seized upon Peel's letter and published it, a businessman who read the story donated £100 towards the idea. It was put into a holding account. It was a long way short of the funding Peel identified (and bush nursing homes were cheaper to set up and run), but it was a start.

Out in the bush, the value of the idea was soon demonstrated in practical terms. In February 1922 pioneer aviator Charles Kingsford-Smith, then a pilot with Western Australian Airways, flew a surgeon from Geraldton 500 kilometres north to Carnarvon to operate on a young girl. The girl survived. Two years later Qantas co-founder Hudson Fysh was asked to make a 100-kilometre dash from Longreach to Corona station to pick up the wife of the manager, who was due to give birth. Fysh knew the woman was the station manager's second wife. He wrote in his book, *Qantas Rising*: 'The extraordinary circumstances of this trip were that some years before, when no aeroplanes were available, Mr Armstrong's first wife was due to have a baby. Down came the floods, cutting them off from medical help, and mother and child died.' The flight passed without incident and the baby was safely delivered at Longreach hospital.

Lack of funds didn't stop John Flynn developing plans for an aerial medical service. He extended Clifford Peel's idea to cover most of inland Australia – from Burketown on the Gulf of Carpentaria in Queensland across to Port Hedland in Western Australia and down to Port Augusta in South Australia. By the early 1920s Peel's original plan for three bases had grown to sixteen. Flynn continued his advocacy of the scheme in the pages of the *Inlander*. He made presentations to church congregations that supported the work of the AIM and lobbied business leaders and politicians. As he travelled thousands of outback kilometres visiting the growing network of nursing homes, from 1925 onwards in a Dodge Buckboard that was to become almost as famous as its driver, he promoted the idea among those who had most to gain from its success.

As time went on, Peel was proved correct in his assertion that civil aviation would be extremely safe. In its first years of operation Qantas was flying 60000 kilometres a month without incident. By comparison, in 1925 there were 700 fatalities in motor vehicles across Australia, 22.9 deaths for every 10000 vehicles (today the figure is around 1.2 per 10000).

One need only refer to some of the previous chapters in this book to understand why the advocacy and planning of an aerial medical service fell to a missionary group rather than federal, state or local governments. When it came to nation building, the sparse outback population was a tiny voice among the competing demands of progress. Sometimes, though, even the little voices got heard. When a group of federal politicians passed through Victoria River Downs station, where a new nursing home was being established, they heard tales of needless death in the outback, and were persuaded to provide £2 for every £1 raised privately. The home was opened in 1923. Subsequently, Prime Minister Billy Hughes offered the same subsidy for all nursing homes in the Northern Territory. Typical of the buck-passing of Australian politics, he regarded nursing homes elsewhere as the responsibility of the states.

It wasn't until 1926 that hopes for an aerial medical service got a much-needed boost. Hugh McKay, founder of the Sunshine Harvesters company and a long-time supporter of the AIM's work, died and his will set up a charitable trust that allocated £2000 ($200000 in present values) for the aerial medical service. The canny McKay made the grant on the condition that the funds were matched by other sources. The effect was to motivate the AIM both to actively fundraise for the service and prepare to launch it.

The following year the General Assembly of the Presbyterian Church authorised the board of the AIM to set up an experimental service. An advisory committee was convened to raise the £7000 thought necessary to run what was called the Aerial Medical Service with one plane and one doctor for a year (by comparison a nursing home cost around £1500 to establish).

The federal government chipped in with £1000 through the Civil Aviation Authority. The Wool Brokers Association did the same. Smaller donations came in from all over Australia, the result of appeals to all levels of society – from big business to schoolchildren. Gradually the funds crept towards the target.

From a short list of half a dozen sites – from Broken Hill in New South Wales to Broome in Western Australia – Cloncurry in western Queensland was chosen as the base for the experiment. The town had well-established medical facilities, a good airstrip and a reasonably well-developed telegraphic and telephony network in the surrounding region. The communications network was a requirement because there wasn't much point in establishing an aerial medical service if no one could call it.

Once the base was chosen, Flynn sent his principal fundraiser, AIM patrol padre Andrew Barber, and his chief medical adviser, Dr George Simpson, on a reconnaissance trip through the area to be covered by the new service. It became an epic 4000-kilometre journey that researched landing sites, identified people who would benefit from the service and explained to them how they could call it for help.

As the two men slogged over rough bush roads in the Dodge Buckboard, they saw first-hand the need for the service. They also gathered further evidence of the impact of the new nursing homes. A woman 200 kilometres from Alice Springs told them how the town's nursing home had greatly reduced the distance she had to travel when she was due to give birth (she had six children). Before it opened she'd had to travel 1000 kilometres by camel train to reach the nearest medical help.

They also saw what people resorted to when they didn't have a medical service. In Katherine they met a young Aboriginal man who'd been gored by a bull out in the bush. The young man had got a needle and curved it so he could use it to sew himself up. He also sterilised horse hair for thread and set about the job, without anaesthetic. A few days later the stitches didn't seem to be holding, so he repeated the operation, doing a better job the second time around. George Simpson examined the wound and found that it was healing well.

Shortly after their arrival in Cloncurry, Simpson was called out on a medical emergency. A miner in Mount Isa had fallen down a shaft and broken his back and pelvis. A Qantas aircraft was called from Cloncurry to evacuate the patient in a flight that would take one hour. The alternative was a 200-kilometre ambulance trip over rough roads. The flight was trouble-free and provided first-hand experience for Simpson's report.

As 1927 passed into 1928, the fundraising stalled just £500 short of the target. Despite this hitch, all of the other elements of the plan were coming together. It was decided that the most affordable way to secure an aircraft was to charter one on an 'as required' basis from Qantas. The fledgling airline was still struggling to stay airborne but Hudson Fysh, now its manager, agreed to provide a De Havilland DH50 at two shillings a mile (approximately $8 a kilometre in present values).

The DH50 was an ungainly looking machine, but it was able to carry a patient laid on a stretcher, plus a doctor and pilot. It gave the service a range that extended well beyond the planned 480-kilometre radius of operations around Cloncurry. The pilot assigned to the service was one of Qantas's best, Captain Arthur Affleck.

Applications were sought for the first doctor to operate the service. The medical qualifications and duties included dealing with accident and emergency cases, touring the operational area providing medical services to locations beyond the reach of conventional medical facilities and providing consultative services to other doctors in isolated locations. A sense of adventure was a given.

The calibre of many of the applicants was exceptional. The qualifications and experience of the successful candidate demonstrated how the proposed service captured the imaginations of many in the medical fraternity. Dr Ken Welch, the first doctor, had a successful practice in Sydney, and a family, but he was prepared to leave all of this for a year to pursue the vision of John Flynn.

The problem of raising the remaining funding was finally solved when Flynn and his principal fundraiser, Andrew Barber, jointly guaranteed the remaining £500. Neither of them actually had the money, but they weren't going to let that stand in the way of the inauguration of the service. Not long after they'd done so, the federal government belatedly appreciated the potential mileage in supporting the scheme and announced it would pay half the charter rate up to the first 40000 kilometres flown.

At last, on 17 May, 1928, the Qantas DH50 named *Victory* rolled out of its hangar at Cloncurry, ready for the inaugural flight of Australia's first official Aerial Medical Service. Captain Affleck taxied across the airfield, opened the throttle and the plane accelerated down the runway. As it soared aloft, the dream of Clifford Peel that John Flynn had then pursued for a decade was finally realised.

The first flight was to Julia Creek, 137 kilometres east, to run a clinic. *Victory* covered the distance in less than an hour. After it landed Dr Welch did two minor operations and saw a number of other patients. When he was finished he and Affleck took off on the return flight. They were back at their base that afternoon.

Now the real work began. The DH50 could cover an area over 725 000 square kilometres, the 'mantle of safety' over the outback that John Flynn had hoped for, but the service still had to be proven. Only then could it extend to other areas. Fortunately, his new Aerial Medical Service didn't disappoint.

Typical of many cases from its early days was that of Jock McNamara. He was mustering in a mountain range on his property 100 kilometres south of Cloncurry when his horse reared and fell. McNamara was crushed beneath it, his pelvis shattered, other bones broken. His cousin, Tom Lucas, was with him when the accident happened. Lucas knew better than to try to get McNamara back to the homestead, so he dragged him into the shade of a tree, gave him a gun, food and water, and rode to call the Aerial Medical Service.

It took Lucas half a day to reach the nearest phone. When Affleck and Welch got the call, they immediately took off and headed for the nearest airstrip. From there they set out for the site of the accident on foot. Meanwhile, McNamara's family and neighbours had improvised a stretcher from an old iron bed and were on their way to him. A day after the accident both parties converged on the place where the stricken stockman was fending off ravening dingoes. He'd been enduring his injuries without pain-killers for more than twenty-four hours.

When Welch arrived he assessed McNamara's injuries and gave him a much-needed morphine injection. Then the members of the rescue party carefully laid McNamara on the stretcher and carried him as gently as they could out of the ranges. They paused only to allow Dr Welch to give McNamara more morphine. McNamara was safely evacuated and made a full recovery. The first thing he did after his discharge from hospital would become a familiar response by those helped by the Aerial Medical Service. He went into his local pub and passed the hat around, soliciting donations. He was adamant that he owed the service his life. McNamara was one of the first people the service saved who would go on to become an active fundraiser.

On another occasion, Dr Welch was called to an emergency near the town of Dajarra. An elderly patient was suspected of having pneumonia, but since the plane was unable to reach the location, Welch made the trip by rail motor, at night. He wrote of the experience:

> The rail motor is a little open truck, and you sit on a petrol case. There is no wind screen, and the wind goes hard in the 'wee sma' hours. We had close calls with numerous stock on the line, and finally hit a large kangaroo full and square – he was dazzled by the headlight. It nearly upset the truck. Last week the truck did come to grief in a collision with a horse. THE PLANE IS SAFER!

In the first year the new service made fifty flights to twenty-six locations, covering more than 30 000 kilometres. Welch saw 250 patients and did fifty consultations with other doctors. Areas for improvement were identified, but the service was regarded as such a success that the decision was made to continue it for another year.

Funding remained an ongoing problem and it didn't help that the service's second year of operation, 1929, coincided with the beginning of the Great Depression. The federal government had to cut its funding, but the Queensland government recognised the value of the service and continued to provide £800 a year. When unemployment spread to a third of the Australian workforce, donations to the AIM shrank. In response, AIM staff who still had jobs took pay cuts. Flynn's dream of expanding the Aerial Medical Service to other centres was curtailed as the Cloncurry service struggled to survive. Flying hours were reduced. Despite being in dire financial circumstances, Qantas agreed to reduce its mileage charges.

Another problem was the poor state of communications in the outback. It often took hours if not days to get to a location that had a telephone or telegraph through which the doctor could be summoned. However, 1929 saw the introduction of the first pedal wirelesses to outback stations (see Chapter 10), the beginning of a communications revolution that eventually facilitated access to the service from even the most remote locations.

Airstrips were few and far between, so pilots were often forced to improvise, landing on salt lakes, claypans or in paddocks that were long, flat and firm enough to support the DH50, whose undercarriage had been strengthened to deal with rough landings. As time went on and station managers realised the importance of good airstrips they started hacking them out of the bush. They erected windsocks to help pilots judge their landing approach and set up kerosene tins to light the runway for night landings. They did their best to stop cattle and sheep running in front of the plane. Some pilots reported dodging mobs of kangaroos. Others attempting take-offs on short airstrips found foliage in the undercarriage after clipping trees while the aircraft fought to gain altitude.

Navigation presented its own set of problems. Many stretches of empty outback had few distinguishing features to steer by, so one of the pilots who succeeded Arthur Affleck, Eric Donaldson, came up with a novel solution. When he spotted a homestead he'd buzz low until someone came outside. Then he'd swoop down, cut the airplane's engine and yell a request for directions. With luck the bemused person on the ground would point the way while Donaldson restarted his engines.

The service continued to struggle for funding until an incident in the early 1930s transformed its profile. In the town of Croydon, 350 kilometres north-east of Cloncurry, a publican named Williamson was working on a kerosene-powered refrigerator when it exploded. He suffered severe internal injuries and burns and was barely alive. Aerial Medical Service doctor Alan Vickers responded to the call. He flew to the nearest airstrip (at Normanton) then travelled overland to Croydon, 150 kilometres away. There he discovered Williamson had inhaled flame and was struggling to breathe. With the help of locals, Vickers got him back to the plane at Normanton.

Dr Vickers realised Williamson's only hope was the hospital in Brisbane, 1600 kilometres away. So the little DH50 hopped from airstrip to airstrip to refuel as it made its epic mercy dash. Williamson's suffering was made worse by heatwave conditions reputed to be as high as 50°C. By the time the plane was approaching Brisbane's Archerfield Airport some fourteen hours later, news of the desperate mercy flight had spread and journalists were waiting to cover the arrival. When the plane finally touched down, the waiting media learned that despite Vickers' best efforts Williamson had died on the final leg of the flight.

Dr Vickers was exhausted, but he still took time to speak to the throng of journalists, giving a detailed account of what had occurred and of the organisation struggling to avert similar tragedies throughout the outback. The story made headlines around the country and gave the Aerial Medical Service much-needed publicity. It also gave the service a flying doctor who was tailor-made for promoting the scheme. Alan Vickers was a down-to-earth, straight-talking medico and John Flynn realised he was the ideal spokesman for the organisation. Flynn asked Vickers to undertake a national fundraising tour.

Dr Vickers proved to be a goldmine. His talks were entertaining, often thrilling, and prompted people to donate to the Aerial Medical Service despite their often straitened circumstances. The promotion of the scheme was also assisted by the 1932 publication of Ion Idriess' book *Flynn of the Inland*. The book became a bestseller and, while it was a romanticised version of the outback and the medical service, it was invaluable in popularising Flynn and the vision he was struggling to realise.

The publicity certainly worked its magic on the politicians. In 1933 negotiations between state premiers and the General Assembly of the Presbyterian Church (the AIM's parent organisation) led to Flynn and the AIM being authorised to form an independent organisation to provide a national aerial medical service. The following year John Flynn presented a draft constitution and plan to the annual State Premier's Conference for an initial network of six bases (including Cloncurry) that would form the basis of the Australian Aerial Medical Service. The Queensland premier was particularly supportive of the scheme, saying that the service operating out of Cloncurry was worth ten times what his government was contributing to it (in fact it was costing ten times what his government was contributing to it, but nobody quibbled).

The motion to establish the organisation was passed. Support for it was so strong that Victoria, a state that couldn't identify a need for its own aerial medical service, agreed to finance the proposed base at Wyndham, Western Australia. This while the nation was in the midst of the worst financial crisis it had ever faced.

Wyndham commenced operations in July 1935, Port Hedland in October 1935, Broken Hill in 1937, Kalgoorlie (where an aerial medical ambulance was already operating and joined the AAMS) in 1938 and Alice Springs in 1939 (helped by funds raised for 'flying sisters' as detailed in Chapter 11). The young Clifford Peel's vision now extended well beyond the three bases he'd envisaged. John Flynn's 'mantle of safety' had been created. In 1942 the AAMS was renamed the Flying Doctor Service (FDS). In 1955 it was granted the use of the 'royal' prefix and acquired the name it retains to this day – the Royal Flying Doctor Service (RFDS).

Throughout the service's development, doctors, nurses, pilots and patients continued to be involved in epic tales of courage, endurance and heroism. In January 1939, an AAMS DH82 Tiger Moth went missing on a flight from Normanton to the Mitchell River Aboriginal Mission (now Kowanyama) on Cape York. On board were the first female flying doctor, Jean White, and pilot Doug Tennant. A search was mounted and the service made headlines once again as the nation's eyes turned to the crocodile-infested wetlands of the Cape. Days passed and there was no sign of the crash site. There were no calls for help from the radio aboard the aircraft. After four days, hopes of finding anyone alive were fading. Then, on an island in the Mitchell River, the crashed Tiger Moth was spotted from the air. Nearby, the doctor and pilot were signalling frantically. They were both alive and uninjured after being forced down by bad weather. The plane had flipped over when they tried to land. Search aircraft were unable to land, so they dropped supplies (including much-needed mosquito repellent). It took a day for a rescue party to reach the pair.

The flying doctor also made childbirth in the outback far safer, although transporting expectant mothers led to at least two midair births. In the 1970s, Robin Miller (a pilot and nurse) was flying a pregnant woman to Port Hedland when the woman suddenly went into labour halfway to their destination. Miller and the woman were alone, but the aircraft had an autopilot. Miller switched it on while she attended to her patient. Throughout the birth she could hear the radio operator at Port Hedland calling the plane and growing increasingly anxious. Miller was too busy to respond. Finally, the baby was delivered and Miller could get back to the radio. She apologised for the delay, and then amended the number of persons on board from two to three. There was a pause while the information sank in, then the operator enquired, 'Boy or girl?'

Not all flying doctor stories had happy endings. On 20 October, 1953, an aging De Havilland Dragon crashed at Cheviot Hills, a cattle station north of Charters Towers. Pilot Martin Garrett was killed, as was a passenger, Elizabeth O'Leary, who'd married flying doctor Timothy O'Leary only six weeks before. O'Leary saw his wife impaled on the aircraft's exhaust pipe, while he and a nursing sister survived.

Less than three years later, the service had its worst crash. At 4.25 p.m. on 4 February, 1956, the call went out for the flying doctor to attend a seriously ill baby on Tableland station, 380 kilometres east of the flying doctor base at Derby in Western Australia. In thundery weather conditions the base's army surplus Avro Anson took off, piloted by Dutch-born Pieter Van Emmerik and with nursing sisters Frances Day and Helen Newman aboard. They reached Tableland just after 6 p.m., and picked up the baby and her father for the return flight. They took off in fine weather at 6.30 p.m., but station hands could see a storm front forming over the King Leopold Ranges, in the direction of the plane's return flight. Shortly after take-off pilot Emmerik reported his flight plan. After that nothing more was heard of the aircraft. It never reached Derby.

The aircraft had a radio beacon, but no signal was picked up as a search was mounted. The weather in the region was diabolical. Massive storms hindered aerial searches for several days while ground searches were hampered by floods. Eventually one of the largest search operations in Western Australia's history developed. It wasn't until eighteen days later that the wreckage was finally sighted in flooded country in the depths of the King Leopold Ranges. The site was only 20 kilometres from Kimberley Downs station, but it took a ground party two and a half days to reach the scene. There were no survivors.

Investigators found that the Anson had hit the ground intact and under full power. They noted that around the crash site several trees had been uprooted by the violent storm. They surmised that pilot Emmerik had fought to keep the plane aloft all the way down to the ground, but had been overwhelmed by the sheer violence of the weather.

The incident prompted a review of flight procedures and the Flying Doctor Service's aircraft. It contributed to the transition from 'seat of your pants' flying to carefully regulated and well-equipped modern operations. The notion of 'mercy flights' also evolved out of the tragedy, whereby aviation rules could only be relaxed in cases of genuine emergency. In modern times aircraft will still attempt landings where there is no airstrip, such as on roads to attend car accidents, but only under specific rules: only essential personnel are allowed on board, all signs and guideposts on the road have to be removed, and the road must be blocked at both ends by police. After that the situation relies on the skills of the pilot to land a plane travelling at 200 kilometres per hour on a 'runway' that may provide less than half a metre clearance on either side of the undercarriage.

The unique service provided by the flying doctor has led to several medical innovations, particularly in remote diagnosis and treatment. In 1942 medical chests containing equipment and medicines were introduced and supplied to stations across the outback, allowing doctors consulting over the radio or telephone to prescribe treatments that were already on hand. Medicines were numbered to make it easier to identify what was required. The system worked so well that it's still in use today, despite the often-told story of a station manager who was instructed to give his wife a tablet from bottle number nine. He discovered they'd run out, so in a moment of inspiration he gave her one tablet from bottle number five and one from bottle four. 'She came good right away,' he told the doctor.

In 1951 Sister Lucy Garlick devised what is now known as the RFDS body chart. It was a response to the usual bushman's answer – 'In me guts' – when asked the location of their pain. The chart is included in every medical chest and overlays a numbered grid on a human torso to allow the patient to be more specific and diagnosis to be correspondingly accurate.

Since the 1930s governments have become far more involved in providing outback medical services like the RFDS, but community fundraising is still vital – everything from car rallies to beauty contests and balls. Some outback pubs have a rule that if you swear, you have to kick a $1 fine into the RFDS swear jar. It's considered 'a bloody good idea', as is the cryptic sign 'YCWCYODFTRFDSTY'. The answer to the question 'What does it mean?' is 'Your Curiosity Will Cost You One Dollar For The Royal Flying Doctor Service, Thank You'.

Today, the forty-seven aircraft of the RFDS are so sophisticated that they're regarded as taking the hospital to the patient. The planes cost millions to buy and equip, but save dozens of lives every year. They operate from twenty-one bases, flying nearly 22 million kilometres annually. They attend 240 000 patients and complete 35 000 aeromedical evacuations. The service has 700 staff (full-time and part-time) and operates from Broome to the islands of Bass Strait.

The fledgling idea of the young pilot Clifford Peel and its realisation by John Flynn has since grown to become the largest aeromedical service in the world. From the country to the city, the drone of an aircraft in the small hours of the night can conjure visions of a mercy flight – a critically ill patient tended by expert medical staff, dim cabin lights catching for a moment the concentration on their faces. Ask the people of the outback what the Flying Doctor means to them and they'll tell you that after they've called the RFDS to a sick child or injured station worker, they strain to hear the distant sound of the approaching plane. When at last it comes, there's no better sound on Earth.

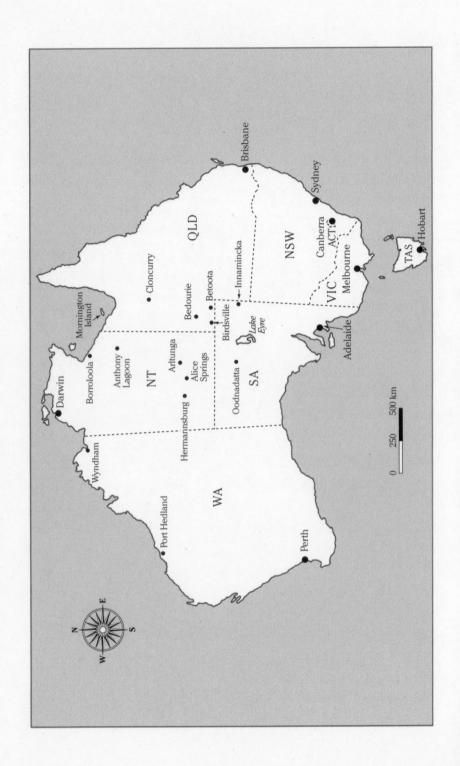

Alf Traeger, 1928
(Photo by John Flynn, National Library of Australia,
[nla.pic-an] 24631139)

10

THE PEDAL RADIO MAN
Alfred Traeger (1895–1980)

If John Flynn had done nothing more than establish the Flying Doctor Service and bush nursing across Australia, it would have been more than enough. However, there was a third pillar to his outback legacy that was perhaps the least visible but arguably the most significant. It came in the shape of a man named Alfred Traeger.

In the 1920s, while Flynn was establishing nursing homes and pushing for the launch of the first Flying Doctor Service, he was also initiating experiments into the use of radio in the outback. It was an extraordinary thing for a minister of religion, charged with the pastoral care of his far-flung flock and the administration of the AIM, to be doing. However, it formed part of a long-term plan to draw together the people of the outback through the miracle of wireless. To this end, in 1925 he and radio technician George Towns were preparing

to leave Adelaide on an experimental expedition that included a visit
to Birdsville's new nursing home (see Chapter 8), when Flynn discovered he had a problem. The electrical generators he'd ordered
from Sydney to power his radios were totally inadequate. Fortunately, Adelaide's radio community was so small that everyone knew
everyone and George Towns learned from Harry Kauper, technical
manager of radio station 5CL (South Australia's first radio station,
established late in 1924), that a young mechanic from a local garage
had tested a 600-volt generator at its workshop a few months before.
Flynn set off to find the fellow.

Alf Traeger was then thirty years old, single and earning a living as an auto-electrician, but his real passion was radio. At the age
of twelve he'd built a telephone that allowed him to communicate
between the shed on his parent's farm and the house. At sixteen he
was enrolled in the Mechanical and Electrical Engineering diploma
at Adelaide School of Mines and Industry. It was there that he and his
fellow students caught the radio bug. His hero was Italian inventor
Guglielmo Marconi and Traeger was soon part of the small and growing band of amateur or 'ham' radio operators who spent every spare
moment building radios, bouncing morse code off various layers of
the atmosphere and being thrilled when they successfully communicated with faraway places. These days they'd be called geeks or
nerds. In 1925, Traeger was in the vanguard.

On 14 June, 1925, Flynn rushed into Hannan Brothers Garage
demanding to see the young radio ham. Did he still have the 600-volt
generator? He did. How much did he want for it? Traeger thought for
a moment, possibly about why a man of the cloth wanted a 600-volt
generator. He eventually parted with the device for £29/10 and an
explanation of the intended use. It involved driving into the outback,
jacking up the reverend's new Dodge Buckboard and coupling the
generator to one of the rear wheels to power the radio.

Traeger may not have been surprised to learn the experiment

was subsequently labelled 'a successful failure'. The power supply from the Dodge wasn't suitable for reliable radio work, communications over long distances (up to 1000 kilometres) were hit-and-miss. Towns, who'd been wounded during World War I, had also found the hard miles of outback travel were affecting his health. In September 1926 Flynn returned to Adelaide looking for a new radio expert. Harry Kauper suggested Traeger.

The second time Flynn went to see Traeger he offered the young radio enthusiast his dream job. Flynn wanted him to solve the great problem of outback communication, with radio. It meant pushing the technology of the day beyond its limits. Flynn was prepared to pay Traeger £6 a week for doing what he loved. Traeger said later he'd have taken the job for £3.

There wasn't a moment to lose. Plans for the Flying Doctor Service were taking form and a radio network was needed to support it. Fortunately, Traeger was soon reaping the benefits of Flynn's extraordinary networking ability. He was given access to radio station 5CL's workshops and the assistance of Harry Kauper. His first job would be the installation of an experimental radio network station at Alice Springs comprising a base station donated by Amalgamated Wireless Australasia's then managing director, Ernest Fisk, and two outpost sets built by Kauper.

In October 1926, only a month after Flynn hired Traeger, he took him to the outback. The key element in their experiments was a new copper-oxide battery that gave a steady power supply to the powerful base 'mother' station. The mother station was also sensitive enough to pick up the weaker signals of the outpost 'baby' stations. A bonus for Traeger was that one of the baby sets was destined for the Lutheran Aboriginal mission at Hermannsburg, 126 kilometres west of Alice Springs. Traeger was a Lutheran whose Adelaide congregation supported Hermannsburg. The other baby set was for the police station at the goldmining outpost at Arltunga, 110 kilometres east of the Alice. The total cost of all the equipment involved was less than £100, a third of Alf's annual income.

It wasn't strictly necessary to do the radio experiments on the outback tours Flynn was conducting (they could have been done just as easily in the vicinity of Adelaide), but they had the advantage of introducing radio to the people who would one day benefit if it worked. It also exposed his radio men to the kind of environments that their equipment would have to survive. In the case of the Alice Springs experiment, this involved a train trip to Oodnadatta then several days bouncing over rough roads and sandhills in the Dodge Buckboard.

On 20 October Traeger arrived at the brand-new AIM nursing home in the central Australian town of Alice Springs, population 350. There were few more exotic places in Australia. Tribal Aboriginal people could still be seen around the town. Camel trains slowly made their way through the red-stone gorge that split the MacDonnell Range. Rugged cattlemen and hard-bitten prospectors strode the streets.

Traeger was soon at work erecting a radio mast behind the nursing home and installing the mother station in the engine room. He rigged up electric lights that were powered by a 5-horsepower generator. It would also keep the radio batteries charged. The mother station's transmitting power was a seemingly insignificant 50 watts – most light globes use more – but it was enough to send morse messages to Adelaide and voice calls to Hermannsburg and Arltunga. The experiment had been given the blessing of the postmaster general's department and the mother station was given the call sign 8AB. Hopes of success were raised when Harry Kauper in Adelaide reported that he'd picked up some of the voice transmissions when 8AB went on the air.

On 11 November Flynn and Traeger set off to install the first of the baby sets – at the Hermannsburg mission. Several hours later they were welcomed by Pastor Friedrich Albrecht and a fascinated group of Aboriginal people who watched as the radio man erected the aerial and started rigging the batteries and radio equipment. On the morning of 13 November everything was ready for the first scheduled communication between the Hermannsburg baby set (8AD) and mother set 8AB (operated in Traeger's absence by a local telegrapher, Maurie Fuss). At the pre-arranged time Traeger transmitted a call in morse code, then waited for an answer. Silence. With Flynn, Pastor Albrecht and most of the Aboriginal community looking on, he called again and again. There was no reply.

Traeger suspected the problem was at the Alice Springs end, where the inexperienced operator Fuss may have been doing something wrong. Why didn't Traeger just get on the phone to suggest Maurie tweak a few things? There wasn't one. Why didn't he jump in the Dodge Buckboard and nip back to Alice Springs to do it himself? It was a hard half-day's drive. A distance of 126 kilometres was nothing in the outback, but Traeger was discovering first-hand what an obstacle distance could be when it came to even the simplest things.

Disheartened but not defeated, Traeger and Flynn spent the next five days at Hermannsburg teaching the missionaries morse code and basic radio operations. When they returned to Alice Springs it was just as Traeger suspected. Fuss hadn't powered up the radio correctly. It only took a moment for Traeger to show him the right way, then they sat down to try to make contact with the new radio trainees at Hermannsburg.

'8AB calling 8AD,' Traeger transmitted, and waited.

Then, they caught a sound – a confused series of dots and dashes, fading in and out of hearing. The inexperienced morse code operators at Hermannsburg were trying to send a reply. It was perhaps appropriate that the baby set's first words sounded like baby talk. With patient coaching from Traeger, Albrecht slowly got the hang of it. Eventually, on 25 November, 1926, he managed to send a short message that was relayed to his wife, who'd gone south to Adelaide to have a baby.

Flynn and Traeger moved on to Arltunga, where they installed the second baby set, 8AC. The three radio sets now formed the first Australian Inland Mission network, communicating haltingly across a span of 236 kilometres of country, establishing the basis of the larger network to come. Although a great deal of experience was gained from the installation, Traeger was unsure whether they'd had a successful failure or a qualified success. Flynn had no doubts. He later said his greatest discovery on the trip was Alf Traeger.

For Traeger the trip to the Red Centre set the course for the rest of his life. He'd met the people he was destined to help. As he and John Flynn left Alice Springs early in December 1926, he knew what he had to do. The mother stations needed to be improved, which was easy. The hard part was the baby set. It had to be simple to use, robust enough to survive outback conditions, have a simple, reliable power supply but be able to transmit and receive over vast distances. It also had to be cheap enough that every homestead or bush camp could have one.

It was quite a wish list, especially at a time when most long-range radio transmitters and their power supplies filled buildings. None of them came cheap. Yet the baby set was regarded as being crucial to the success of the Flying Doctor Service, whose inaugural flight was then less than eighteen months away.

On his return to Adelaide, Traeger became the Australian Inland Mission's Radio Engineer. He was probably the only person in the world who was employed by a missionary organisation in that capacity. The first thing he did when he got home was go to church with his parents. Then he went to work.

Working day and night, month after month, through 1927, Alf took Flynn's vision for radio and applied his practical knowledge and newly gained experience to realising the dream. He redesigned everything – aerials, transceivers, power supplies. He made cheap and easily assembled aerials from interlocking bicycle tubing. He built radio after radio, smaller and smaller, with parts donated at cost from AWA and ideas refined in brainstorming sessions with Kauper.

For the crucial power supply he didn't like the idea of rechargeable batteries or the jacked-up rear wheel of a Dodge Buckboard. He wanted to produce the required steady electrical current as simply as possible. While pondering the problem, his eye fell on an emery grinder, a common tool in machine shops for smoothing rough edges. They can be hand cranked or externally powered, but once you get the grinding stone spinning, it tends to keep rotating at a fairly constant speed.

It was the kind of constant speed Traeger was looking for. Could the principle of the emery grinder be used to generate a steady electrical current? Traeger set about building a generator based on what he had in mind. When it was finished, he connected it to an electrical meter to measure the power output and started turning the generator by hand. The needle slowly rose. Then it paused. As he continued turning the generator at a steady pace the needle confirmed that the power output remained constant. Traeger had just become the first person to generate a steady electrical current by hand. It was the equivalent of discovering fire. Eureka? For some maybe, but Traeger knew the idea needed refinement.

After only nine months working on the myriad problems of outback wireless, Traeger believed he had the basis of a working baby set. He started pressing Flynn for another field test. By then Cloncurry had been chosen as the site for the first flying doctor base. Traeger wanted to go there. In October he and Flynn set off once more. As they drove north Traeger gleefully sent morse code messages on the new baby set while Flynn turned the hand generator. They received replies in both voice and morse code. The set worked so well that by the time they reached Cloncurry, Flynn was convinced Traeger had cracked the problems of outback radio.

Traeger disagreed. Everything worked well in the hands of an

expert, but it wouldn't be anywhere near as easy for an inexperienced operator. His opinion was reinforced by his experiences on the
rest of the trip.

Flynn had arranged to visit Mornington Island, where a handful
of missionaries were working with one of the most remote indigenous communities in the country, the Lardil people. On their way
they passed through the Kidman-owned Augustus Downs station,
earmarked by Flynn as the site for the Cloncurry network's first baby
set. The men there weren't keen on the idea of learning morse code;
they thought their women would be better at it. At the Gulf of Carpentaria, Traeger, Flynn and the baby set boarded a fishing boat for
the sea voyage to Mornington Island. It was a grand adventure for
Traeger, but now salt air and tropical damp joined the list of environmental extremes his baby sets had to survive.

At Mornington Island, memories of the murder of head missionary
Richard Hall by members of the indigenous community just ten years
before were still fresh. Hall's assistant had been seriously wounded
and both men's wives and children forced to barricade themselves
inside the mission home. They were trapped for ten days with no
way of calling for help. It wasn't until the mission boat returned that
they were rescued. Accordingly, Mornington Island was high on John
Flynn's list for a baby set and a way to communicate with the outside
world.

The radio man and the reverend made it back to Cloncurry early
in November 1927, just in time for Traeger to delight the locals by
tuning in to a call of the Melbourne Cup, the first time anyone there
had heard it 'live'. The next night he set up a base station, running
it off the power supply for the shire hall's electric lights. When he
called Harry Kauper in Adelaide, 2500 kilometres away, the reception was crystal clear. It was a perfect demonstration of the power
of radio to overcome the great distances of the Australian continent.
It was also an excellent publicity device for the imminent Flying

Doctor Service and the radio network that would support it. The next day the Shire Clerk agreed to set up the local Aerial Medical Service committee.

If Traeger thought he'd been busy in 1927, it was nothing compared to 1928. He now had to take his ideas and turn them into a baby set simple enough for anyone to use. Morse code was a drawback, but it was the most reliable way of getting messages through. The big problem was still the power supply. Traeger and Flynn had found the generator worked best with one person winding and the other sending morse code. Traeger could do both on his own but he knew it would be a different story out in the field. He could easily imagine a man or woman struggling to call for help while one of their loved ones was tapping out a different code on death's door.

In May 1928, when the first Flying Doctor Service took to the air, Traeger was still refining the baby sets. The need was more urgent than ever. That month Alf hired two assistants (young men from his local congregation) to help assemble the baby sets. Traeger was working almost ceaselessly. His strong religious upbringing meant Sunday was his day of rest, so after working for six days straight, he'd go to church then sleep the rest of the day away. His father, Johann, often came down to the workshop to help out in any way he could. His brother Jack worked with the two assistants building cabinets for the almost-finished baby sets.

Traeger still wasn't happy with the hand-operated generator. It worked perfectly, except that it meant performing two manual operations at once. It was like trying to rub your stomach while patting your head, with the added complication that you were trying to tap out morse code.

On 2 August, 1928, Alf celebrated his thirty-third birthday. It wasn't a Sunday, so he was hard at it in the workshop, as usual. At lunchtime he took a moment to gulp down a sandwich. As he did so he was still chewing over ideas for generators. Suddenly, he stopped eating. His brother Jack later recalled that Alf stood up, sandwich in hand, and declared, 'I am going to buy bicycle pedals.'

Later that year, John Flynn was invited to a special occasion in Alf Traeger's Adelaide workshop. In his letter to his boss, Traeger noted that the first flying doctor aircraft had been named *Victory* and then wrote with unrestrained pride, 'Come and see the real victory.' On 17 November Flynn arrived and was shown the first complete baby set. It was unlike anything Flynn (or anyone else) had seen before. The radio was fairly remarkable – compact, robust, stripped back to the basics – but what was really extraordinary was the power supply. It was bolted to the floor and looked like a prototype for an exercise bike. In fact it was a pedal-operated generator geared to spin at a constant 1000 rpm while the operator pedalled at a leisurely 60 rpm. Its power was further regulated by an idea Harry Kauper contributed – 'crystal control' similar to the highly accurate quartz crystals in modern watches. The generator could be turned by hand or foot.

Traeger demonstrated how easily the radio could be operated by a single person. When he was finished John Flynn said in typical Australian style, 'Big mobs of thanks.' He then asked Traeger to go home and put on his best suit. 'I want to take a very important photograph,' he said.

Flynn's years of patrolling the outback, followed by his administration of an organisation that reached out to its loneliest and furthest corners, put him in the ideal position to appreciate the historical importance of the photo he took on 17 November, 1928. It shows the inventor Traeger with the device that gave a voice to the outback for the first time in its history – the pedal wireless.

By April 1929 Traeger had ten baby sets and the Cloncurry mother station ready to go. The baby sets were despatched from Adelaide and transported by ship to Brisbane, then by rail and road to Cloncurry, arriving there on 28 May. Traeger followed closely behind.

Radio operator Harry Kinzbrunner had been hired late in 1928 to become the radio operater for the mother station (call sign VJI), a role that required great communication skills in every sense. He had to direct traffic on the fledgling network, nurture the radio skills of the beginners and solve the problems of inexperienced operators spread far and wide across the outback. Above all he had to remain calm and efficient in every emergency. VJI went on the air with considerable ceremony on 6 June, 1929.

The first baby sets ended up costing £33, the equivalent of a month's salary at the time. The first were provided to the outback stations free of charge, paid for by Sidney Kidman (one of whose stations got the first), the Country Women's Association and donations to the AIM. On 18 June Alf set off from Cloncurry with local AIM patrol padre George Scott to install the first set at Augustus Downs, 300 kilometres north, as promised nearly two years before. The following day Gertrude Rothery, the station manager's wife, sent the first message from baby set number one. With Alf at her side she started pedalling. Then she tapped on the morse code key:

Dot-dot-dot-dot . . . dot . . . dot-dash-dot-dot . . . dot-dash-dot-dot . . . dash-dash-dash.

It was the word 'hello'. After Kinzbrunner replied, Rothery painstakingly transmitted a telegram to be forwarded to John Flynn: 'Greetings by wireless service from Augustus Downs. First station installed. Manager family and station deeply appreciate service rendered.'

Years later Rothery told of the quiet patience of the shy Traeger in helping her to master the baby set. She regarded being able to call the flying doctor and send and receive messages as the biggest thing that ever happened in her life in the outback. At the other end, the waggish Kinzbrunner suggested the first word she'd sent hadn't been 'Hello'. He reckoned it was 'O hell'.

Over the next few months Traeger and Padre Scott crisscrossed the outback, installing pedal wireless baby sets at Lorraine, Gregory Downs and Corinda stations, the Aboriginal community at Mornington Island and the AIM nursing home at Birdsville. By the end of the first six months the network extended over 1000 kilometres from north to south. Feedback was soon coming in from the field. Kathleen Burnett, eighteen-year-old daughter of the owners of Lorraine station and the youngest operator on the network, reported that termites were eating the wooden cabinet housing the baby set. From then on, all cabinets were made of metal.

Early in 1930 Alf returned to the location of his first experience in outback radio, Hermannsburg, to install a pedal wireless that was now well beyond the experimental. It was rapidly becoming famous as the potential of its revolutionary technologies was appreciated. On the same trip Traeger installed radios at Innamincka Hospital, at the Bedourie Hotel and at the police station at Borroloola. When the police commissioner in Darwin suddenly found he could communicate directly with his officer there, he wrote a cheque for another radio for the remote outpost at Anthony Lagoon. As each baby set went in, it communicated with the base station at Cloncurry, whose area of coverage now extended 800 kilometres north-west (to Borroloola) and 1000 kilometres south-west to Hermannsburg. The baby sets could communicate over greater distances, but in the case of Hermannsburg there were simply no more settlements between it and the Western Australian deserts.

Everywhere they were installed, the sets were almost universally welcomed. According to *Flynn of the Inland* author Ion Idriess, when one drover found he could check on his ailing wife through the combination of the pedal wireless at Birdsville and the telegraph at Cloncurry, and get an answer back in only in two hours, he declared 'the bush is done'. There was nothing for it but to go 'further out'.

By 1931 twenty pedal wirelesses were operating across Queensland, the Northern Territory and South Australia, with more on the way. That year the wireless at Hermannsburg was used to coordinate the search for members of Harold Lasseter's ill-fated gold-prospecting expedition. Lasseter perished, but the rescue of three others was attributed to Traeger's invention.

While Traeger was covering enormous distances crisscrossing the outback, he was also continuing to make improvements to the pedal wireless. In 1931 he devised an ingenious morse keyboard that allowed letters to be pressed that then produced the appropriate morse signal. As soon as he unveiled it he was given an order for twenty.

That year Alf also got first-hand experience of how one of his radios could be a life-saver. A radio had been sent to the tiny settlement of Betoota, 120 kilometres east of Birdsville. When it got there, Traeger decided he'd drive up through the sandhill country of South Australia and Queensland to install the set and others that had been shipped to destinations further north. He loaded up Flynn's Dodge Buckboard and set off, reaching Innamincka without incident. From there to Betoota it wasn't particularly far (about 300 kilometres) but in places the road existed in name only. After several days had passed and he still hadn't arrived in Betoota his increasingly concerned family contacted Cloncurry. There was no word. It turned out Traeger didn't have a pedal wireless with him.

After seventeen days everyone feared Traeger had met with a terrible accident. If he was lost there was a limit to how long he could survive. Then, when all hope seemed gone, Traeger chugged slowly into Betoota at the wheel of the battered Dodge. He was dishevelled, sunburnt and his shirt had no buttons. It turned out he'd been bogged in a sand dune for three days. Then he'd damaged the suspension on the rocks of the Sturt Stony Desert. Traeger snatched an hour's sleep before setting up the radio equipment. When the aerial was erected the following morning, Alf could finally transmit the news of his survival.

It was good news for the whole outback of Australia. As the number of pedal wirelesses increased and Traeger constantly improved them, their value became increasingly clear. Emergency calls to the Flying Doctor Service took precedence, but the AIM base station was also permitted to relay messages that could then be telegraphed anywhere in Australia or the world. Through an arrangement with the post-master general, the AIM earned a small amount from every telegram sent through its network, assisting with funding the service. Before long thousands of words were being transmitted every month. Meanwhile, the pedal wireless operators quickly discovered they could talk to each other, breaking down the isolation that was such a curse in the outback. They also learned to relay messages if they could hear a distant baby station struggling to contact the base station.

In 1932 patrol padre Kingsley Partridge asked Traeger if it would be possible to have a portable baby station that he could take in his car when he toured his central Australian region. It took only a year for Traeger to present him with the first of a new set of pedal wire-lesses that would make outback travel safer than it had ever been. To this day radio sets are standard equipment for outback four-wheel drive enthusiasts.

Orders for pedal wireless sets were pouring in to Traeger's workshop but Traeger was already focussed on one remaining challenge – pedal radios that could transmit voice instead of morse code. Only then could the voice of the outback really be heard. With morse code, a good operator like Traeger could achieve speeds of twenty words a minute; the best could transmit up to thirty-five words. By comparison the average person speaks at 150 to 200 words per minute.

By the mid-1930s, Traeger knew voice transmission was feasible, but he realised it would involve the considerable expense of replacing all the old sets with new ones. He decided it would be far better if the existing sets could be upgraded instead. By September 1934 he'd worked out how to take newer components and 'reverse engineer' voice transmission into existing sets. As he explained it:

The idea is a B class modulator fitted on to the standard transmitter with the improved type of transmitter valve fitted. The microphone currents are amplified and drive the modulator which in turn modulates the carrier wave supplied by the transmitter. All you have to do is to talk into the microphone while pedalling.

Installation of the new technology started in what was a momentous year for outback radio and the AIM. In 1934, baby sets installed in aircraft led to the first medical consultation while the doctor was in the air. The Cloncurry base station was upgraded and the network passed the milestone of fifty pedal wireless outposts scattered across the eastern section of the outback. The Australian Aerial Medical Service was created out of the original Cloncurry medical service, and new base stations for wireless networks and flying doctors were soon established in Western Australia at Port Hedland and Wyndham. Traeger was effectively part of the new organisation, but actually remained on the payroll of the AIM until 1937.

During 1935, Traeger received a letter from the nursing sisters at the AIM nursing home in Birdsville. Could they have some stronger wires for the connection from the home to their wireless's 20-metre aerial outside? The galahs that flocked to the waters of the Diamantina River were also flocking to the wire and using it as a perch. In fact, there were so many galahs that the wire kept breaking. The sisters also asked if they could conduct daily radio sessions with women in the Diamantina region to exchange news and information. 'Go ahead,' Traeger wrote back, while sending a package with stronger wire, 'the Post Master General says you can transmit on 148 metres if you fix your times with the base station in Cloncurry – and what about making your chatter to one another just like the galahs on your aerial.'

The slightly condescending humour masked a profound step forward for the use of the pedal wireless. It allowed the isolated women

of the outback to become a community. Every morning at 7 a.m.
the vast stations and small towns of far-western Queensland – Clifton
Hills, Pandie Pandie, Monkira, Birdsville, Betoota, Bedourie and
others – engaged in what has been claimed as the first talkback radio
in the world. The ability to pass the time of day with one's neighbour
is taken for granted all around the world but the Galah Sessions,
which soon spread across the outback with the introduction of voice
pedal radios, afforded the same opportunity to people who sometimes didn't communicate with another human being for weeks on
end. There are stories of people who wept when they finally got a
pedal wireless and heard the mother station, a voice from the outside
world, for the first time.

Another story from the 1930s is of a group of children who were
taken on a trip to the seaside from their stations in far western
Queensland. It was a 2000-kilometre journey there and back, and
their parents only let them go because the vehicle that was transporting them had a pedal wireless.

While installing new sets and continuing to develop the pedal radio,
Traeger also found time to woo and marry Olga Schodde, a woman
from his Adelaide congregation. On his wedding day, in 1937, tele-
grams of congratulations came from pedal radios across Australia.
The same year he became an independent contractor, building and
servicing radios for the Australian Aerial Medical Service and cus-
tomers across outback Australia. By then some outback people had
been operating pedal radios for nearly ten years. They quipped that
they couldn't hold a conversation unless their legs were going up and
down.

Use of the pedal wireless started to fade after 1939 when Traeger
introduced 'vibrator' power, which utilised the 6-volt batteries found
in the increasingly ubiquitous motor car. Electrical generators were
also becoming increasingly common and affordable. By then there
were 200 baby sets installed across the country.

It was through the baby sets that much of the outback learned of the commencement of World War II. Unlike the outbreak of World War I, they did so at the same time as the rest of Australia. Despite his German heritage, Traeger's skills in radio made him highly sought after for the war effort, as were the radio operators in remote northern locations where the baby-set network could provide forward listening posts for the nation's defenders. Throughout the war and beyond, the networks continued to expand. By the end of the 1960s, when the baby sets switched to single sideband (a more efficient method for radio communication that utilises only that part of the radio wave that carries the voice signal) and utilised transistors instead of valves, there were twelve mother stations and 5000 transceivers in the field.

When John Flynn died in 1951, his ashes were interred near Alice Springs in the heart of the outback he'd worked to make a better place. Alf Traeger died in 1980. He was not as well known as Flynn, but he was revered by the people of the outback who knew what a difference baby sets, pedal wireless and Traeger radios had made to their lives. Monuments and memorials were erected to both men across a grateful outback, but one need only look as far as the current Australian 20 dollar note to be reminded of their legacy. It features an image of John Flynn and several of the iconic elements of the Flying Doctor Service. The De Havilland DH50 *Victory* is easily recognisable. An image of a patrol padre mounted on a camel refers to Flynn's early years trekking across the outback ministering to an incredibly isolated congregation. Lucy Garlick's pain chart is there. And so is a strange bicycle-like device – Alf Traeger's pedal radio generator. Most people couldn't tell you what it is, but the people of the outback recognise it immediately. It's the machine that broke the silence of the outback and finally gave them a voice.

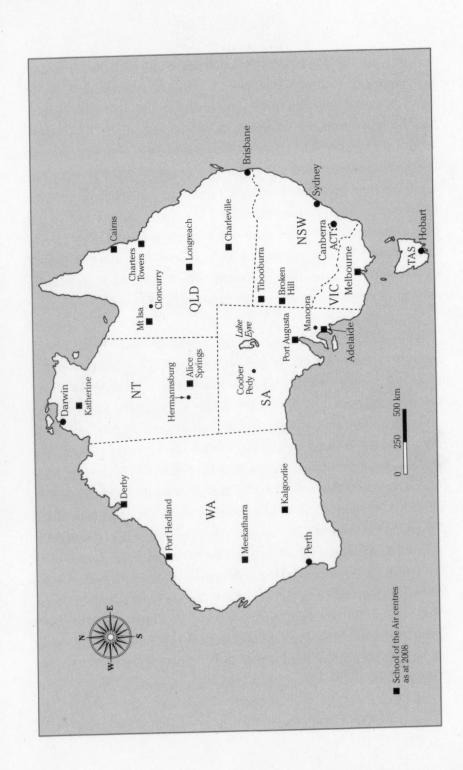

School of the Air centres
as at 2008

Adelaide Miethke, circa 1930s
(National Library of Australia,
[nla.pic.an] 24618898)

I I

THE SCHOOL OF THE AIR
Adelaide Miethke (1881–1962)

If the story of Adelaide Miethke is anything to go by, you're never too old to become an outback pioneer. In 1944 she was sixty-three years old, a retired inspector of schools and former teacher living in Adelaide. She was also on the board of the Alice Springs Flying Doctor Service she'd helped to establish, even though she'd never set foot in the town of Alice itself. It was only when a visiting English parliamentarian, Dr Edith Summerhill, got in touch with the Flying Doctor Service to ask if she could see its Alice Spring facilities, that Miethke got her chance. Summerhill was hoping to establish similar services in other parts of what was then the British Empire and Miethke agreed to accompany her. As Miethke later recalled:

I went by plane. These far northern parts were new to me and I was tremendously interested in the country. Our first stop was Mt. Eba [a station 150 kilometres south-east of Coober Pedy] for luncheon. I looked around at the hard brown gibbers, at the scanty trees of the distant bush country, and then noticed a hen searching for food among the gibbers and the thought came, "People live here!" Then I caught sight of two sober little faces peeping round the corner of a building. Children! I gave a friendly smile. The faces instantly vanished. When I looked again they were back, watching eagerly. Thinking to make friends, I slowly moved in their direction. Quickly they sensed my intention and fled in panic. I retraced my steps, and when I looked back they had reappeared. The picture of those two children, too shy to meet any stranger outside their own limited world, stayed with me.

The children became faces of a problem that Adelaide Miethke eventually realised extended across the outback. In 1945 she managed to have a 'flying sister', Myra Blanch, appointed to the Alice Springs FDS with the intention that she'd fly from station to station and provide woman-to-woman advice on basic health issues. Blanch soon found it easier to drive an old utility on her rounds, and as she got to know her region she grew increasingly worried about the condition of the children she encountered. Some were undernourished. Many weren't getting a proper education. Half the children who were supposed to be doing their schooling by correspondence were missing out entirely.

In 1946 Miethke became the first woman president of an FDS branch, which meant more frequent visits to Alice Springs to develop her understanding of the services' operations and the area's needs. Soon she was seeing for herself how children of outback workers struggled to understand their correspondence lessons and how their sometimes poorly educated parents struggled as well when they tried to help them. The academic and social gap between children who could get to the school in Alice Springs and those far out in the bush was plain to see. For the retired educator it was a situation that cried out to be addressed.

During one of her visits to Alice Springs, Miethke got talking to the director of the FDS base, Graham Pitts. Pitts told her about a nursing sister who used to give health talks to outback mothers over the air. They'd been popular sessions until the woman had moved on. As Pitts continued, something in Adelaide's mind clicked.

'Did you say she talked to mothers?' she asked.

'Yes.'

'All at the same time?'

'Yes.'

Graham continued talking about mothers, but Adelaide was thinking about children.

'If you could talk to mothers all at once, couldn't you talk to children?' she asked. Pitts agreed that it should be possible, and the germ of an idea was born. In fact the concept of using the flying doctor radio network to broadcast lessons to children had been floating around since the days when John Flynn and Alf Traeger set up the first network in the late 1920s. It hadn't happened, mainly because it was a formidable undertaking. Fortunately, Adelaide Miethke was the right person for the job.

Miethke was born in the South Australian country town of Manoora, 120 kilometres north of Adelaide, in 1881. She was the sixth of seven girls and three boys. Her father Carl, like many South Australians, was a German immigrant but as a lad he'd run away to sea, become a goldminer, then a mercenary in the American Civil War. When he returned to Australia he became a schoolteacher and eventually the headmaster at Manoora. He married Adelaide's mother, Emma, when she was only fifteen; Carl was thirty-five. She started having children while barely out of childhood herself and died, worn out from years of child rearing and hard work, when she was only thirty-seven. At the time Adelaide was eleven.

Carl had been devoted to Emma and never remarried. Instead he raised his children with the same strict discipline he applied in his school. Legend has it that young men who called on the attractive Miethke girls were sent on their way by their stockwhip-cracking father. All the children were brought up to high moral standards and were also encouraged to think independently. Whether influenced by their father's iron rod or their mother's difficult life, none of the Miethke girls married. Only one of the boys tied the knot.

Adelaide Miethke eventually followed her father into teaching and became active in the teacher's union. There she campaigned for better pay and conditions, particularly for women. During World War I she organised fundraising through the South Australian Children's Patriotic Fund and coordinated the sewing of 50 000 fly veils to protect the eyes of the horses of the Australian Light Horse. In 1915 she became founding president of the Women Teacher's League and the following year the first female vice-president of the South Australian Public School Teacher's Union.

Miethke was a born communicator, a teacher with a natural authority whose students didn't get away with much. 'Tough but fair' was the verdict. Her friends and colleagues variously described her as 'buxom' and 'outspoken', with a sense of humour. Some noted that she worked to such high standards that she inspired everyone around her to greater efforts. She could also be a formidable adversary. In 1919, at a union conference, she flayed the South Australian government for its treatment of teachers. One fiery speech was punctuated with applause from her colleagues throughout.

Shortly after, the politically savvy director of education, W.T. McCoy, recognised she was the kind of person who could get things done and promoted her to headmistress of the girls' section of Woodville High. There was some irony that Miethke, a career woman, was responsible for turning out the housewives of South Australia, but typical of her style she aimed to prepare students so that their homes didn't become their prison. Eventually, this led to the organisation of junior technical schools for girls where Miethke introduced progressive teaching methods and business-oriented studies.

In 1936 Miethke was nearing the end of an impressive career, and compulsory retirement at age sixty, when she became president of the Women's Centenary Council formed to raise funds for South Australia's centenary. The council brought together dozens of South Australian women's groups to raise funds to create a fitting memorial to the pioneer women of the state. The idea they liked most was to employ a 'flying sister' who could support the current generation of pioneering women and help break down their loneliness and isolation. It was such a good idea, and Miethke was such a good fundraiser, that they quickly amassed £5000.

When the Australian Inland Mission's Reverend John Flynn heard about the money, he immediately saw a different way it could be spent – setting up an Alice Springs branch of his fledgling Flying Doctor Service. He decided to pay Miethke a visit.

The meeting between Flynn and Miethke was like the clash of two great forces of nature. The determined women's advocate had spent a lifetime fighting tooth and nail for every small advance, and wasn't about to give her windfall away to a talker like Flynn, no matter how persuasive he could be. Besides, Alice Springs wasn't even in South Australia. For hour after hour Flynn extolled the virtues of the flying doctor and the contribution the women of South Australia could make. As Miethke recalled:

> He told us of his own Inland experiences, passing from hut to homestead, from lonely settler to distant mining camp, by any and every kind of transport available, roughing it through the outback to reach his various destinations. He told of men, women or children who had sickened and died between the period of one visit and the next, and of the suffering endured for lack of medical attention. He told of agonies

suffered during the long, rough jolting journeys by any conveyance at hand in trying to reach medical aid.

Throughout it all Miethke defended her plan for a flying sister and the right of the women of South Australia to spend their hard-earned funds as they chose. It was after midnight when Flynn left, empty-handed. All he'd managed to pry out of Miethke was an assurance that she'd think about his proposal. In a lot of cases that would have been the polite brush-off that ended the matter, but Miethke was true to her word. She decided to put Flynn's suggestion to the next meeting of the centenary council. Predictably, it didn't go down well. Then, to the surprise of many who were there, Miethke got up and fought for the idea as hard as Flynn had done. She'd realised it was the right thing to do. She argued it was exactly what the pioneering women of South Australia would have chosen for their sisters in central Australia. She made such a strong case that the proposal was referred to a subcommittee to examine in detail. Miethke was its chair.

The Alice Springs base for the flying doctor commenced operations in 1939 (a Pioneer Women's Garden of Remembrance was also opened in Adelaide) and a grateful John Flynn gave the Women's Centenary Council two seats on the Alice Springs FDS board. It was a decision that eventually introduced Adelaide to the outback and set her on a course to create an educational institution that was the first of its kind anywhere in the world.

After her meeting with Graham Pitts in 1946, Adelaide Miethke started thinking about how she could create a school around a radio network. That year she also started and edited *Airdoctor*, a magazine for the FDS, in which she outlined her ideas. A radio school would create a classroom that would bring children out of their isolation, give them access to trained teachers and help them understand their correspondence lessons. 'As well as bringing colour to their lives, interest, diversion and expectancy – could their lessons be supplemented?' she wrote in *Airdoctor*. 'Ideas were crowding in: scripts, stories, lessons, friendly talks.'

The challenges in creating such a school were both educational and technical. It wouldn't work if children had to get a radio operator's licence before they learned the alphabet. Reception was also an issue – lessons would soon break down if half the class didn't hear what a teacher said and it had to be repeated over and over. Nevertheless, Adelaide knew she was on to something. She set up a meeting with the head of the Alice Springs School, Leslie Dodds, and FDS Director Graham Pitts. As she wrote in *Airdoctor:*

> The idea was unfolded.
>
> First to Mr Pitts. 'Can it be done? Technically, is it practicable?'
>
> 'Sure. It means sustained transmission, though. We'd need new equipment – stronger, clearer, more powerful.'
>
> 'Will you work on it?'
>
> 'Sure.' Already his mind was at work.
>
> And then to Mr Dodds. 'Suppose I prepare the talks, who could give them?'
>
> 'Let me think it over,' he said, 'but, of course, I'd like to help.'

Dodds went to talk to his teachers. Pitts went to talk to his radio men. Miethke started talking to parents around Alice Springs. Not surprisingly, the teachers thought it was a great idea. The parents welcomed the possibility of having real teachers involved in their children's education. They also hoped a school community would help their shy children improve their social skills. Miethke was pleased to discover that using radio was less of a problem than she'd imagined. Most children could already operate them because they'd long ago become the hub of outback communications.

That just left the bureaucracy of the South Australian Education Department – Miethke's old stamping ground. The retired inspector

of schools tapped into her old networks and employed her considerable arm-twisting skills to get the government to agree to a trial.
Unfortunately, Miethke didn't document the trials and tribulations
of motivating the department to try a radically new approach to
education. However, the time gap between the original idea and
its realisation – roughly six years – suggests she'd had to drag the
bureaucrats the whole way.

At least the delay gave Graham Pitts time to gather the necessary equipment to upgrade the radios both at the Alice Springs FDS
base and among the baby sets that would be used by the children
around the network. In the years immediately after the war, supplies of almost everything were scarce. Ironically, production of the
latest radio equipment was lagging far behind demand, while older
army surplus radios were being discarded and left to rot. Pitts, who
was as good a radio man as Alf Traeger, scavenged and cannibalised
anything he could lay his hands on. He was driven by his passion
for Miethke's idea, but it still took him until 1950 before he'd got
the equipment up to the standard he considered necessary for the
school.

When everything was ready he laid cable from the radio room of
the FDS base to Alice Springs school, where the staffroom was converted into a temporary studio. It meant the teachers had to eat their
lunches out on the school verandah with their pupils, but it didn't
particularly bother them – thirteen had volunteered to be part of the
experiment. At last everything was ready for the first test broadcast.

On 20 September, 1950, the first lesson went to air. The name of
the teacher isn't known, but it may have been Leslie Dodds or the
teacher who coordinated the experiment, Tom Kissell. The classroom
measured over a million square kilometres and had an indeterminate
number of pupils. It was a one-way communication – the teacher
delivered the lesson, the children only listened in. Parents then
reported on the quality of the reception – both of the radio signal and

on the part of the audience. Some children, unfamiliar with what a classroom meant, took some time to get used to the idea. Others could barely hear what was being said. Nevertheless, the school started broadcasting three teaching sessions a week.

Behind the scenes considerable effort went into solving the teething problems. Curiously, the baby sets closest to the base station were finding it hardest to pick up the signal. Those furthest out (over 400 kilometres away) were getting good reception. Eventually Pitts realised that he'd chosen a broadcasting frequency that worked best over long distances. The solution was to broadcast on two frequencies, the second one being more suited to short range.

Within a year of the trial beginning, the sessions were increased. During 1951 they started being broadcast daily. When it was practical to do so, the lessons were followed by question-and-answer sessions so students could clarify anything they hadn't understood. The teachers and technicians pushed the technology to include singing lessons and music. When it was noticed that having several teachers was too confusing for the children, it was decided that all lessons would be given by just one voice. Initially, the job fell to the Alice Springs school's Tom Kissell.

As Miethke celebrated her seventieth birthday, she also oversaw events to mark the official opening of what was now being called the School of the Air. The title was reputedly coined by one of Adelaide's colleagues, mathematician and CWA stalwart Dorothy Dolling, who also worked as a writer under the pseudonym Eleanor Barbour. On 8 June, 1951, (a month after the death of John Flynn, who was buried on the outskirts of Alice Springs), education officials and School of the Air supporters gathered at the Alice Springs FDS base. Miethke wrote in *Airdoctor*:

Microphone, amplifier and chairs on the lawn, last minute testing in the transmitting room. On the verandas and in the lounge the sound of hurrying footsteps. In the studio of the Alice Springs Higher Primary School some distance away, the leader of the broadcast team sat ready, script in hand. At their transceivers, at individual outposts, the children and parents outback waited.

Following a number of speeches, the time came to demonstrate the school in action to the visiting dignitaries. Visitors at the Base listened attentively to the "roll-call" and the responses by the children. There followed a spelling test from pages previously assigned for study, each word being appropriately used in a sentence; an outline of social studies; an introduction with regard to the term's literature. Then, by way of entertainment to celebrate the occasion, children from Alice Springs School sang to the children outback, and were answered by a chorus from Hermannsburg Mission station. Other children were invited to contribute, and two timid solos and a quavering duet came in answer to this impromptu invitation, while from a distant mission station childish voices offered to say their "two times tables" as they didn't know any songs.

The disembodied children's voices were sometimes barely audible over the hiss of static and unsteady radio signals. For the assembled media, the poor sound quality emphasised the immense distances that were being overcome. The compelling story of those faint voices talking over the airwaves, connecting with their teachers in a way that had never been done before, was reported worldwide. It was one of the great achievements in the history of the outback.

While the School of the Air focussed on primary-school students, Miethke also sought ways to improve services for secondary students. Outback children who wanted to continue their education usually had to go to a boarding school in a larger town or a city, such as Adelaide. So when the South Australian government enquired what Miethke wanted to do with the remaining money she'd raised with her Children's Patriotic Fund during World War II, she replied: 'What I would like is a school hostel in Adelaide for my country girls who cannot get board when coming to the city to study. My country children raised much of this money and this could be their reward.'

The government liked the idea so much that it built four hostels. Over her objections they named one of them Adelaide Miethke House and unveiled a plaque that explained the reason for the name. It reads: 'Children loved her.'

In 1952 Molly Ferguson was appointed the first full-time teacher of the School of the Air. In many ways her contribution to the early development of the scheme was as significant as Miethke's. Apart from her broadcasts she also took the school to her pupils, travelling far and wide to visit them, give them personalised attention and help their parents organise their study environment. While on the road, she broadcast lessons from whatever baby set she happened to be near. The signal was then relayed to the rest of the network.

Graham Pitts was also busy around Alice Springs. Anything that operated with electricity had the potential to affect the quality of radio transmissions and he worked assiduously to eliminate every source of interference. Eventually, it became clear that a radio facility was needed outside the town. Pitts chose a site for a base station at Wigley Hill, 6 kilometres away. A landline was laid back to the Alice Springs school. The trench for the line was dug by prisoners from the local jail.

When it began, responsibility for the operation of the School of the Air was spread across three organisations: the South Australian Education Department's Correspondence School, the Alice Springs school and the Royal Flying Doctor Service. Miethke, who was still on the FDS board despite her advancing age, acted as the liaison officer between all three. The school was literally under her wing, and as editor of *Airdoctor* she publicised each new development. One of the most significant developments came during the term break of May 1955. She wrote:

Meanwhile, the children's interest in one another was growing too. They
longed to put faces to the voices which joined in the daily sessions. And
teacher, too! A "Get Together" was planned, and across the distance
came the children, travelling toward the centre at Alice Springs. What
an exciting experience! For a whole week individual help with correspondence lessons each morning; in the afternoon, excursions, with
talk and play and discussion to their heart's content.

Thereafter, in the daily sessions, voices recalled faces, personalities,
friends. School of the Air was fulfilling an ideal, and the "Get Together"
had to be an annual event.

In 1955 Molly Ferguson retired to get married (she became Molly
Healy). She was awarded an MBE for her role in the development
of the School of the Air. She was succeeded by Margaret Stiller, who
wrote of her experience in *Airdoctor*, '1956 has been the happiest
year of my life.'

Stiller's tenure included a visit from the Duke of Edinburgh, who
spoke to the pupils despite sunspot activity affecting reception. The
Get Together was held in Adelaide, in three cottages belonging to the
CWA. During 1956, enrolments increased from twenty-nine to fifty, in
part the result of Stiller contacting parents to encourage them to get
their children to participate. She, too, toured the region and 'gained
a much better understanding of the children, their environment, the
problems of the pupils and supervisors in correspondence lessons, as
well as getting to know each other in person'. Stiller also noted that
the school was developing its own support skills. 'Sometimes when I
am not able to hear a station clearly, everyone is immediately ready
to pass on the message if they can hear it.'

She was also responsible for further initiatives:

There were one or two children of pre-school age listening to some of
the sessions, and as an experiment I decided to devote one afternoon

lesson each week to them. The idea caught on immediately, and many parents have told me how much the little ones enjoy their own special session. Almost weekly we have someone new joining in with sessions for the little ones.

It was part of Miethke's management style to provide the framework for others to build on, and it must have given her great satisfaction to see how quickly the School of the Air grew – a library service, teacher patrols and new schools opening in other regions. By the time Adelaide Miethke died, in 1962, more schools were operating in Broken Hill (1956), Port Augusta (1958) and Cloncurry (1960). Kalgoorlie School of the Air opened in 1962, Port Hedland in 1964 and Katherine in 1966. Most were administered by their respective state and territory education departments, and while they may have developed independently (although many operated with the support of the Flying Doctor Service), they shared a common experience. The exchange of ideas relating to 'distance education' continues to this day.

For many years most of the schools operated as a supplement to correspondence courses. However, the experience of schools like Alice Springs showed that correspondence courses were part of the problem. Postal services were often slow. Marking work involved sending it to the state's capital, processing it and then mailing it back. The procedure could take months. In 1974 the Northern Territory School of the Air became an autonomous educational organisation, responsible for all aspects of its operation. Prior to that year, enrolments stood at around sixty. The following year there were 123 students – tuning in from cattle stations, mining camps and Aboriginal communities too small to have their own school.

School of the Air services cost about twice as much per student as regular schools and they cannot completely overcome the disadvantages that isolation creates for the children of the outback. Yet every state with children living in remote areas values its Schools of the Air so highly that at last count there were sixteen schools and branches servicing areas ranging from 400 000 to one million square kilometres.

There are few memorials or monuments to the 'outback pioneer' who started them all – there's Adelaide Miethke House in Adelaide and Miethke Place, an unremarkable cul-de-sac in the Canberra suburb of Flynn. However, Miethke wasn't the kind of woman who sought recognition. She was more interested in getting the job done, and in creating a unique education system that has improved the lives of thousands of outback children she certainly succeeded. Her name may be all but forgotten, but she left a legacy no monument could ever hope to match.

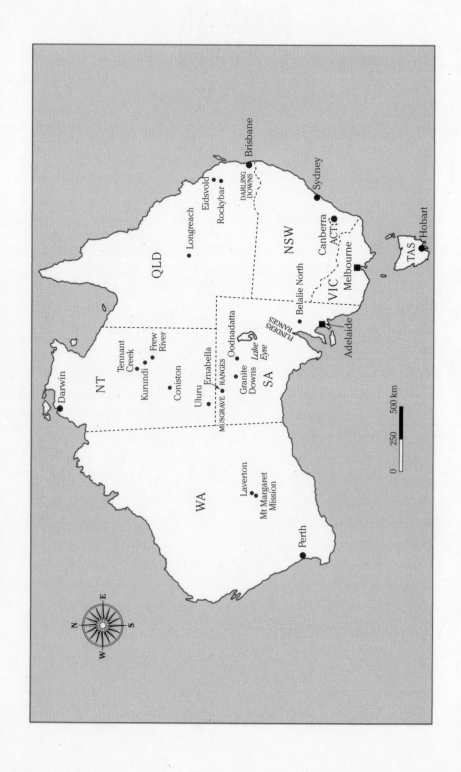

R.M. Williams, 1988
(National Archives of Australia)

12

THE LAST BUSHMAN

R.M. Williams (1908–2003)

In an almost forgotten book, *Exploring in the Seventies,* outback pioneer Alfred Giles bemoaned the inadequate equipment supplied to the team sent across central Australia in the 1870s to establish the route for the Overland Telegraph. He wrote:

> The packbags were made of a poor canvas with short flaps that would not cover the contents in the bags when full . . . The bags were constantly being ripped in the scrub or bumped against tree-trunks or anthills . . . Our water-bags were just plain canvas, nor were they fitted with a neckshape to fasten around the horse's neck . . . and often when full it was our horror, when longing for a drink, to see a packhorse bump in between two trees, squash the bag, and throw up a jet of the precious fluid that we expected to have on reaching camp.

Giles's lament was all too common. Just as the outback is a great test of character, it also exposes any weaknesses in equipment. The difference between 'rough-and-ready' and 'the best money can buy' sometimes becomes a matter of life or death. Under such circumstances the demand for the best-quality equipment was driven by far more than simple economics.

On 24 May, 1908, a child whose name would come to be associated with high-quality equipment and many of the other qualities that are valued in the outback was born at the small South Australian country town of Belalie North, 200 kilometres from Adelaide. His name was Reginald Murray ('R.M.') Williams.

His early life was typical of many bush kids. He grew up sleeping on the verandah of his parent's cottage in all weathers, winter and summer. His father was a horse trader who could shoe horses and make and repair all the paraphernalia for horses, buggies and carts – in leather or at the blacksmith's forge. Williams spent much of his time at his father's side, watching and learning how to make almost anything by hand. In the early 1920s his family moved to Adelaide to ensure that he and his two sisters (Daisy and Effie) got the best possible education.

Williams thought he was already learning everything he needed in the bush and was bitterly unhappy at his city school. His parents may have hoped to nurture the lad's sharp intelligence, but he preferred to learn his lessons the hard way – in the school of life. At age fourteen or fifteen (accounts vary) he told them he wanted to leave school. His parents were adamant that he should stick with his studies. Defying their wishes, the headstrong youngster packed his meagre belongings, including a Bible his mother convinced him to take, and set out on foot, a swagman, in search of a job. The adventurous youngster picked up odd jobs until he eventually landed work as a lime-burner at a mission property on the edge of the Gibson Desert in Western Australia. To get to the site, at Mount Margaret

Mission near Laverton, he crossed the Nullarbor by train on the recently completed Trans-Australian Railway (see Chapter 6).

Lime-burning is a labour-intensive technique for extracting lime from limestone. The lime can then be used to make concrete. The work kept Reg busy for several months, at the end of which he was put to work building a concrete tank for the mission's water supply.

The Mount Margaret Mission had been established to address the needs of the region's indigenous population, many of whom were still living close to their traditional lifestyles. For Williams the experience of living among Aboriginal people left a deep impression. He made friends with a half-caste named Sandy, who developed Williams' skills in tracking and hunting. He was allowed to witness some of the ceremonies of Aboriginal people who'd had almost no contact with Europeans when they came in from the Gibson Desert. The impressionable youngster didn't know it at the time, but he was witnessing cultural practices that would soon be gone forever.

Williams' own bush skills so impressed the missionaries that when the work on the tank was finished, they asked him if he'd be interested in working as a camel boy on a government census of the Aboriginal population of central Australia. No one was really sure how many people were out there, so it was proposed to send Williams with a missionary named Bill Wade to find out. Williams knew almost nothing about camels, but he was a fast learner. Soon he knew how to pack, track and work with these sometimes recalcitrant animals.

The census was an extraordinary job for a teenager. It was also fraught with danger. The pair sometimes faced hostile tribes. They travelled vast areas of utter emptiness where they searched desperately for water, knowing that if they didn't succeed they were certain to perish. They operated beyond roads, rail and telegraph; they had no radio with which to summon assistance; and there was certainly no hope of aerial rescue or supply drops. The job gave Williams firsthand experience of the pre-requisites for outback survival: skill, good equipment and a hefty dose of basic commonsense. It turned him into a resourceful young man confident in his own ability while respectful of the dangers that could make the unwary pay dearly for a moment of complacency.

He loved the outback life. He befriended Aboriginal groups who took him on hunting expeditions and introduced him to a life and culture that existed in harmony with the environment. He camped under skies hung with a multitude of stars that burned more brightly than any he'd ever seen. He saw landscapes of desolation alongside places of extraordinary grandeur – most of them rarely if ever seen by other Europeans. He learned that in such places he could be free in a way he'd never known before. When the census ended, he didn't want to leave.

He worked on a number of stations in the area, all the time learning bushcraft from the people he worked with and absorbing their experience. He eventually took up dingo-scalping with another man, Gordon Billings. At that time most Australian governments regarded dingoes as vermin (they attacked stock) and paid a bounty on every one killed. The pair worked out of Oodnadatta, ranging far into the desert regions to the north, east and west. In 1928 Williams decided to try trading steel spear tips with Aboriginal people in return for dingo scalps. When word of what he was doing reached the police, they sent out a search party in pursuit of him.

Unfortunately, Williams' entrepreneurial initiative coincided with what became known as the Coniston Massacre. Aboriginal involvement was suspected in the murder of a Northern Territory prospector, and in a reprisal raid by police as many as fifty Aboriginal men, women and children were slaughtered. As word of what had happened spread, fears of further killings gripped the white people in the outback. The idea of someone arming the indigenous population with steel spears was too much for the officers of the law.

When Williams heard of the plan to arrest him, he took flight into

South Australia's northern wilderness, trying to put distance between himself and Oodnadatta's Sergeant Virgo and the police trackers. With a team of camels the twenty-year-old started from Granite Downs station, 250 kilometres west of Oodnadatta, and headed 150 kilometres further west to Ernabella. He continued another 100 kilometres along the southern side of the Musgrave Ranges, then picked his way through a narrow gorge to the northern side, and almost on to Uluru, more than 50 kilometres away. He made the journey while the country was considered extremely dangerous to Europeans, especially those travelling alone. Yet the young man had confidence in his ability to maintain good relations with the indigenous population. He was far more concerned about what the police, especially the feared Sergeant Virgo, would do to him.

Williams eventually backtracked to Granite Downs and station-owner Mick O'Donohue's roughly made homestead. There he surprised a stranger, a stockman named Brown. The man was highly suspicious of Williams, particularly of his story of being on the run, but gradually tensions eased and he allowed him to camp near the homestead. Brown shared his meagre dinner and afterwards settled down to pass the time with his hobby, leatherwork. As Williams watched the older bushman at work, he became fascinated. He later recalled:

He was making an intricate water-pouch worked from a single strand of kangaroo hide. I had seen and admired something of the sort before and was immediately interested in his technique. He showed a lot of patience once he sensed my admiration and showed me the turns and convolutions that comprised the plait. He showed me other knots too, and though I did not master them for many years that evening turned out to be the inspiration of my later life, a starting point of my interest in making bush things.

The experience helped Williams realise that the things he'd learned at his father's knee were a small part of a much greater body of bush knowledge. Not surprisingly, the people of the bush could not only repair the equipment they depended on, they could also improvise many of the things they needed from whatever materials happened to be at hand. Indeed, it's part of outback lore that there's almost nothing that can't be fixed with a length of fencing wire.

Williams left Granite Downs and eventually turned himself in, having led the Oodnadatta police on a 1000-kilometre wild-goose chase. He escaped punishment, but realised it might be prudent not to push his luck with Virgo for a while. He returned to Adelaide where, too proud to go back to his parents, he set up a bush camp on the property of a friend in the Adelaide Hills. He soon found work as a labourer and on 25 May, 1929, the day after his twenty-first birthday, he married the girl who'd been his sweetheart since his early teens – Thelma Mitchell. Thelma's visions of wedded bliss may have suffered a setback when he moved his new wife into his bush camp – there was no electricity and no running water – but it was the life her new husband was used to and she adapted as best she could.

Not long after his marriage, Williams was faced with another of life's hard lessons. This time, though, it was an experience he shared with many other Australians. In September the Great Depression descended and millions were thrown out of work. Williams was proud of his ability to turn his hand to anything, but now he discovered he had as much to offer as many thousands of others. In his search for work he joined the swarms of swagmen trekking hundreds of kilometres looking for anything that might bring in some income. In his case he needed money to support his now-pregnant wife. On 5 July, 1930, Thelma left their bush camp to go to Adelaide's Salvation Army Hostel and have her first child. When she was discharged, mother and baby returned to the rough life of the camp. Now, as Williams travelled the outback, often it was with his wife and daughter, Diane, in tow.

Williams eventually found work digging wells by hand, an occupation his grandfather had once followed. It was appallingly hard work, coupled with the ever-present danger of a cave-in. While digging wells for an Aboriginal mission in the Flinders Ranges, north of Adelaide, his worst fears were realised. A wall collapsed and he was almost completely buried under tonnes of earth. Williams credits his young wife's quick-thinking and digging in the right spot for saving his life.

All too soon, the well-digging work ran out and Williams was reduced to doing anything going on the surrounding stations in return for subsistence wages. His wife and daughter remained at his bush camp beside a waterhole on the Aboriginal reserve. As things grew desperate he swallowed his pride and accepted handouts of flour sent by his parents.

It was while Williams was at his bush camp that life threw him an unlikely lifeline. It came in the form of a rough-looking stranger who turned up one night in a buggy drawn by two mules. The driver asked if he could stop the night by Williams' campfire. Williams noted later that the bloke looked like the type who wouldn't take no for an answer. His name, he said, was Dollar Mick Smith.

Dollar Mick was a disreputable character who'd had more than a few run-ins with the law. During the Depression he'd been reduced to doing whatever he had to in order to survive. Rather than move on the next morning, he stayed, and it wasn't long before he'd educated Williams in some of his schemes and dodges for earning a few pennies. He taught him how to steal chickens, avoid being arrested for vagrancy and much more besides.

In the camp at night, Smith and Williams passed the time trying to come up with new ways to make money. The best ideas they had were for necessities that people couldn't make themselves. Gradually, it dawned on them. Smith and Williams were both raised in the bush, and had been learning how to improvise various bits of bush gear for years. There weren't a lot of people around who could do it, but they could.

They started scrounging materials and turning out station equipment – saddle bags, pack saddles, bridles – anything anyone wanted. Their work wasn't much to look at, but they knew what they were doing and their buyers knew what they wanted. As word of their abilities spread and orders trickled in, the bush camp in the Flinders Ranges became more permanent and the range of goods the pair were producing slowly increased. They soon discovered that even in the midst of the Great Depression there was still a market for quality – meaning it could be relied on to do the job it was made for.

It was obvious, though, that they were never going to get rich with a business that barely qualified to be called a cottage industry. Things came to a head when Williams, Thelma and their son Ian (born August 1932) came down with sandy blight and the mission authorities demanded that they vacate what was meant to be Aboriginal land. Ian's eyes were so bad that Williams realised he needed hospital treatment. He and Smith parted ways, Smith to continue his life knocking around the outback, Williams to return to Adelaide.

Williams' fledgling business with Dollar Mick had given him confidence in his ability to make a range of bush products, but he knew he'd have to do a lot more if he was going to make enough money to support his family (and more immediately, pay for Ian's eye treatment). Never one to shrink from seizing a bull by the horns, the 24-year-old Williams went to see the 75-year-old cattle king, Sir Sidney Kidman.

Williams asked Kidman to let him make pack saddles for the Kidman stations. Kidman said he could already get good pack saddles. Then he asked Williams why he thought his were better. It was all Williams needed:

For answer I gave him a quote from his old manager at Anna Downs, Archie McLean: 'Some day a better pack will be built using a higher

fork in the steel, a deeper side, and rigged with double girths instead
of carrying breast-plates and breeching. And the bags will have special
gussets for items that have to be kept upright.' . . . I did not tell Sir Sidney that his own man had been my teacher.

Kidman was sufficiently impressed that he decided to give the young
bushman a chance. When he took delivery of the pack saddles he
liked what he saw and told Williams to send him the bill. Instead,
Williams demanded money up front. At the time Kidman was one of
the richest men in Australia. If anyone could be trusted with credit
for thirty days, it was him. Then Williams explained that he was
broke and wouldn't have the money to buy materials for the next lot
of pack saddles until he got paid. Kidman wrote out a cheque on the
spot. Williams, the young entrepreneur, was on his way.

His next lesson was in the power of advertising. Back in the Flinders
Ranges bush camp, Dollar Mick had needed a pair of riding boots.
He and Williams had experimented until they'd produced something
that suited Dollar Mick perfectly. The boots they came up with had
elastic sides, rather than laces, which meant stockmen could pull
them on quickly if they were roused from their swags when their
mob of cattle rushed in the night.

Williams thought such boots might be a good new line for his tiny
operation and spent sixpence on an ad in the *Adelaide Courier*. It
read: 'Elastic side boots made to order. Twenty shillings. Cash with
order. 5 Percy Street, Prospect.' After the ad appeared it took as long
as it takes a letter to be mailed for the first order to arrive. It was the
first of what would become ten million pairs of boots, and rising.

The Percy Street address had its own significance. It was the
address of a workshop belonging to Williams' parents that sat alongside their house. The prodigal son had returned and Williams proudly
recalled that his father used to sit quietly at his side, watching him
for hours as he skilfully turned out the leather goods of his growing

business. The address eventually became famous, thanks to another brilliant business move. The tags attached to the uppers of the boots (to assist stockmen with pulling them on) were all embroidered 'R.M. Williams, 5 Percy Street, Prospect.' Out in the stock camps, when someone swore by their R.M. Williams boots, those same boots carried the answer to the question, 'Where can I get a pair?'

Williams was now in his mid-twenties. The days of the bush camps seemed to be behind him as he became a businessman, managing a company that was employing increasing numbers of people. As it grew, Williams was able to put a proper roof over his young family's head, a fine home in North Adelaide that was originally the South Australian governor's residence. Later, in 1945, he was in a position to purchase the opulent mansion Neidpath. By then the former kid from the bush was doing extremely well. He and Thelma went to garden parties and rubbed shoulders with Adelaide's elite. Williams swapped stock horses and camels for polo ponies. He took an interest in a goldmine near Tennant Creek and cattle stations at Kurundi and Frew River. He helped establish the Australian Rough Riders Assocation and published its newsletter, which eventually became the magazine *Hoofs and Horns*. He published a guide to leather and bush crafts called *The Bushman's Handbook*.

It seemed Williams could do no wrong, but life had yet another lesson to teach the now forty-something lion of business. In 1952 he had what he later described as a 'nervous breakdown'. His marriage was failing and the 'castle' at Neidpath had become more like a prison. Thelma loved living 'to the manor born', but for the middle-aged man who'd lost the uncomplicated life of the bush camp, the trappings of wealth came at a high price.

The nature of his problem was far from simple. In his oblique references to what happened, Williams mentions loneliness and a sense of personal failure. In his biography it appears to have been so serious that he contemplated suicide. He mentions having 'an overcrowded mind which almost persuaded me to shut off the whole hectic scene'. With regard to his personal life he described himself as 'a scoundrel' and noted that 'what most, if not all, women need is to be loved and for their loved ones to be faithful'.

On the surface, Williams had it all. His company, whose slogan was 'the bushman's outfitter', was thriving. His goldmine had struck a rich vein and was making him incredibly rich. His cattle dealing extended across the country. Williams got to the point where he couldn't face any of it and he all but barricaded himself in his room, refusing to leave or to see any visitors. The fact that his companies continued operating perfectly well in his absence probably did not help matters.

Williams eventually fled his marriage, family and business, and embarked on a global odyssey – a lost man in search of himself. In Calcutta he witnessed the worst extremes of poverty. In Hong Kong he met Australian author Alan Marshall, a man who overcame the crippling effects of polio to lead a rich and colourful life. While there he also dined with Winston Churchill. He explored the social and political philosophies of thinkers as diverse as Gandhi, Karl Marx and Sun Yat-sen.

Yet the answers he sought lay 'further out'. On his return to Australia, Reg 'went bush'. By then his marriage was over and he moved into a tiny cottage on Northfield, a property he'd bought just outside Adelaide. From there he focussed on his cattle dealing and made a point of joining the drovers when he could, returning to the life of the bush camps and the stock routes. It was in the peace around the campfire that he discovered what he was missing. It was the outback.

In 1955 he remarried. With his new wife, Erica Nunn, he bought Rockybar, a property near Eidsvold in central Queensland. It was a place that had been hacked out of the bush by hand many years before, the pioneering work still in evidence to a man like Williams who had an eye for the raw products of basic bushcraft. Williams and Erica lived there for fifteen years. Williams' love of the place ran so deep that he wrote of its almost mystical qualities years later in his book *I Once Met a Man*. In a cave on the property he'd found Aboriginal art that preceded the date carved by the first white settler, in 1874. The settler's grave was on the property. He'd died in 1942.

Williams' businesses continued to prosper, but gradually he and Erica grew apart. His second marriage ended in 1972. By then he was sixty-four and old enough to be philosophical about the ways of the human heart. He certainly wasn't as shattered as he'd been when his first marriage failed. At that point he should have been contemplating retirement, but there remained one great task for him to do. As a teenager, Williams had experienced much of the life of the outback pioneers. Now, in his later years, he realised that many of the experiences he treasured were slowly fading from the nation's memory. The terrible isolation had long since been overcome by Traeger's radio, the Flying Doctor Service and even the Country Women's Association. The great cattle drives of old had been replaced by road trains. Even mustering was done with helicopters and planes. Williams realised that many of the skills he'd learned in the bush camps and the experiences he'd had of outback life would disappear forever when the last of his generation passed away. Something had to be done to preserve those memories.

Through the pages of *Hoofs and Horns*, Williams had long been supporting outback poets, illustrators and storytellers as a way of keeping memories of the bush alive. In 1974 the painter Hugh Sawrey suggested to Williams that Australia should have something like the American Stockmen's Hall of Fame. Williams thought it was an excellent idea. He embraced the project with his extraordinary energy and enthusiasm, and was soon utilising his extensive network of people in business and politics to promote the project.

It took a few years, but a committee was formed and eventually a site for the Stockman's Hall of Fame was chosen, on the outskirts of the western Queensland town of Longreach. Now the problem was raising the money to get construction under way. Public donations flowed in, corporations were supportive, but the Hall of Fame needed government backing if it was ever going to happen. Like many of the people in this book, Williams soon discovered that when it comes to the bush, politicians can't be relied on for much. By 1980, fundraising for the Hall of Fame had stalled.

Williams decided it was time to stir people to action. In his typical bushman's style, at the age of seventy-two he went to Longreach and set up a bush camp on the proposed site of the Hall of Fame. He informed curious media that he intended to start work on the first building – an information centre and caretaker's cottage – and build it with his own two hands. To most people it looked like a publicity stunt, but for Williams it was a chance to return to the outback camps he'd grown up in from the deserts of Western Australia to the Adelaide Hills. The millionaire who'd become a household name really only needed a rough shelter, a pile of firewood and a few simple comforts.

The camp worked like a magnet. Craftsmen and labourers came from far and wide to lend a hand – hewing stone, carving timbers, living rough while working hard. Longreach mayor James Walker dropped in from time to time for a yarn and a tot of rum. Journalists came from everywhere to tell the story of the wealthy old man building a museum by hand, camped in a paddock in the middle of Queensland. Gradually the message permeated to the senior levels of government that a group of Australians were determined to preserve a vital part of Australia's heritage even if the government wasn't. It could be that nothing galls a politician more than someone else pioneering great things in spite of them. As the building at Longreach neared completion, the celebration of Australia's 200 years of European settlement, the 1988 Bicentennial, appeared on the horizon.

The federal government seized on the opportunity to provide funds (in addition to the amount Williams and the Hall of Fame committee had raised) for the main museum building.

The Hall of Fame is now housed in the kind of soaring edifice politicians think impresses an electorate. It was completed in 1987 and opened by Queen Elizabeth II in 1988.

The structure Williams built from locally sourced stone and timber stands nearby, hardly noticed by most visitors. Compared to the main building it's the sort of unpretentious construction that outback pioneers might be more accustomed to. It houses the museum's extensive library of books and documents on the outback and country life. It's a place where passing researchers can discover the many voices of the outback in an environment more in harmony with their tone. One of those voices belongs to Williams. The building itself is one of his stories and a fitting if understated monument to his legacy. His respect for the qualities admired in the outback made him a handsome living, but his desire to preserve and celebrate those qualities has ensured that they're still understood and valued today. Without that, books like this might never get written.

On 4 November, 2003, at the age of ninety-five, R.M. Williams died at his home on the Darling Downs. Tributes to his almost legendary status poured in from everyone from politicians to business moguls, stockmen to stockbrokers. Williams' life spanned an era of extraordinary change in the outback, reaching back to the days when camel trains still crossed the empty stretches of wilderness and Aboriginal people were still experiencing their first contact with the rest of the world. Williams saw and did things no one will ever experience again. Along the way, life taught him many lessons. In the end it gave him the wisdom to do his part in preserving the best of them for future generations.

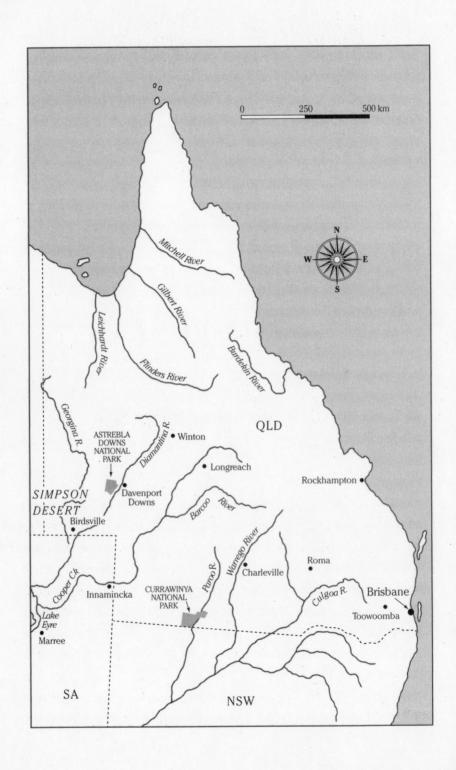

Frank Manthey, 2007
(Planet Press EnviroPrint)

Peter McRae, 2007
(Michelle Havenstein)

13

OUTBACK RESCUE

Peter McRae (1951–) and
Frank Manthey (1938–)

The previous chapters in this book have explored the lives of men and women who've transformed the outback experience. They've tamed it, shaped it, settled and civilised it, and in the process discovered the beauty and terror of this extraordinary country – some developing an appreciation and connection akin to that long held by indigenous Australians. This chapter is about two men whose love of the outback is as strong as all those who have preceded them. The difference is that they've been motivated to try and return the outback to the way it once was.

Zoologist Peter McRae and former roo-shooter Frank Manthey's story reaches back to 1975, to a time when the empty gibber and sandhill country west of the Diamantina River was being swept night after night by powerful spotlights. Out in the region known as Heartbreak Corner, a search was being conducted for an almost mythical creature thought to be on the brink of extinction. It looked a bit like a rabbit, but moved like a kangaroo. It had grey fur but, for no obvious reason, its tail was black and white. The bilby (*Macrotis lagotis*) hadn't been seen in Queensland for years.

Teams of scientists went out for a month at a time, four times a year, for four years, searching for bilbies. They were there as part of a massive fauna survey being conducted by the newly formed Queensland National Parks and Wildlife Service (NPWS). The service had previously been part of the state's forestry department, where its work was so undervalued that no one even knew what wildlife existed in the state's many varied habitats. Throughout the late 1970s and early 1980s the Queensland NPWS combed the state, shire by shire, compiling an inventory of animals from the deserts of the far west to the jungles of the tropics and on to the Great Barrier Reef.

Out in the 95 000-square-kilometre region beyond the Diamantina the news for the bilby wasn't good. Despite the intensive survey work, not a single bilby had been sighted, let alone caught. The researchers saw burrows and evidence of digging, hoping it was done by bilbies, and locals said they occasionally saw bilbies on the roads, yet still the traps came up empty; the spotlights scoured Diamantina Shire in vain.

When the fauna survey ended, so did the search for the bilby, but the hope that they were still out there remained. In 1987 Greg Gordon, principal scientist at the NPWS, managed to get enough money out of a mining company, Delhi Petroleum, to have another go. He rang NPWS zoologist Peter McRae to see if he was interested in spending three years in the middle of nowhere looking for bilbies.

'Yeah, count me in,' came the reply.

Together with Rob Atherton, one of the original survey scientists,

McRae started work in 1988. The pair went through the records of
the fauna survey to find possible bilby locations. They used helicopters to assess places for closer study and finally settled on a site on
Davenport Downs station, which straddles the Diamantina River 250
kilometres north-east of Birdsville. They set up camp and started
spotlighting, night being the only time the strictly nocturnal bilbies
left their burrows. They went out night after night without success.
They searched for weeks – so long that they began to doubt their
ability to even recognise a bilby if they saw one.

'We knew what bilbies looked like,' McRae recalled in an interview
with this author. 'Apart from seeing pictures, we'd looked at museum
specimens, but until you actually see one in the wild, you don't know
what it's going to look like. Elephants are different because if you see
an elephant you'll know it's an elephant. At night when you've spent
four or five hours spotlighting you don't know if you're missing them.
Have they got eye shine? Do they crawl along the ground? Do they
walk around upright? What do they do? You really can't anticipate
that thing until you experience it.'

To cover more territory, Atherton would go spotlighting in one
location, McRae in another. At 3 or 4 a.m. they'd meet up again to
compare notes, but night after night they had nothing to compare.
Then came a night that was different. It was raining. Out along the
Diamantina, on the fringe of the parched Simpson Desert, rain is a
rare event. It did nothing for the comfort of the two scientists, but it
was just what they needed. At around 2.30 a.m. both men were peer-
ing into the unusually misty night in separate locations when both
thought they'd spotted something. McRae remembered:

I thought, Is this a bilby? It's not a rabbit. Bilbies don't have eye shine.
If they do it's a very very faint pinkish glow. It's not something that
stands out obviously like koalas, cats or foxes. You're actually looking for a shape with ears, a body shape. It's a bit like a rabbit but once

you've seen both you'd never confuse them. I just got so excited and
then I saw another three in the next hour and unbeknownst to me, we
met up again at 3 or 4 in the morning and he'd seen a similar amount.
We were just ecstatic. These things do exist!

Finding the bilbies was a great leap forward, but the discovery only
marked the beginning of years of intensive study. Almost nothing
was known about the species and the pair virtually had to start from
scratch. It was a massive undertaking, but in 1990 Rob Atherton's
health took a turn for the worse. He'd been diagnosed with a brain
tumour a few years before. It had been in remission but now it was
back. When it didn't respond to treatment Atherton resigned from
the NPWS to spend what time he had left with his wife and children.
It was to be only six months.

As McRae mourned the loss of his colleague and friend, he was
left to continue the bilby study on his own – hard and often thank-
less work in one of the loneliest places in the country. His study site
is now part of Astrebla Downs National Park:

It's flat, treeless, Mitchell grass plains. It's so flat you can see car lights
from 70 kilometres away. It's featureless, sort of moonscapey without
the craters, and in summer 55°C and in winter zero. It's a really harsh
environment and no evidence of anything being there. Nothing alive,
not even plants. Dead plants litter the surface and that's most of the
time. It can be five or six years. You go out there and you think, 'Nothing could live here. There's nothing. There's just dirt.' And yet bilbies
are racing around all over the place digging holes.

What kept him going over the next decade was an insatiable desire
to find out how the bilbies were doing it. The questions were endless:
'It eats subterranean termites; why does it eat them? Because they're
full of carbohydrates and fat. How do the termites get there? What are

they doing? What are *they* living on? The more you learn, the more you want to really understand what's going on with these things.'

The biggest question was: why were the bilbies endangered? Historically they'd been found as far east as the Darling Downs, on the inland side of the Great Dividing Range. Now they were down to fragmented populations scattered over 150 000 square kilometres in western Queensland, west of the Diamantina River. There was another remnant population in Western Australia's Great Sandy Desert, where they were down to 5 per cent of their original habitat range. In Queensland it was only 2 per cent.

As McRae sought answers he began to understand just how tenuous the bilbies' existence had become. What was particularly worrying was that of all Australia's fauna, bilbies should have been the *least* threatened. Bilbies are generalists. Unlike fussy eaters such as koalas, echidnas or numbats, bilbies eat almost anything – insects, ants, termites, grasshoppers, beetles, small lizards, small mammals, bulbs and roots. They also don't need to drink water. They can get all the moisture they need from their food. That means they can live in areas where it's bone dry almost all the time.

Compared with other marsupials, bilbies have a high reproductive rate, too. Females generally produce two young, four times a year, and bilbies live for seven years in the wild. So they have the potential to increase their population very quickly. Bilbies also have the second-shortest gestation period known for any mammal – twelve to fourteen days. McRae regards that as miraculous:

> When you think about it, to go from two cells to something that's got brains, kidneys – sure it's in this undeveloped state, but it's got the workings of a living, breathing bilby – and it crawls out of the birth canal and attaches onto the nipple in the pouch and it spends eighty days in there, two cells to something as magical as life in less than two weeks is just amazing. There's a lot of magic in that.

The bilby's habits also enhance its chances of survival. Being strictly nocturnal, they are out of reach of daylight predators such as wedge-tailed eagles. They can also burrow up to 2 metres underground, far enough that other predators can't dig them up.

To McRae's way of thinking, the bilby should have been the mar-supial equivalent of the rabbit. 'We should be almost running over them on the road. They should be pests. So if we're losing a species like that we're doing something drastically wrong. You can under-stand losing something that is highly specialised – if it only likes this type of community or this soil type or this tree – but bilbies can be anywhere.'

As McRae developed his understanding of the types of habitat that most favour bilbies, he was shocked to realise that the region where they *were* surviving wasn't one of them. Other species such as kowaris (*Dasycercus byrnei*) and hopping mice (*Notonmys fuscus*) are arid zone specialists. Bilbies aren't. 'In terms of habitat, for them it's sub-optimal or at least very marginal. That's the toughest place you can be if you're not an arid zone specialist. They're handling it, but it's not ideal.'

With Queensland's bilbies pushed to the very edge of their tra-ditional range, the question arose: Why? Intensive agriculture was responsible for some habitat destruction, but in the mulga coun-try west of Roma land clearing hasn't been as widespread. The bilbies have still disappeared. Rabbits don't compete directly with bilbies for food, but it's a different story when it comes to burrow-ing sites. Without burrows the bilbies don't stand a chance against predators. McRae identified three main threats – dingoes, foxes and cats – except bilbies have coexisted with dingoes for thousands of years. It was only when he examined the impact of all three species combined that he began to understand why his bilbies were only just 'hanging on' in the desert.

Dingoes have been the top predator in the outback for about 6000 years, having displaced the Tasmanian tiger (*Thylacinus cynocephalus*) and Tasmanian devil (*Sarcophilus harrisii*) and pushed both to extinction on the mainland. While bilbies are on the dingo's menu, their burrows afford some protection and the two species established a balance long ago.

The two newcomers to the equation, foxes and cats, were another story. When foxes were introduced, the country had already been overrun by rabbits, so with plenty to eat they quickly spread throughout the mainland. When domestic cats escaped into the bush, their supreme hunting skills made them lethal to everything in their path and they've been sighted in every habitat in Australia. McRae knew that dingoes, foxes and cats all eat bilbies, but in hard times dingoes will also eat foxes and cats. Just as they'd done with Tasmanian tigers and devils, dingoes keep cats and foxes in check.

Unfortunately, dingoes also prey on lambs and calves, and the graziers' war on the dingo has given foxes and cats enough breathing space to wipe the bilbies out of the cattle and sheep country. West of the Diamantina, dingoes are still plentiful which goes some way to explaining why the bilbies were still there. Another clue came with a plague of rats:

It's a boom and bust system out there. And in the booms, the population of native rats [*Rattus villosissimus*] can just explode. There's thousands and thousands of square kilometres where the population of these native long-haired rats, the classic desert rodent, erupts almost overnight and there are thousands per square kilometre eating everything. When you get those really good periods and there's plenty of food around out on the open plain, that's when things like cats can move out of their usual habitats around rivers and start preying on native rodents.

That's what happened in 1992 – a series of wet summers and winters led up to a huge rat plague and all these cats turned up out on the

open plains. At my study site you'd never imagine a cat could live out
there, but in September 1992 there were cats everywhere. (We ended
up getting the army out. A platoon of snipers from Enoggera Barracks
in Brisbane came out for four days and they shot 417 cats within 20
kilometres of my camp site.) What happens in that situation is that the
rat population can crash overnight. That's when they put pressure on
the native species like bilbies.

McRae realised the bilby was hanging on by the weakest thread. Its
survival depended on one of its predators, plus the terribly hard conditions, keeping another of its predators under control. Unfortunately,
the pulses of boom and bust were taking their toll. McRae's population surveys revealed that bilby numbers were slowly but steadily
declining. Another boom like the one in 1992 could spell the end for
his bilbies. At that point he was probably the only person in western
Queensland who ever prayed for drought.

In an effort to buy time, McRae decided to attempt a captive breeding program at his base in Charleville, 800 kilometres east of his study
site. The idea was fraught with danger, particularly as it involved
removing some of the remaining population of an endangered species from the wild. The experience gained with other species had
shown that captive breeding can be spectacularly unsuccessful. Pan-
das are a classic example. They have highly specialised needs and
even then reproduction rates are very low. What McRae quickly discovered was that bilbies are the opposite:

> They don't need anything special. I just give them dry dog biscuits and
> budgie seed and they do fine on that, and because it's dry food I give
> them water. The simple fact is that they breed crazily. There are no
> dramas with them. You don't have to wear white coats and sterilise
> anything, speak softly and play music or anything like that.

Relieved that Queensland wasn't about to lose the species, he was now faced with a new problem – what to do with all the bilbies in his captive population. He was reluctant to release them back into the wild in far western Queensland because he was now sure it was far from ideal bilby habitat. A better idea was to release them into an area where they were once found that provided better conditions. If it worked, the exercise would also provide valuable insights into what bilbies, and other endangered species, really need to survive.

'The only way to do that is to build an enclosure,' McRae says. 'We've been trying to get cats and foxes out of areas for a long time and you can bait and trap and poison and stuff but you never get them all. People had done it before, fenced off areas to create sanctuaries – there's one at Heirisson Prong in Shark Bay in Western Australia. So I figured let's do it here.'

The idea meant returning part of outback Queensland to the condition people like John Wilson (see Chapter 1) had found it in. After more than 200 years of trying to tame the outback, it was time to appreciate and value what it once was.

In the mid-1990s, McRae sat down to work out the details. He decided Currawinya National Park, 300 kilometres south-west of Charleville on the Queensland–New South Wales border, was the perfect place. The 151 300-hectare former sheep station on the Paroo River was ideal bilby habitat. Its semi-arid mulga scrublands were still intact and there were park rangers on hand to manage the enclosure.

The snag came when he worked out the cost. The enclosure he envisaged wasn't something you'd see in a zoo. It involved a 20-kilometre fence enclosing an area 29 square kilometres. He estimated it would cost $300 000. It was a lot of money for just one species, even if it was endangered. He had no idea how he could go about raising an amount like that.

The solution came from an entirely unexpected direction. Enter

Frank Manthey. He was everything the science-trained McRae wasn't. He was your standard-issue, solid country bloke. Born and raised in the bush, he'd left school at the age of thirteen and went to work on cattle stations, then as a roo-shooter, in western Queensland. He'd married an Aboriginal woman and together they'd raised five sons and a daughter who cherished the sort of bush life they both knew and loved. When he decided it was time to settle down, he took a job as a park ranger. The job wasn't particularly challenging – collecting fees, making sure people camped in the right places, persuading people who were like he used to be that their activities weren't appropriate in a national park.

Then, after forty years of marriage, Frank's wife developed a heart condition. When she had a heart attack and died, everything Manthey lived for seemed to go with her. The sense of emptiness and loss almost overwhelmed him, but in the midst of his grief he noticed McRae. Compared to Manthey's job, McRae seemed to be doing important work, but Manthey knew how tough McRae was doing it out at his desolate study site, and the frustrations he'd endured over many years.

'Peter said come out to Astrebla, do some cooking,' Manthey recalled in an interview with this author. 'I've got a bit of a reputation as a bush cook. So I went out there and one blurry night I saw a little female bilby. It changed my life. I said, "We'll build that fence." I didn't know how, but I was determined that's what we'd do.'

Throughout his life Manthey hadn't had much time for doing things by the book. If the NPWS didn't have the money for a bilby fence, they'd get it from someone who did – the Australian public. Once again it was up to volunteers to do what governments couldn't or wouldn't do. Manthey started running bilby shows. After he finished work, four or five nights a week in the meeting room of the NPWS office in Charleville he gave talks to the public about saving the bilby. Afterwards he took whoever had turned up out the back to see the captive bilbies in their enclosure. It helped that bilbies are drop-dead cute and soon the talks were a must-see attraction on the Charleville tourist circuit.

Manthey was a born communicator. The former roo culler discovered he could also shoot from the lip, and he was almost always on target. As he recalled, 'Once we'd started the shows, all I had was a dream out in the distance – to build this fence. Every night I talked to people who didn't know about cats, foxes and endangered animals. After an hour with me they believed in me. They left wanting to help and they started spreading the dream.'

All Manthey asked of people was a gold coin donation, more if they could afford it. If thirty people turned up, they might make $50. At that rate it would take decades to raise enough money to build the fence. The answer was merchandise. McRae remembers Manthey's first attempt:

> We started off with little foam coolers that cost about twenty cents – the cheapest, nastiest, white, throw-away thing. We got a mate to do up some Save the Bilby stickers and Frank and I paid for it, and we stuck them on these white coolers that would have cost us forty cents all up and we sold them for four dollars or something like that. That was the beginning of the commercial side of it. As we started to get a bit more money we thought, let's get jackets, hats, all these sorts of things.

It still wasn't enough. Manthey decided that they needed to launch an appeal. To his way of thinking the maths was simple. The proposed fence comprised 15 000 panels. Each panel cost $20. If they could get 15 000 people to donate $20 each, they'd get the money. Again there was a snag. McRae and Manthey were government employees. They had no authority to do what they doing, let alone launch a bilby fund, but Manthey refused to give up. The big-hearted bushie had found something that gave his life meaning once again. He was determined that the bilby fence was going to happen.

Early in 1999 he arranged a meeting with the then head of the
Queensland NPWS, Barry Carbon. It was a bold thing for a mere
park ranger to do, but Carbon had already heard about Manthey.
His fundraising was already looked upon as 'highly adventurous' by
those in the NPWS. That's the phrase bureaucrats use when they
don't want to say 'doomed'. Even Manthey and McRae knew it would
be a nightmare if they got the appeal going, raised say $100000,
then the appeal stalled. What would they do with the money? Send
it back? For Carbon the standard procedure in such a situation was
to give Manthey a sympathetic hearing then warn him not to let the
door hit him on his way out.

Then the bureaucrat met the man. As Manthey laid out the problem, detailed the plan to solve it and handled every obstacle put
before him, Carbon may have reflected on what it would be like if all
his staff were like him. The proposal was risky, but if anyone could
make it work it was Manthey. Carbon became a convert. In March
1999 Environment Minister Rob Welford launched the Save the Bilby
Fund. (Manthey now credits the support of these and subsequent
directors and ministers as being crucial in what he and McRae have
been able to achieve.)

There was a good immediate response, but when interest began to
stall Manthey took the campaign to the people. He hit the road doing
media interviews, shopping centre displays and talks to schools. He
set up a bilby booth at the Ekka Agricultural Show in Brisbane and
the Royal Easter Show in Sydney. His star attraction was a young
female bilby named Dawn. She became an extremely well-travelled
little bilby as she and Manthey crisscrossed the country raising funds.
A growing band of Charleville volunteers helped run the bilby shows
and fund-raising administration while he was on the road.

The hard work had some unexpected rewards. On one occasion
Manthey opened an envelope and rolls of money fell out – all old-
style 10 and 20 dollar notes. A pensioner had been saving them for

years and decided the best thing to do with the nest egg was to help save the bilby. Manthey counted the money. It came to $7800.

Manthey's ideas for saving the bilby grew increasingly ambitious, and involved targeting the Easter Bunny. In a country where rabbits cost more than $600 million in lost agricultural production it made no sense that chocolate bunnies are what we reach for to celebrate Easter. As far back as the late 1970s the bilby had been seen as the perfect indigenous alternative. It's still got the big floppy ears and hops, but it has a more finely featured face and a cuter little pink nose.

Making, distributing and selling chocolate bilbies was a daunting prospect, but it was then that Manthey's promotional work paid an unexpected dividend. He was being interviewed on the radio and mentioned his frustration with trying to get major chocolate companies interested in supporting the bilby. He threatened to bring chocolate bilbies in from China. One of his listeners didn't like the sound of that. He was a former manager at Darrell Lea chocolates, an Australian company battling to survive in a market dominated by the giant international companies. He called his former colleagues at Darrell Lea and suggested they give Manthey a call. The deal they subsequently brokered was a win–win for all. Darrell Lea took care of all the production. The Save the Bilby Fund got a percentage of all chocolate bilby sales. Darrell Lea also got the kind of publicity money just can't buy. When the Easter Bilby was launched, the new minister for the environment, Dean Wells, got up in state parliament and told his fellow parliamentarians:

> We have a perfectly good native species in the bilby, which has big ears
> and a very high reproductive rate. Further, being a marsupial, it comes
> armed with a pouch with which it can carry Easter eggs. It's also noc-
> turnal which means its habits of daily life make it much more suitable
> for delivering Easter eggs than the rabbit. I would urge all members

of this house to promote the Easter Bilby. Don't be a rabbit. Invite the
Easter Bilby this Easter.

His words were reported around the nation, and with 50 cents per
bilby going into the fund its coffers grew as fat as the consumers who
switched to eating 60000 to 80000 chocolate bilbies a year. Other
activities were bringing in about the same amount. Unfortunately,
as the money pile grew, so did the cost of the fence. When McRae
had first worked out the cost, it was $300000. By the time they were
getting close to collecting $300000, the cost had risen to $450000.
Nevertheless, $300000 was enough to get started.

As the first of 4100 fence spikes went into the ground in September
2000, McRae and Manthey discovered that the bureaucratic controls
the NPWS had insisted upon during their fundraising actually had
an advantage. They'd been required to keep the details of all donors
to the fund (just in case). It now gave them a mailing list they could
use to call for volunteers. Other environmental organisations were
enlisted to assist and soon a small army converged on Currawinya
National Park.

The fence had to be built in such a way that no predatory animal
could get past it. It was to be more than 2 metres high and electri-
fied. To stop a determined predator climbing over it, the top section
was suspended from hand-cut supporting wires woven by hand
through the wire mesh. That made the top section floppy enough
that the weight of the predator would pull the mesh above it down,
effectively trapping it outside the fence. Between that and an electric shock every couple of seconds, they'd eventually let go. On either
side, mesh 1 metre wide was to be buried 15 centimetres down to
prevent anything burrowing underneath.

The job was incredibly labour-intensive but once again the Bilby
Brothers, as they'd become known, got to see human nature at its
best. People answering the call for help came from all over the world.

After only a year, the fence was complete. To celebrate the opening, hundreds turned up to a party at the old Currawinya Woolshed. Afterwards, Manthey and McRae, their volunteers and the rangers at Currawinya set about making sure they got rid of every rabbit, fox and cat within the fenced area. Manthey's old skills as a roo-shooter were called upon as they went out on nightly patrols in the 29-square-kilometre area. One of the worst droughts in Currawinya's history added to the pressures on all the animals in the enclosure, but any that weren't supposed to be there also met with 'a severe response'.

As the European animals that had done so much damage gradually disappeared, a small piece of the outback slowly reverted to the conditions that had once existed over the entire continent. The drought meant that it was 2004 before it was possible to release bilbies into the enclosure. Among them was a little female bilby who'd shouldered much of the burden of raising funds to build the fence. Dawn was released into the enclosure, free at last.

The Save the Bilby Fund has now raised more than a million dollars. It's an independent nonprofit organisation with goals that have since expanded beyond its original objective. As McRae explained, 'We've started to give money to other endangered species projects – hairy-nosed wombats, kowaris – and for bilby research. We're hoping to be an organisation that can disperse funds to other less publicly embraced species that are struggling for research funds.'

According to McRae, the bilby enclosure has also provided valuable information that may help ensure the bilby's survival:

Fences aren't the answer, but they can tell us the answer. The thing about a big exclosure [sic] like that is that it lends itself to lots of opportunities for research into a whole range of ecosystem processes. The fence is providing insights into what needs to be done for bilbies to survive in their normal range. That means controlling foxes, cats and rabbits. You'll never get the last one but if you can keep densities down the effects can be minimised. Doing that requires funding and vigilance from the federal level down to the grazier looking after his or her patch of the outback.

Where cats are concerned, McRae believes we have to start by changing the way we keep them as pets. He isn't entirely anti-cat, but he believes we need to regulate who you can get a cat from and have every pet cat de-sexed and registered. When you know there are no breeding cats in a community, targeting wild cats then becomes more effective. 'If Fluffy is de-sexed and registered and Fluffy eats a bird in your garden fifty times a year, that's your problem,' he says. 'You're losing those birds. This will inevitably occur in urban environments but at least Fluffy's not getting out and having kittens which are getting out into the desert.'

McRae realises he's talking about a major shift in attitude, but there are some encouraging signs. The federal government has proposed spending five million dollars on a bilby centre for Charleville. McRae has invited architecture students to submit designs and hopes it will re-create the bilby's world and reveal to visitors the rich interactions between all the species of the arid zone. While plans for the centre are slowing moving forward, McRae is still spending long periods at his remote research camp at Astrebla Downs National Park.

Manthey is still touring the country talking to schools and running stalls at agricultural shows. He's managed to have the second Sunday of September, at the end of threatened species week, declared National Bilby Day, and bilbies now have a website (savethebilby.com. au). Neither McRae nor Manthey are young men, although both have the kind of energy that makes you think they'll go on forever. Manthey hopes he can keep going long enough for people to see that the bilby is a way to save a lot of other species. McRae doesn't know who will carry on his research and the work of the Save the Bilby Fund:

To date we haven't got too many people who are driven like Frank and I were. If you look at those big, powerful, talented communicators who can change the way big parts of society think – Nelson Mandela, David Suzuki and even Al Gore – they don't come along very often. You need someone who can get the message across. If we're really going to change the way society looks at the landscape and our place in it, we have to know how important the Australian landscape is.

It sounds like a job description for the next outback pioneer. The challenge is every bit as daunting as those faced by the pioneers detailed throughout this book. How do you save endangered species? How do you eradicate feral predators? How do you get people involved? Could you get the traditional custodians of the land to help and create meaningful employment for indigenous communities across the country? How would you fund something on such a scale? Could you ever get politicians to appreciate an idea so remote from their constituents?

The easy answer to all these questions is 'too hard'. Except that's what they said about crossing the Blue Mountains, blazing stock routes from one side of the country to the other, building the Coolgardie Pipeline and the Trans-Australian Railway, establishing the Flying Doctor Service and the School of the Air, and improving the lives of women in the outback. Every one of the people in this book has faced their particular challenges with determination, resourcefulness and unfailing energy. Young, old, male or female, they've been enthralled by outback Australia and given their all to make it a better place for everyone. If there's one thing that unites them all and provides a source of hope for the future, it's this: there's no such thing as impossible for an outback pioneer.

SOURCES

Chapter 1: John Wilson
Blaxland, G., *Journal of a Tour of Discovery Across the Blue Mountains*, Sydney University Press, Sydney, 2004.
Collins, D., *Account of the English Colony in New South Wales*, Cadell and Davies, London, 1803.
Cunningham, C., *The Blue Mountains Rediscovered*, Kangaroo Press, 1996, Kenthurst.
Price, J., Hand-written manuscripts of his journeys with John Wilson in 1798, held among the papers of Sir Joseph Banks, State Library of New South Wales. Digital scans can be viewed on the SLNSW website. Partial transcriptions can be found in several volumes, notably Cunningham's *Blue Mountains Rediscovered*.
Watson, F. (ed.), *Historical Records of Australia*, Library Committee of the Commonwealth Parliament, Sydney, 1915.

Chapter 2: James Tyson
Anon., 'The Tyson Interview', The *Brisbane Courier*, 8 December, 1893.
Anon., 'Tyson', *The Bulletin*, 17 December, 1898.
Anon., 'With the Cattle King', The *Adelaide Observer*, 28 July, 1928.
Denholm, Zita, *T.Y.S.O.N.: The Life and Times of James Tyson, Pastoral Pioneer*, Triple D Books, Wagga Wagga, 2002.
Paterson, Andrew 'Banjo', 'T.Y.S.O.N.', *Australasian Pastoralists Review*, 18 December, 1898.
Peck, Harry H., *Memoirs of a Stockman*, Stockland Press, North Melbourne, 1942.

Chapter 3: Nat Buchanan
Anon. (Gordon Buchanan), 'Pioneers of the Far North', *Sydney Stock and Station Journal*, November 1921–May 1922.
Anon., *Northern Territory Times*, 7 February, 1896.
Anon., *The Bulletin*, 9 July, 1881.
Buchanan, Bobbie, *In the Tracks of Old Bluey*, Central Queensland University Press, Rockhampton, 1997.
Buchanan, Gordon, *Packhorse and Waterhole*, Angus & Robertson, Sydney, 1933.

Chapter 4: Dervish Bejah
Farwell, George, *Land of Mirage*, Cassell, Melbourne, 1950.
Heyer, John, *The Back of Beyond*, Shell Film Unit, 1954 (available on DVD through the RFDS).
Madigan, C.T., *Crossing the Dead Heart*, Georgian House, Melbourne, 1946.
Wells, L., *Journal of the Calvert Scientific Exploring Expedition, 1896–7*, Government Printer, Perth, 1902 (facsimile edition published by Hesperian Press, 1993).

Chapter 5: C.Y. O'Connor
Carnegie, D., *Spinifex and Sand*, C. Arthur Pearson, London, 1898.
Constructing Australia – Pipe Dreams, Film Australia, 2007.
Tauman, M., *The Chief – C.Y. O'Connor*, University of Western Australia Press, Perth, 1978.

Chapter 6: The Trans-Australian Railway

Anon., 'East-West Railway, 350 Men Paid Off', *The Argus*, August 20, 1917.

Anon., 'Scene At The Linking Up', *The Kalgoorlie Miner*, 26 October, 1917.

Burke, D., Road through the Wilderness, New South Wales University Press, Sydney, 1991.

Flynn, John (ed.), 'Spanning a Continent', *The Inlander*, Vol. 4, No. 2, 1917–1918.

Chapter 7: The Country Women's Association

Arthur, R., 'A Bushwomen's Conference', *Sydney Stock and Station Journal*, 6 September, 1921.

Country Women's Association of Australia, *Getting Things Done: The Country Women's Association of Australia*, CWA, Cherrybrook, 1986.

Gordon, Florence (ed.), 'Our Home Page', *Sydney Stock and Station Journal*, September 1921 – June 1922.

Lawson, Henry, 'Borderland', later renamed 'Up the Country', *The Bulletin*, 9 July, 1882.

Paterson, Andrew, 'An Answer to Various Bards', *The Bulletin*, 1 October, 1892.

Stevens-Chambers, Brenda, *The Many Hats of Country Women: The Jubilee History of the Country Women's Association of Australia*, CWA Australia, Brisbane, 1997.

Chapter 8: Grace Francis

Batstone, K., *Outback Heroes*, Lothian Books, Melbourne, 2003.

Francis, G., *The Diary of Sister Grace Francis MBE, Birdsville Nursing Home, September 1923 to August 1925*, AVC Printers, Brisbane, 1957.

Rudolph, R., *Flynn's Outback Angels*, Vol. 1, Central Queensland University Press, Rockhampton, 2001.

Chapter 9: John Flynn

Australian Transport Safety Bureau, *Road Crash Casualties and Rates, Australia, 1925 to latest year*, Australian Transport Safety Bureau,

Canberra, 2005.

Batstone, Kay, *Outback Heroes: 75 Years of the Royal Flying Doctor Service*, Lothian, Melbourne, 2003.

Fysh, Hudson, *Qantas Rising*, Angus & Robertson, Sydney, 1965.

Idriess, Ion, *Flynn of the Inland*, Angus & Robertson, Sydney, 1932.

Job, M., *The Origin of Mercy Flights*, <www.airwaysmuseum.com/Mercy%20Flights%20article.htm> viewed 28 November, 2007.

Marsh, Bill, *Great Flying Doctor Stories*, ABC Books, Sydney, 1999.

McKay, Fred, *Traeger: The Pedal Radio Man*, Boolarong Press, Moorooka, 1995.

Miller, R., *Flying Nurse*, Rigby, Adelaide, 1971.

Sutherland, S.K. & Tibballs, J., *Management of Snake Bites in Australia and Papua New Guinea*, RFDS, Brisbane, 2002.

Welch, K., *Aerial Medical Service*, AIM, Sydney, 1928.

Chapter 10: Alfred Traeger

Batstone, K., *Outback Heroes*, Lothian, Melbourne, 2003.

Idriess, I., *Flynn of the Inland*, Angus & Robertson, Sydney, 1932.

McKay, F., *Traeger: The Pedal Radio Man*, Boolarong Press, Brisbane, 1995.

Chapter 11: Adelaide Miethke

Alice Springs School of the Air <www.assoa.nt.edu.au/> viewed 1 December, 2007.

Ashton, J., *Out of the Silence*, Investigator Press, Adelaide, 1971.

Miethke, A., *Airdoctor*, various editions, FDS, Adelaide.

Rudolph, I., *Flynn's Outback Angels*, Vol. II, Central Queensland University Press, Rockhampton, 2002.

Chapter 12: R.M. Williams

ABC Online, *R.M. Williams* <www.abc.net.au/schoolstv/australians/rmwilliams.htm> viewed 1 March, 2008.

Williams, R.M., *Beneath Whose Hand*, Macmillan, Sydney, 1984.

Williams, R.M., *I Once Met a Man*, Angus
   & Robertson, Sydney, 1989.

**Chapter 13: Peter McRae (1951–)
and Frank Manthey (1938–)**
Manthey, F., Interview with author,
   Sydney, March 2008.
McRae, P., Interview with author,
   Charleville, May 2007.
Stevens, J. (director), *The Bilby Brothers*
   (documentary), Gulliver Media,
   Brisbane, 2002.